Possessions

Indigenous Art/Colonial Culture

INTERPLAY

THEORY ARTS HISTORY

Possessions

Indigenous Art/Colonial Culture

Nicholas Thomas

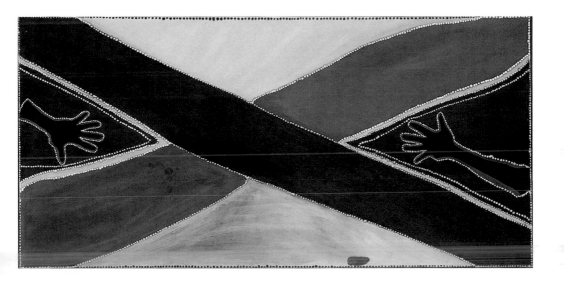

With 183 illustrations, 20 in colour   T&H   Thames and Hudson

For John Pule

Frontispiece: ROVER THOMAS Roads Meeting, 1987

© 1999 Thames and Hudson Ltd, London

British Library Cataloguing-in-Publication Data
A catalogue record for this book is available from the
British Library

ISBN 0-500-28097-5

Printed and bound in Singapore by C.S. Graphics

Contents

1 PAUL KANE Medicine Mask Dance, 1847

I

The modernist art of the twentieth century was marked by unprecedented engagement with 'primitive' art. Europeans such as Picasso,
Matisse, Ernst, Pechstein, Nolde, Brancusi and others responded to
masks, sculpture and diverse other genres of tribal African, Oceanic and
American art. Though fraught with contradictions, their interest has
long been celebrated as a cross-cultural discovery. Recognition of the
power of the indigenous forms led not only to radical shifts in European
artists' creativity, but also in some degree to an acknowledgment of the
richness and complexity of non-European cultures.[1]

For better or worse? In the aftermath of the postwar epoch of decolonization, the cultural dominance as well as the political and economic
hegemony of the West was challenged. In the 1960s, anti-colonial cultural criticism, exemplified by the work of Frantz Fanon, was at first
directed against racist mentalities in the broadest terms. From the 1970s,
however, writers such as Edward Said drew attention to links between
imperialism and high culture. Though his influential study, *Orientalism*,
was concerned with academic writing and literature rather than visual
art, the vigorously anti-imperial spirit of his book made it inevitable that
positive assessment of modernist interest in tribal art would give way to
contention. Had European artists simply appropriated the forms and
aesthetics of other cultures, reinvigorating their own practice while
giving nothing in return? Were they essentially colonizers in the domain
of art, retailers of primitivist stereotypes? Were their interests in tribal
culture merely projections of Western fantasies that reflected no deep
understanding of any particular non-European tradition?[2]

It is easy to suggest that neither uncritical celebration nor categorical
condemnation is a sufficient appraisal of any particular art work or
oeuvre, or for assessing what might be called the politics of primitivism at
any particular moment. Argument about these dimensions of modernism
has inevitably continued, provoked notably by the 1983 exhibition
'"Primitivism" in 20th Century Art' at the Museum of Modern Art in New

York. But at the same time the grounds of debate have been shifting. Until relatively recently, the whole issue was assumed to lie in the fact that 'primitive' art inspired modernists; the possibility that cross-cultural fertilization was a two-way affair received little attention. Indigenous art, however, was always more than an object of colonial spoliation, more than a passive reference point. Tribal arts, though often discussed as if they belonged to the remote past, are not static. In much of Asia and Africa, colonial visual culture and commercial iconography stimulated the emergence of radically innovative popular genres.[3] Though this material lay beyond the vision of European curators and art-historians, over the 1970s and '80s the pre-eminence of Europe and the United States in modern and contemporary art was gradually called into question. No doubt the status and authority of European art remained undiminished in many quarters, but African and Asian artists were nonetheless increasingly represented at the Venice Biennale and in similar exhibitions, and indeed biennales themselves proliferated in places outside Europe and the US: in Havana, Cairo, Sydney, Seoul, São Paulo and elsewhere.

By the 1990s, it had become fashionable to suggest that old relations between centres and peripheries had been superseded. It could be claimed that contemporary African artists were doing the same thing to Western culture that Western culture had done to their traditions. Art was moving beyond the antagonism between colonialism and anti-colonialism, and toward a new cosmopolitanism marked by flows of ideas and influences in many directions.[4] Globalization emerged as a theme that loomed large in cultural criticism and curatorship; it has become something of an art-world cliché. To be sure, the fact that a much wider range of art might be included in international fora and discussed in leading art journals is only positive. But this book is written against the simplistic evocations of globalization, which suppose that art today is defined by the links between all parts of the world. Transnational interactions have, to be sure, been of profound significance, but cultures and cultural relations in particular regions and nations continue to be deeply shaped by more local factors. It is naive to believe that colonial inequalities and asymmetrical relations between countries and continents are somehow being dissolved through cosmopolitanism.

This book re-examines both European engagements with indigenous art and the presence of indigenous art in the contemporary art world. It does so not from a European perspective or a global one, but from a distinctive, local vantage point, one that is at a remove from the centres of Euro-American culture yet not in the Third World either. It addresses the interplay between indigenous culture and colonial art in

2 LAWRENCE PAUL YUXWELUPTUN Scorched Earth, Clear Cut Logging on Native Sovereign Land. Shaman Coming to Fix, 1991

settler countries – countries, like Australia and unlike India, in which considerable numbers of Europeans made their home, dispossessing and eventually outnumbering indigenous people. In some settler colonies, such as the United States, the overwhelming nature of immigration and the diversity of the immigrant population meant that the division between indigenous natives and white colonists has been displaced by a more complex pattern of diversity. In others, the binary opposition between natives and settlers has remained highly conspicuous. Irrespective of these variations, the distinctive feature of settler colonialism was the sustained and direct character of engagement between indigenous and European cultures. Colonialism thus consisted of more than relations between Europe and distant regions, just as the art of colonialism consisted of much more than the responses of European intellectuals to objects from places they generally had little knowledge of and never visited. Colonial relationships were also made through direct contacts and local interactions. This book explores the most fraught and sustained of such interactions, in the arts of colonies of settlement.

Settler colonies differ from those based in trade, or the exploitation of native labour and natural resources. Throughout the Americas, and in Australasia, southern Africa, and at certain times in many other places, colonizing populations established themselves and became settlers on indigenous peoples' lands. The indigenous population, in theory, was to be supplanted rather than exploited. The commitment to acquire the land typically led to piecemeal dispossession through direct appropriation, campaigns of forcible removal and genocidal terror, and subsequently to programmes of assimilation which subverted indigenous culture to the same degree that settler appropriations of land had subverted subsistence practices. Though these strategies were frequently abetted by disease and depopulation, their effect was typically highly uneven. In each settler-colonial theatre, certain native groups were all but eliminated, while others, thanks to their remoteness, active resistance, or canny accommodation to the emerging colonial regime, remained strong and retained lands and some degree of local autonomy. Hence, in the United States, the indigenous peoples of the densely settled northeast have been as radically marginalized as those in urban southeastern Australia, while those in Australia's central deserts and remote north retain country and culture, as do those in the American southwest. These contrasts are obviously crude: what people have lost and retained or recreated varies, as do the causes of defeat in some cases and survival in others. I hasten to add that even those groups who have been most marginalized have often lost knowledge of particular customs and traditions, rather than 'culture' itself. 'Culture' is not tradition but what people do, whatever that happens to be.

Diverse as its manifestations have been, dispossession looms large in all settler-indigenous histories. The process stands, ironically, as the dark side of a story that has often been narrated as a progression from darkness to light. Some colonists saw the new societies they were founding as the culminations of civilization, as 'last nations' that extended European progress beyond the congestion of Europe. Yet these utopias were to be created on the lands of peoples who have subsequently often affirmed their special spiritual attachments to the land, and their precedence, by claiming the title of 'First Nations'. In the nineteenth century, when evolutionary thought postulated radical distance between the civilized and the savage, between modernity and the dawn of time, colonists and natives were close; they shared the very ground that they struggled over. Though this coevality was consistently denied in settler ideologies, contacts were in fact sustained rather than episodic and were marked by a singular kind of antagonistic intimacy.[5]

Most forms of colonial government have given way to political decolonization, though the process of national liberation has been notoriously accompanied by persisting economic and cultural inequalities. When settler colonies become settler nations, however, the colonial relationship endures. In global terms, the 'colonial age' may be a thing of the past, but this is not true in Canada, Hawaii, New Zealand or Australia; nor is it for that matter in Taiwan, Japan, Scandinavia or in much of Latin America, where native peoples' movements are increasingly conscious of their affinities with those of other aboriginal peoples such as indigenous Australians and Maori. In many places, times have changed since the nineteenth century, and for that matter since assimilationist thinking dominated government policy in the 1960s, but there has been no decolonization, except in the sense that nations such as Australia and Canada are no longer British colonies or dominions. The colonial nationalism of white settlers accomplished its purpose, but native peoples experienced no independence from their immediate colonizers. To be sure, if settlers withdraw, or if indigenous peoples are eliminated altogether, a settler colonial society may, in principle, be transformed into a polity of another kind, but in general the histories of settler nations have not led to either of these extreme outcomes. In places such as Canada, New Zealand and Australia, indigenous peoples survive, while settlers remain dominant. In recent decades, indigenous cultural and political renaissances have taken place, and questions of indigenous rights are persistently troubling, and frequently debated. To varying degrees, efforts have been made to transcend the injustices of invasion, to restore rights to land and to redress manifold forms of discrimination. But the intimate connection between the foundations of settler societies and the dispossession of prior occupants makes any larger resolution elusive and intractable.

Settler misgivings are a recurrent feature of colonial history, and are present in visual art from the beginnings of colonization. Native peoples have been denigrated and misrepresented, but rather more enters into their representation than stereotypic, often racist expectations. Actual encounters between colonists and natives have also profoundly shaped those representations; some settler artists, such as Paul Kane, were captivated by indigenous objects and performances, and communicate their visual drama, even if they lacked understanding of their ritual significance. Encounters were marked by moments of awe, respect and partial understanding, as well as misrecognition and hostility. It is this uncertain combination of acknowledgment and denial that has characterized the settler-indigenous relation in general.

The ambivalence of settlers toward natives was sharpened by an emerging preoccupation with national identity. This was conspicuous in British dominions such as Australia, Canada, and New Zealand from the 1890s, if not somewhat earlier. The discovery that national (and other) identities are 'inventions' has become a hallmark of recent scholarship, but long ago artists and writers in those countries just mentioned presumed that the nation lacked an identity, and that it was their task to invent one. In doing so, producers of culture – such as designers in various media as well as painters and poets – frequently turned to what was locally distinctive, either in the natural environment or in indigenous culture. The deep association between indigenous people and the land provided strong and condensed reference points for a colonial culture that sought both to define itself as native and to create national emblems. Settlers also, of course, frequently wanted to emphasize their modernity and their connections with Britain and Europe; hence the use of native reference to proclaim a distinctive culture was never the sole basis for declared identity, but rather one strategy that was often inconsistent with others.

Indigenous reference has been far more conspicuous at certain times than others, but it has often been prominent, and has had paradoxical effects. While indigenous people's claims to the land are being denied or forgotten, elements of their culture are being prominently displayed and affirmed. The 'native' status of the new settler nation is proclaimed in a fashion that perforce draws attention to real natives who are excluded. The effort of certain settler artists and designers to localize settler culture thus animates a powerful but unstable set of terms, which I want to characterize as a 'native and/or national' identity. Over time, or indirectly, local signs could be (and have been) reappropriated by natives, to draw attention to their precedence, and to reassert indigenous sovereignty – perforce at the expense of the legitimacy of the settler nation. The 'and/or' in this relation is central to this book, as it is to the interplay of dispossession and repossession that defines the history of settler societies.

Primitivism in settler culture is therefore something both more and less than primitivism in modernist art. There is a general affinity, in the sense that the motifs and forms of 'primitive' art were drawn upon in 'modern' art in the context of ideas that valued the 'primitive', or at least regarded it as an object of special interest. Settler primitivism is not, however, necessarily the project of radical formal innovation stimulated by tribal art that we are familiar with from twentieth-century modernism. It was, rather, often an effort to affirm a local relationship, not with a generic primitive culture, but a particular one – for example, that of Australian Aboriginal people, or the Maori of New Zealand, in the cases that I treat as paradigms here. In settler art and design, the incorporation of forms, styles and motifs abstracted from these indigenous cultures might well proceed in the service of a native and/or national identity without reference to European avant-garde modernism. Modernist art in these societies was often not internationalist in orientation, but rather looked awkwardly toward nationalism and cosmopolitanism at once.

Despite its singularity, indeed its peculiarity, settler art can add something to the larger debate concerning indigenous and modern art. The situation of indigenous people within rather than beyond the settler nation can be conducive to a stronger and more definite indigenous presence in art and in other forms of culture than in Europe or elsewhere – though the contrasts between settler societies are also striking in this respect, Maori being persistently more visible than indigenous Australians or North Americans, for reasons that are explored in the chapters that follow.

Indigenous peoples are, as we shall see, conspicuous in settler art in the eighteenth and nineteenth centuries, well before modernism made its belated impact on conservative antipodean art milieux. In countries such as New Zealand, Australia, and Canada, indigenous motifs and references moreover feature in settler design, in architecture, on stamps and currency, in fashion, and in conservative as well as in innovative works of art. Indigenous reference has thus been a widely visible, public phenomenon in settler culture, one sometimes promoted by government initiatives, as well as one present in the work of individual artists and in commercial iconography. It has been something broader than an avant-garde strategy in art, or a gesture in acknowledgment of critical intellectual rhetoric. Settler primitivism therefore often lacks the

3 AUSTRALIAN $1 NOTE issued between 1966 and 1984, based on a painting by David Malangi

subversive aspirations which typify the European avant garde. For if the latter has become susceptible to the charge of recapitulating old racial stereotypes, nevertheless it often started from some degree of estrangement. In its radical moments, settler modernism shared this awkward relation to broader values, but cultural expressions that drew upon native imagery were more often supportive of settler nationalism, not hostile to it.

This book is not a study of colonial images of indigenous people, but a cross-cultural art history that includes indigenous narratives and art works. Such a history must trace moments of dialogue and exchange, but must also acknowledge that colonial relations have often been marked by misconstrued dialogue or forced silence. Indigenous people may inhabit a cultural domain that is largely unrecognized by colonizers; indigenous representations and self-representations are shaped by particular understandings of history, cosmology and land that often lie beyond settler vision.

Colonial imaginings of place, past and future also have their own mythic proportions, and their own cosmological coherence; settler and indigenous visions alike affirm attachments to land, but in terms that are all but incommensurable. Yet art objects that emerge from profoundly different ground are found side by side in museums and in other public situations in settler societies. In art galleries, romantic colonial landscape paintings and white modernist works may be found alongside indigenous art objects in an arrangement that echoes the strange proximity, the antagonistic cohabitation of country, that marks these societies' histories. In settler museums, the jostling of 'modern' and 'primitive' objects does not so much display the affinities of form that have interested art historians like William Rubin, curator of the '"Primitivism" and 20th Century Art' exhibition mentioned earlier. Instead, this jostling points unavoidably to rival attachments to country, and competing imaginings of the nation. In these societies, cultures, motifs and art forms count as possessions, as things that are lost, stolen, recovered and represented.

This is not to say that aesthetic issues are irrelevant to the appreciation and significance of indigenous art. The sheer power of indigenous painting, sculpture and work in fabric and fibre has commanded respect, not only for the art itself, or for the artists, but for indigenous culture in a broader sense. And the affirmation of indigenous culture, which is displayed in many contexts for tourists and shown in prestigious national cultural institutions, unavoidably translates into recognition of native people, if in a partial and uncertain way. Indigenous political claims in

New Zealand and Australia have over the last thirty years attracted wider understanding and support for a range of reasons, among which the interest in art has loomed surprisingly large. But support for indigenous claims only goes so far. While – to cite just one example – the Canadian government delivered in early 1998 a formal apology for historic injustices to native peoples, in Australia much contention and bitterness has surrounded the government's unwillingness to do the same.

This book is concerned with shifting settler views of indigenous art, and settler argument about the business of colonizing and nation-making. But it is equally concerned to explore the actions, voices and cultural expressions of indigenous peoples themselves. Their artifacts and art forms, from the beginning of colonization to the present, embody stories that ought to be part of a cross-cultural history. This history does not simply have two sides: one cannot juxtapose a native perspective with a colonial one because, as I noted, there has been no single dialogue, or no single experience or exchange, that can be told from one 'side' or the other. There have instead been multiple encounters, and many situations in which there has been an encounter, often a tragically harmful one, without much exchange of meanings. Some indigenous cultural expressions lie beyond, or seem remote from, the zone of contact that colonialism creates. They speak not to the struggle over land and sovereignty, but to rituals, customary practices and mythic imaginings that appear to have nothing to do with recent history. But indigenous culture has also been refashioned historically, under colonial circumstances, and much indigenous art is marked by those circumstances; much indeed seeks to condemn them. If settler culture is destabilized by the 'and/or' of native and/or national reference, contemporary indigenous culture is fractured and strained by its groundings in tradition and/or modernity.

To a substantial degree, this conflict of terms may be imposed by outsiders, who have generally valued indigenous art (or at least that perceived to be untainted by colonial influence) as an unambiguous expression of 'primitive' culture. Since the serious study of First Nations' material culture began in the late nineteenth century, scholars and connoisseurs have generally paid attention only to pieces they regarded as traditional. New genres of indigenous art were emerging, which borrowed colonial media and representational styles to express new Christian beliefs, and to record the colonial experience. But art forms of this kind, often made as tourist souvenirs as well as for local use, were typically derided by ethnologists as adulterated expressions of cultures on the wane.

The preference for 'traditional' art has carried over into the present, even though the purist aesthetic has been criticized on many grounds, and is at last now generally discredited among curators and scholars. This is so in part because a broader audience retains an appetite for a pure 'primitive' culture that can be romanticized. The notion that indigenous art sustains mystical values was, for instance, central to the celebrated 1989 Paris exhibition, 'Magiciens de la terre'. The most conspicuous strand of contemporary primitivism is New Age or environmentalist in orientation. Tribal peoples are seen as sources of ancient wisdom, their lifeways exemplifying harmony with nature. This evocation is one that many native peoples have themselves seized upon. The grounding of contemporary life in tradition and in the ways of ancestors is reaffirmed, as is the depth of indigenous spirituality. These claims may be apt enough, for indigenous worldviews were and are distinguished by the significance of ancestral dreamings (in Australia) or genealogy and *mana* (spiritual power and efficacy) among Maori. But the expression of these values in non-indigenous public milieux may entail their translation into stereotype. A culture that may indeed be distinctively spiritual, and shaped by long occupation of the land, may be rendered as mystical or 'cosmic' and archaic. Contemporary New Age settler primitivism and indigenous 'auto-primitivism' affirm each other, but indigenous cultural pride always carries a political edge that gives this dialogue an unpredictable character. In other words, those who view romanticizations of indigenous culture cynically may be surprised by their effect.

In recent years, critics, art historians, and curators have become increasingly interested in indigenous artists who do not work in traditional media or styles. A significant group of contemporary native artists have emerged, in North America as well as in the Australasian settler societies, who in many cases have art school training. Their art practices draw heavily on contemporary international art, though they may also affirm the inspiration of indigenous forms, references and values. The work of Lawrence Paul Yuxweluptun, for example, like that of many other practitioners, is informed by contemporary postcolonial theory, and particularly by the critique of colonial images; much is also inspired by contemporary writings on identity, which typically insist upon the the mixed and displaced character of modern selves and cultures.

In certain art milieux, this kind of contemporary, overtly hybrid indigenous art is embraced, and traditionalist work disparaged. In others, traditionalist work possesses distinctiveness and authenticity that contemporary art, indigenous and non-indigenous alike, has lost. This book rejects this kind of opposition. The crucial point is that indigenous cultures are simultaneously 'traditional' and 'contemporary'. They are 'traditional' in the sense that distinctive views of the world remain alive, but they are also 'contemporary' in the sense that they belong in the present. The traditionalist strands of indigenous art reflect certain dimensions of indigenous life, and the avant-garde strands others. The spectrum as a whole manifests the degree to which indigenous peoples have been neither fully absorbed by, nor excluded from, modernity. They have at once sustained a degree of cultural autonomy, and been compelled to interact with colonial cultures and institutions. There has no doubt been more loss than gain. The upshot of the history, however, is a contemporary indigenous culture that is extraordinarily challenging. This culture belongs to the present, but also lies beyond it – beyond, that is, the space and time of colonial modernity and post-modernity. Maori art, for instance, is created in and out of genealogical time and tribal histories constituted by ancestral acts. It appears as a disturbing interruption in the modern colonial nation, but is not encompassed by that nation's homogeneous, linear modern time.

Indigenous art, moreover, enables us to see the contemporary world as replete with such paradoxes. The new intensity of travel and communication does not lead to standardization, or to a mere proliferation of identities that have the same form but different content. It leads, rather, to interactions between cultures that may remain on radically different ground. Mutual contact produces mixing, perhaps, but it also makes visible profound differences that resist fusion. Indigenous peoples, among others, insist on their distinctiveness, even as they experience globalization, and gain a small voice that is too rarely heard in the cacophony of global cultural 'dialogue'. Within the settler-colonial societies themselves, however, that voice has become increasingly articulate and insistent. If the settler nations have been persistently 'unsettled', they are more so, and irreversibly so, today.

If its subject-matter is cross-cultural traffic, *Possessions* itself manifests a kind of intellectual exchange, between anthropology and art history. I have avoided burdening this book with an extended discussion of these disciplines, or any programmatic statement about what might be gained by joining or blurring them. This is a topic that much has been written about; more importantly, much productive blurring is currently being done.

Though my interest here is in doing anthropological art history, rather than in describing it, it may be worth setting out, briefly, the approach I have tried to adopt. While anthropologists have frequently taken art works essentially as illustrations or expressions of social relations, religious symbols, or other meanings external to the objects themselves, I have presumed that art is effective in defining those social relations and meanings, and may radically redefine them. If this were not so, there would be no special reason for approaching the larger issues of cross-cultural history, of the painful dialectic of dispossession and repossession, through art. I have therefore shifted between discussion of particular works and their situations. I avoid saying 'between content and context' because the term 'context' is a problematic one, suggesting as it does that a social and historical field simply contains art. As I have suggested, I try to see this relation more interactively: objects and contexts not only define each other, but may change and disrupt each other.

Because settler-colonial society is built on contradictions, objects and their situations are very often at odds with each other. I am concerned not only with the particular properties of art works, but with their success and failure, with the ways in which they are presented to audiences to be debated, celebrated, or perhaps ignored. Fieldwork anthropology of the conventional kind may not be conspicuous in this book, but its anthropological perspective may be seen in these emphases: I prefer to analyse the workings of art through local responses rather than sociological abstractions.

It is important to stress that this is a partial account in a number of senses. I do not provide anything like a full chronological survey of the art histories of all colonial societies, or of either of the two countries, Australia and New Zealand, on which I have chosen to focus my discussion. Their histories suggest paradigms for the tensions between indigenous art and colonial culture in other settler societies, though some cases, such as Canada, fit closely, while others do to a more limited degree. The use of nativism in Latin American nationalism is for example broadly related to the tendencies in the British colonial sphere, but of course emerged from different contexts and had different effects. While these broader parallels may be suggestive, I must make it clear that I do not attempt to offer a fully representative account even of the two case studies. My nineteenth-century Australian examples are for instance all drawn from the east of the country, and do not necessarily reflect developments in the other Australian colonies, which remained separate until Federation in 1901. Although I do trace themes from the beginnings of colonization to the present, I do so in a highly selective way; I have extracted the works, developments and events which tell us most about the content and limits of cultural exchange at particular times. My discussion incorporates several shifts of focus, which are intended to provide complementary and cross-cutting perspectives. Chapters Two, Three and Five consist of wide-ranging surveys of settler landscape, settler design and indigenous modernism respectively; Chapters Four and Six each present more sustained analyses of two artists, settler modernists in Chapter Four, and contemporary indigenous artists in Chapter Six. Chapter Seven presents a more anecdotal, diary-like account of contemporary developments in New Zealand, while Chapters Eight and Nine integrate further contemporary examples with interpretive reflections. (I would have taken a less idiosyncratic approach, were more general works not readily available by Tim Bonyhady, Wally Caruana, Vivien Johnson, Joan Kerr, Ian McLean, Andrew Sayers and Bernard Smith and many others, on indigenous and settler Australian art; and by Leonard Bell, Michael Dunn, Sidney Mead, Roger Neich, Rangihiroa Panoho, Francis Pound and Cliff Whiting, again among others, on Maori and settler art in New Zealand).[6]

There is a further important sense in which this book's partiality must be signalled. Its writer is a white Australian. I attempt to discuss both colonial and indigenous traditions in a broadly balanced way, and write about native work on the basis of sustained inquiry, interviews with artists, and the like, but it must be conceded that I do not write from an insider point of view. The anecdotal character of sections of the book aims to remind readers that this discussion is not simply an expression of detached theorizing or expertise, but also the upshot of research experience and personal interaction; it is motivated not only by abstract intellectual questions, but by the fact that I happen to live in a particular part of the world. I am not so much concerned to 'come to terms' with this in a personal sense as to illustrate why the region's history makes 'coming to terms' always an incomplete business: one that is necessary, awkward, rewarding and also improbable.

Yet my aim is not primarily to make exclusive claims about what is distinctive to a particular part of the world, the 'antipodes', nor even about settler-colonies in general. My conviction is rather that these societies enable us to see global processes of cultural exchange in a focused way. The sustained character of interaction in these situations makes it all the more striking that dialogue has proceeded in fits and starts. This halting process has not led inexorably toward commonality. Histories – of travel, colonialism, nationality and culture – become mutually mired rather than shared. Yet the interactions have been, and are, fertile as well as fraught. This book is not exactly a vindication of cross-cultural art; it is rather an expression of astonishment before its risks and its promises.

II

Presence and stillness

Around 1967, Colin McCahon (1919–87), the pre-eminent figure in postwar New Zealand art, produced a series of north Otago landscapes, stark paintings of the stark hills of the South Island. In these works, the horizon is typically high in the painting, and parallels an equally firm line that marks the base of an escarpment. The viewer looks across a horizontal plain toward a near-vertical slope, and above and beyond that to the sky. This is immediately recognizable as a landscape, rather than as three bands of paint, because the diagonal slash and associated tonal complexity give shape to an abrupt ridge, which descends directly and steeply from the upland behind.

4 COLIN McCAHON North Otago, 1967

5 DORIS LUSK Canterbury Plains From the Cashmere Hills, 1952

These paintings recall earlier landscapes by McCahon, such as *Takaka: Night and Day* (1948, fig. 7) and *6 Days in Nelson and Canterbury* (1950), that are among his most frequently reproduced works. What is arresting in all cases is the grasp of the land's substance, and its vacancy. To adopt an old-fashioned vocabulary which probably remains current to those who most admire these works, there is a sense of truth to the shape of the land. The country evoked is sometimes spiritually pregnant, foreboding or purely strong; but it is also absolutely devoid of artifice, uninscribed and uncultivated. McCahon's immediate predecessors and contemporaries were rarely concerned to depict such profoundly evacuated land; 'regionalist' landscape painters of the nineteen-thirties, forties and fifties in New Zealand were interested in the characteristic forms of hills, to be sure, but they typically put the run-down or unpretentious structures associated with rural settlements in the foreground. They more or less deliberately gave their paintings historical specificity by introducing such subjects as railways, wartime exercises or developments around ports or mines. These were paintings of modern life, albeit in the antipodean backblocks.

Canterbury Plains from the Cashmere Hills (1952) by Doris Lusk (1917–90) invites direct comparison with McCahon's *Takaka*. The most prominent geographic element in each painting is a valley flanked by a succession of spurs, seen from an elevated, almost aerial vantage point. Lusk's fertilized tract of pasture, which extends down the length of her valley and part way up its gentle sides, is sharply differentiated from the higher ridges, but even the latter have plainly been touched by settlement: a rough track extends up through a pine plantation across the foreground, and presumably zig-zags up to the point from which the view is taken. There is a small town at the mouth of the valley and beyond that the plain is divided by fences. This countryside is at once extensive and bounded; it is not virgin land but land appropriated and reshaped by settler agriculture.

McCahon's topography is also reordered, not by these manipulations of the environment, but by artistic licence: his valley is more an enclosed hollow than a river's true cradle; it lacks the predictable shape that would be provided by a steep head or broad opening. This non-naturalistic view seems to be from one high tract of land into another, though the artist's vantage point is not revealed topographically, as it is in the composition and even the title of Lusk's painting. The space between foreground and horizon is at once filled with hills, and empty of features. The simultaneity of 'night and day' underlines the work's spiritual burden; here as elsewhere in McCahon, a lapse into pomposity is barely avoided.

In a settler colonial world, the evocation of an empty land awaiting some sort of meaningful inscription or spiritual definition cannot be seen as a purely pictorial or aesthetic statement. One could say that McCahon was more of a modernist than Lusk because he subordinates content to form more vigorously; and his work could indeed be understood to move from one effort of reduction to another, as he subsequently moves away from any sort of figurative painting, and away from colour. Talk of this kind would, however, obfuscate questions that are fundamental for a settler culture, and for the motivation and reception of paintings such as this. Arguably, if white people are to define an alien land as their own, they are bound to dispossess its prior occupants, and establish and celebrate their own investments of labour and sentiment in it.

The effort of aesthetic colonization worked at both particular and general levels. Many nineteenth-century painters in New Zealand, Australia and North America idealized settlement, and celebrated the specific accomplishments of the squatters and farmers whose newly-established properties they depicted. Though remote in many respects from such works, Lusk's affectionate evocations of countryside and country towns could be seen as latter-day reiterations of the theme. She does not declare possession of a land half-won, but unselfconsciously describes a Europeanized country and a secure European presence. She refrains from the romantic excesses of the nineteenth-century painters,

6 TYREE BROTHERS General View of Takaka, c. 1878–94

but nevertheless reaffirms the comfort, peace and security of an agricultural region. There is no sense of conflicting claims to the land. If, in other work, Lusk presents a countryside newly altered by industrial technologies, she does not register the earlier irruptions that produced this not-so-old geography. If the view of the Canterbury Plains historicizes or moralizes, it does so by looking through a valley that opens up and expands; prospects are wide and the future is predictable.

McCahon works at a different register. While Lusk presents the outcome of a history of settlement and cultivation, McCahon's appropriation is more generalized and comprehensive. While Maori are simply not visible in Lusk's painting, the landscapes of *Takaka*, *6 Days*, and *North Otago* are primal and pre-social. It is almost a shock to be told, by a turn-of-the-century photograph from the Takaka area, that barrenness was not an original condition but an effect of a rapid and devastating process of deforestation. As the New Zealand critic Francis Pound has noted, McCahon's insistence upon the silence and emptiness of the land 'in effect, and doubtless unintentionally, echoed the colonialist erasure of Maori voice...and served to declare New Zealand a *terra nullius*.'[7] White pioneering, too, is brushed away, but the larger effect of these erasures of history is to permit the affirmation of profound attachment to the land on the part of the artist as an individual, and more significantly, on the part of the settler nation, for whom the artist may presume to speak. Landscapes, whether peopled or unpeopled, would seem unavoidably implicated in the culture of colonialism.

This is to presume some collusion between the creative project of an individual painter and the collective efforts of a settler population to establish a sense of place and identity. However dubious the assumptions behind such identifications, they are often made, and McCahon's achievement has been characterized in precisely these terms. The most substantial publication on the artist to date, by Gordon Brown, opens by insisting upon the unique character of his stature and vision. He is described as the 'most articulate' of modern New Zealand painters, and this is what he is supposed to have articulated:

> McCahon considered the imagery given to the New Zealand landscape and revitalized its forms. He has reassessed the uninviting wilderness and what looks ordinary about the land and given it a new meaning by simply pointing to its physical presence. If we are to possess the land, we must first come to terms with living on it and, above all, love it as if the land were part of what we are. For McCahon the land becomes an expression of vast geological forces that result from the creative will of God; the same will that unites with the urge to live, and in this way helps to shape and sustain humanity.[8]

There is a slippage here between a singularly prophetic and religious attitude, concerned to depict forces that bear upon humanity in general, and a 'we' that appears particular and in fact *national*. Another critic has made this understanding of the painter's accomplishment more explicit: 'His oeuvre…does attain real credibility as a Pakeha [white New Zealander] claim to the right to stand on the land, and claim spiritual appreciation of the forces which govern the Antipodean universe.'[9]

Stated crudely, McCahon effected through high art what settlers did or desired to do in practice. As colonists bought, captured or confiscated the land to turn it to their own ends, the artist declares it vacant and proceeds to colonize it at the level of meaning. McCahon's advocates do not use the word 'colonize', but they do refer directly to possession of the land. In a settler colony, possession of the land is the issue. White societies in Australia and New Zealand depended not on the exploitation of indigenous labour on plantations or the mercantile extraction of precious commodities, but on the replacement of indigenous landowners by settlers.

7 COLIN McCAHON Takaka: Night and Day, 1948

8 COLIN McCAHON Urewera Mural, 1976

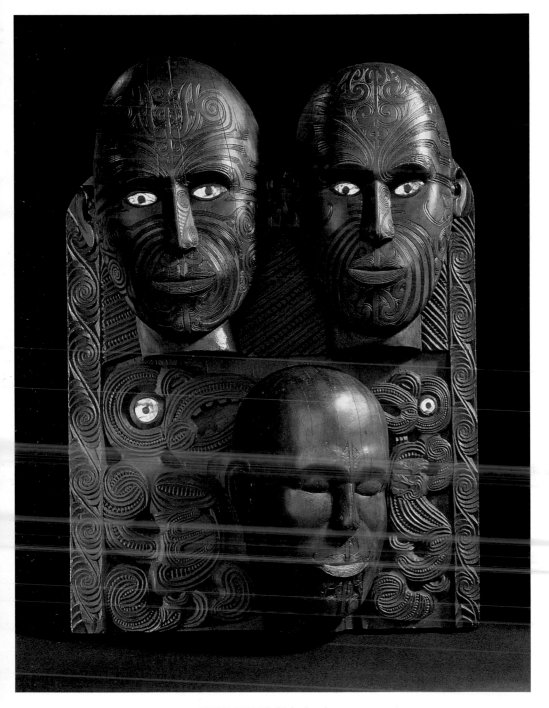

9 TENE WAITERE Ta Moko Panel, c. 1899

10 AUGUSTUS EARLE Distant View of the Bay of Islands, 1827

11 EUGEN VON GUERARD Panoramic View of Mr Angus McMillan's Station, Bushy Park, c. 1861 (details of fig. 35)

It is striking that if McCahon's landscape art really did engage in this sort of appropriation, the operation could be explicitly commended as recently as the 1980s. For commentators such as Gordon Brown, who can be described as cultural nationalists, art should express something distinctive to New Zealand, and supply New Zealanders with a sense of place and identity; and McCahon's status as the pre-eminent New Zealand artist of the second half of the twentieth century is assured because this is what his work does.

I have, in effect, adopted the argument but altered its values, by insisting that the process of nation-making has a negative dimension in the dispossession of the land's prior inhabitants. This is now a familiar line of argument in talk about culture and cultural politics in both Aotearoa New Zealand and Australia, and it is an argument that I am concerned both to extend and to qualify in this book, not least because it comes unstuck in interesting ways in the case of McCahon. Whether one celebrates or condemns his 'revitalization' of the land, the account I have sketched out is credible for only some of his paintings. It might be argued that important bodies of his work are simply not concerned with locality or nation at all; other series can be seen directly to reverse the aesthetic colonization of the stark landscapes, by explicitly affirming the indigenous presence that seems elsewhere to be so profoundly denied.

In the late sixties and early seventies, the texts that McCahon inscribed on his canvas, which were already something of a hallmark of his work, expanded to take up the whole painting; many are biblical passages or transcriptions of verse, others appropriate the simple arithmetic of the blackboard, and a number of major works feature Maori inscriptions, genealogies and slogans. I suggest that these words do something very different to the Maori motifs that McCahon employs in certain earlier and contemporaneous works. While the *koru*, the stem-bulb forms derived from Maori rafter painting, seem somewhat arbitrarily introduced, and carry an ambiguous mixture of decorative effect and symbolic potency, the texts speak powerfully and authoritatively. Their strength and directness has much to do with McCahon's relentless aggrandizement of art and self-aggrandizement, which may be understood less as an expression of personal arrogance than an effort to give painting a novel degree of public authority in New Zealand. McCahon produced paintings on a scale that was unprecedented in the country, a scale that presupposed institutions and a public, rather than an audience of friends and private collectors. He invested in his work a spiritual content that elicits a devotional attitude toward God – yet also toward the practice of painting and his own paintings in particular. The prophetic style delivers a message, but serves also to confer authority upon the speaker, upon 'the Artist' as a figure, and so upon McCahon himself. Pedagogic intent and content indeed come together in paintings such as *Teaching Aids* (1975); the look of the blackboard, and the simulation of wiped-out chalk in many of the later white-on-black works, are too obvious to remark upon.

McCahon's claims may work for some viewers and not others. A McCahon painting that stands alone, that is seen by an American or a European viewer, may be pretty easily walked past, noticed no less fleetingly than so many other canvases on gallery walls; yet sustained exposure to the oeuvre teaches a person to listen to the text's painterly intonation, to pause before it and meditate. If McCahon's wider reputation outside New Zealand and Australia has been and will be slow to grow, his authority in his home country has become very considerable. This is specifically important when McCahon's painterly pronouncements display Maori history. The artist no doubt intended his works to affirm the indigenous subjects they alluded to, but the question of whether appreciation was also appropriation could and did arise in connection with his works and with many others to be discussed in this book. With respect to a multi-panel transcription of the Tainui genealogy, the prominent Maori art historian Ngahuia Te Awekotuku demanded some years ago to know what right McCahon had to write out in paint the succession of names.[10] That charge arises precisely because the painting is powerful, and amounts to something more dramatic and compelling than the printing of the same genealogy in a book. The list is not simply a text, but a display or performance; writ large it becomes a declaration, an announcement, an advertisement or a sign. Printed transcripts of Tainui genealogies remain available in many books and in libraries, but McCahon's painting is now thought to be so contentious as to be 'virtually unexhibitable'.[11]

If one accepts that the painting of names or culturally-specific motifs entails artistic appropriation, it is hardly surprising to find art works of this kind censured by critics conscious of cultural property. But what the 'appropriation' does is to deny the premise of settler culture (that was also, as we have seen, a premise of some of McCahon's own work): it proclaims that the land is not unwritten. To the contrary it is burdened with a history, a history to be evoked not in a single painting but in a succession; in a series of panels that cannot be absorbed in a glance, but instead require a sort of journey through its pauses and stations.

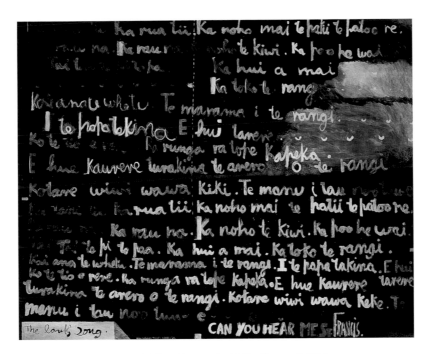

12 COLIN McCAHON The Lark's Song (a poem by Matire Kereama), 1969

Possibly the most complex of McCahon's Maori history paintings is the *Urewera Mural* (1976, fig. 8), a large work commissioned for the visitor centre of the Urewera National Park. As in the earlier north Otago and Canterbury landscapes, there is an emphasis on ridge lines that establish the body and the substance of the land; but in this case, and in contrast to the earlier paintings, that land is replete with inscriptions. Maori histories in the South Island were not well known to Pakeha in the 1960s, but Tuhoe country was famous for the prophets of the late nineteenth and early twentieth centuries, and especially Te Kooti and Rua Kenana. Te Kooti was both a warrior and the founder of the independent Ringatu church. Rua Kenana was a visionary who anticipated the departure of all settlers and the return of the land; the builder of a New Jerusalem on the sacred Tuhoe mountain of Maungapohatu; and an agitator against discriminatory legislation. Both were notable for their efforts to hold fast to land and preserve Maori autonomy after the setbacks of the land wars of 1860s, in a period of depopulation and rapid change. They fashioned not only new religions but a new visual culture that drew upon icons of Pakeha authority such as flags, as well as Christian crosses, stars, and the diamonds and clubs of playing-cards. This syncretic Maori iconography turned colonial artifacts and symbols to new purposes, which often remained obscure and threatening to the missionaries and other colonizers: the rule of their language and law was prejudiced by the prophets' unruly and esoteric appropriations.

A great deal might be said about what these millenarian movements and their leaders attempted and accomplished, but the key point in this context is that they stand not for pre-European Maori tradition, but for a 'tradition' of innovation and resistance. Even if McCahon was drawn to the prophets' spirituality rather than their politics, these dimensions of their practice were so intimately intertwined that any affirmation of one can only be a celebration of both: religious authority and the campaign against colonial encroachment are perforce commemorated together.

The *Urewera Mural* is dominated by the central form of Tane, the god of the forest, here rendered like a vast life-giving tree trunk, in gilt paint with all its unavoidable religiosity. Inscribed equally brightly are the names of the prophets and that of the tribe; the prominence of TUHOE, UREWERA and THE LAND in the lower right-hand portion of the work binds the people and the geography; a multiplicity of other names suggest particular sites, while the names of the sacred mountain and the people are conspicuous to the left. Associated, smaller-scale works make the point still more simply and directly, even if they lack the mural's key location in the National Park, as a kind of caption to the country itself. *A Poster for the Urewera* (1975) carries the text 'Tuhoe are the people/Rua is the prophet'. The bright background colours are luminescent: the presence and power that settler colonialism must deny are categorically reaffirmed, on a 'poster' that disavows its art-status while appealing to the masses who might pass it in the street.

Or so one might have claimed. McCahon's *Urewera Mural* was reappropriated, 'heisted', or 'stolen' from the National Park by, it is alleged, two Tuhoe men, early in 1997. Although police believed that they had quickly identified the perpetrators, they failed to locate or recover the painting for almost eighteen months, during which time there was apparently no demand for any political or financial ransom, though negotiation led to the work's return in August 1998. Interpretations of the motivations for the action were predictably various and irreconcilable. Some claim that the Tuhoe regarded the painting as a valued expression of their own heritage, and that they were pre-empting the proposed relocation of the work out of their tribal land to Te Papa, the new national museum in Wellington. Others (more correctly, as it turns out) suggested that the activists' attitude was more negative, that the action sought to refute McCahon's attempt to depict Tuhoe history and by implication the sovereignty of white art in the representation of New Zealand. One Maori activist allegedly described the mural as 'just another fucking colonial painting'; it was proposed that a work painted by a Tuhoe artist might occupy the space in the visitor centre vacated by the McCahon.

Even if Maori personae, texts and histories become prominent in McCahon's work of the 1970s, for better or worse, there is no simple linear progression and certainly no overt disavowal of the earlier landscapes. A semi-abstract work of 1975 incorporates a stark and empty plain reminiscent of 6 Days and reproduces a text McCahon had inscribed on a waterfall mural of the mid-sixties: 'As there is a constant flow of light we are born into a pure land'. It is the choice of the text that is especially striking: the Edenic associations of an empty, promised, virgin or uncultivated land were continually restated in the settler responses to New Zealand and Australia, as they had earlier been in North America too. Despite one's simultaneous awareness of another people and another culture, the PURE LAND seems burdened neither with other presences nor the history of one's own transactions with them. As there is a constant flow of light... was executed over the same period as the preliminary studies for the Urewera Mural.[12]

What I find intriguing about McCahon amounts to one of the themes for this book: this is his lurching between two attitudes that can at no time be reconciled. These are also reflected in the contention around in his work and in the two readings of the Tuhoe reappropriation. Some earlier and subsequent artists celebrate the settler accomplishment categorically; some take possession of particular tracts of the landscape; some discover a larger affinity and intimate engagement with the whole. Some are preoccupied with issues of form or technique and could be seen to effect these appropriations only implicitly; others are overtly preoccupied with the quest to define their locality and nationality. Some artists, again of both the nineteenth and twentieth centuries, worked toward a local visual idiom through an engagement with indigenous culture rather than the natural landscape. For some, native people amounted to little more than local curiosities or sad relics of an epoch that was necessarily passing, but for others Aboriginal people, Maori and Native Americans were actors with whom they had to reckon. The moral complexities of conflicting claims to the land were made explicit; travel and exchange were fraught.

To put things in these terms is to acknowledge that not one but several related shifts took place: in the work of individuals, among settler artists of the same generation, and over time. Some denied an indigenous presence which others acknowledged, but those who acknowledged that presence did so in different ways. Some framed it nostalgically and sentimentally; some romanticized the colonial endeavour; others acknowledged its imperfections and struggled with the question of dispossession. I do not wish to reduce these complexities to a single model, though I concede that they may amount to much of a muchness for the Maori activist who is simply offended by McCahon, or at any rate by his status. I am interested in drawing attention to a basic, multifaceted ambivalence around the denial and affirmation of the indigenous presence, around the virtue and illegitimacy of colonial settlement, that runs deep. If I am to suggest that this ambivalence is foundational in settler culture, it makes sense to go back to one of its earliest expressions. Let me step backwards to a past that troubles the present in antipodean historical consciousness.

Colonialism

As every Australian child learns at school, Botany Bay was the site proposed by Joseph Banks for the penal colony of New South Wales; but Governor Arthur Philip, on his arrival there in January 1788, found it unsuitable, and investigated the drowned valley to the immediate north, Cook's Port Jackson, that was to become Sydney Harbour. In his *Account of the English Colony in New South Wales*, the most informative of the early accounts from the settlement, David Collins tells us that as Philip's boats proceeded up the coast, they:

> attracted the attention of several parties of the natives…who all greeted them in the same words, and in the same tone of vociferation, shouting every where 'Warra, warra, warra', words which, by the gestures that accompanied them, could not be interpreted into invitations to land, or expressions of welcome. It must however be observed that at Botany Bay the natives had hitherto conducted themselves socially and peaceably toward all the parties of our officers and people with whom they had hitherto met, and by no means seemed to regard them as enemies or invaders of their country and tranquility.*[13]

This is almost Collins' first reference to the Aboriginal people, and it could be seen to inaugurate not only his own discourse but that of white Australia in general. The footnote flagged by the asterisk reads: 'How grateful to every feeling of humanity would it be could we conclude this narrative without being compelled to say that these unoffending people

13 PORT JACKSON PAINTER Three Natives Attacking a Sailor (also known as The Hunted Rushcutter)

had found reason to change both their opinions and their conduct!' It is clear that the Aborigines along the coast had already decided that the British were not to be welcomed; but Collins treats this as an exception to their hitherto peaceable conduct, manifest from such encounters as had taken place around Botany Bay. That sociable disposition stemmed from a sense that the British were neither enemies nor invaders, but the implication in the main text that this generosity was ill-founded is borne out: the Aborigines were soon compelled to regard the colonists as the enemies and invaders they in fact were.

What is striking is this writer's propensity to regard the indigenous people as both essentially benevolent and fatally unknowing, at the same moment as he reports their actual belligerence. This hostility presumably followed from the realization that the British really were a threat; resistance to intrusion was expressed through words and gestures even before the site of settlement was fixed upon.[14] Collins scrupulously reports many subsequent incidents – straying convicts, in particular, were prone to get themselves speared – but never makes resistance a theme. He anguishes rather over the fact that the goodness that Aborigines had manifested was betrayed by the conduct of the white settlers.

Pristine nature was to be similarly ruptured. Ground was cleared around a:

> run of fresh water, which stole silently through a very thick wood, the stillness of which had then, for the first time since the creation, been interrupted by the rude sound of the labourer's axe, and the downfall of its ancient inhabitants; a stillness and tranquility which from that day were to give place to the voice of labour, the confusion of camps and towns, and the busy hum of its new possessors.[15]

The natives, whose suffering of an unjust invasion occasioned a poignant footnote a couple of pages before, are now forgotten, or rather erased. Collins elsewhere illustrated and wrote of 'the Mo-go, or stone-hatchet' that had 'an edge fine enough to divide the bark of such trees as they take their canoes or hunters' huts from, and even the shields which are cut from the body of the tree itself;'[16] but these axes and the labour of their use are suddenly silenced in the primordial tranquility of a forest. 'Stillness' was subsequently taken to be a quintessential feature of the Australian bush, and might be seen as a trans-Tasman antecedent of the silence and vacancy that later haunted McCahon and many other cultural commentators on the New Zealand landscape. If, in 1788, Sydney Cove really was quiet, that would have been so because it had been evacuated by Aborigines who were avoiding the immediate vicinity of the settlement. But the native landowners in fact frequently made their presence felt. In September, 1788, Collins reported that 'The natives continued to molest our people whenever they chanced to meet any of them straggling and unarmed'[17] and his two volumes are replete with particular cases of convicts being killed, beaten, stripped or harassed, in some cases in direct reprisal for the theft of Aboriginal artifacts; crew on the vessels returning home sought profit from these implements as curiosities.

Despite all this it was evidently important to understand the ground of the colony as a virgin tract. What is interesting are not the pretty obvious associations between colonization and sexual conquest, but the understanding of the enterprise as one that has a kind of pure beginning. Collins evokes this origin, only to acknowledge its illusory character.

> That these ['new possessors'] did not bring with them, 'Minds not be be changed by time or place,' [sic] was fervently to have been wished; and if it were possible, that on taking possession of Nature, as we had thus done, in her simplest, purest garb, we might not sully that purity by the introduction of vice, profaneness, and

14 PORT JACKSON PAINTER
Balloderree

immorality. But this, though much to be wished, was little to be expected; the habits of youth are not easily laid aside, and the utmost we could hope in our present situation was to oppose the soft harmonising arts of peace and civilisation to the baneful influence of vice and immorality.[18]

While acknowledging and regretting that the settlers were invaders of the Aborigines' 'country and tranquility', Collins advertised in his preface the benefits that ought to follow from Governor Hunter's just administration. His 'well-known humanity' would induce the 'savage islander' 'to participate in the enjoyments of civilized society; and instruct him to appreciate justly the blessings of rational freedom.'[19] The approbation of authority is typical of eighteenth-century prefaces, and certainly conventional enough to be parodied. And it is hard to see that Collins was not being ironical in suggesting that Aborigines might acquire some sense of 'rational freedom', confronted as they were by a penal colony in which convicts were often fettered, and were uneasily controlled by men themselves subject to military discipline. The anxiety of the colony's rulers to familiarize Aborigines with their civility, to create channels of intercourse with them, led them to kidnap a few individual natives, who were then also chained up, though not always securely enough to prevent them running away. A satirical performance intended to show up 'the blessings of rational freedom' could hardly have featured grosser contrasts.

What is foundational in Collins' account, then, is a set of confusions. These confusions were not haphazard or accidental, but were inherent in the contradiction between the practical character of this particular colonial endeavour and the moral imperatives it carried; the sheer conflict between circumstance and rhetoric. In principle, Aborigines were savages, yet as individuals they might be recognized as dignified and estimable people. On the one hand an Aboriginal presence was real, and it had to be reckoned with; on the other hand, it had to be imagined away. It was plainly appreciated in principle that the settlers were in a direct contest with another people, whose land was being invaded. That general condition was persistently manifested in violent acts and in words such as 'warra, warra, warra', whose overall intent was clear, as their particular meanings, like those of the local languages and cultures in general, were mostly obscure. Conflict was continually experienced yet, it would seem, denied; the reality of Aboriginal resistance was in rhetoric eclipsed by a sort of innocence whose violation occasioned settler guilt.

I too lived at Berowra (Et in Arcadia ego)

When I was a teenager, in the mid-1970s, my parents had a weekender on Berowra Creek, a tributary estuary of the Hawkesbury River, north of Sydney. Although there were perhaps fifty houses in the area along the shore from a car ferry and teashop, most were accessible only by boat, and further development was restricted by national park regulations. Although this was also the site of one of Sydney's elite restaurants, and thus hardly in the wilderness, one had only to travel for an hour or so in a rowboat or canoe to sense that one had been disproportionately removed from civilization into a domain of absolute tranquility. In the narrow tidal creeks off the broad estuary, the wilderness was at once originary and vibrantly present; in the heat of summer, particularly, the cicadas were deafening, the perspiring eucalypts screened even nearby ridges with a blue haze that shimmered palpably, the tides were fast and audible, the sandbanks shifted, and the mullet jumped and ran.

The closest of these places, and that which I came to know most intimately, was Calabash Creek. Though the bay itself was pretty well frequented by people fishing, once you were a few hundred yards up one of the several creeks that led sinuously into the mangroves, you had the

15 MARGARET PRESTON Calabash Bay, Hawkesbury, c. 1939

sense that the place belonged to you alone. I only discovered later that the locality featured in some widely reproduced works by Margaret Preston, who entitled another work *I Lived at Berowra*. At the time I was not interested in how the place might be represented but simply in being there: in fishing for mudcrabs, in scrambling up the waterfalls around steep-sided gullies, in following the ledges of Hawkesbury sandstone that were burnt orange beneath weathered overhangs and mottled with lichen and native orchids above. Never turning into true caves, breaking slopes rather than forming high cliffs, the lines of rock shelters and bluffs followed the contour produced by the harder layers in the horizontal sedimentary strata; on the exposed slopes the scrub could be severe, dry and spiky, though the gullies were moist and heavily shaded. This was the area I first camped alone, where I acquired a sense of autonomy.

At the same time I became interested in conservation, and joined a bushwalking club that took me elsewhere – to places that really were isolated, in the Blue Mountains and the Colo wilderness, to the west and northwest of Sydney, and in various areas further afield. Through this experience I became more deeply attached to Calabash Creek in particular and to the eastern Australian bush in general. Walking often, you got to know certain mountains well; not only the steeper and gentler phases of the ascent, but the form of a cluster of ridges seen from a distance, and the different appearances from a variety of vantage points. One of those that always stood out was Pigeonhouse, in the Budawang ranges close to the coast, a few hundred kilometres south of Sydney. This conical mountain, solidly green save around its sandstone summit, was visible from the sea, and was one of many coastal features that had been named by Cook in 1770. I had been subjected to rather too much of Captain James Cook at school to want to know more about his exploits, but did become curious about a later phase of the history of white engagements with these tracts of bush.

In the State Library of New South Wales, then as now a haven for all manner of eccentrics and homeless people as well as scholars, I began a sort of undirected research, through old magazines and newspapers, into the origins of the walking clubs. This was also the prehistory of Australian environmentalism, and very much part of the history of Australian art: bushwalking began with the plein-air sketching parties led by people such as Frederick Eccleston DuFaur in the 1870s, who also campaigned for the declaration of nature reserves.[20] Kuringai Chase, around the estuary adjacent to Berowra Creek, was among the earliest, but the National Park (gazetted 1887), immediately to Sydney's south, had been the second in the world after Yellowstone (1872). It was a small source of pride to Australian conservationists, I think, that on this point the marginal antipodean nation might be almost first rather than last, though the later change of name to the Royal National Park testified to the persisting power of the imperial connection. I was hardly theorizing the issues at the time, but questions of what was national and what was colonial, of affection for the land, of biography, art and attitudes to nature, were emerging and interweaving.

Conservation issues were frequently debated during meetings of the bushwalking club to which I belonged, and the National Parks and Wildlife Service was jocularly known as 'the Enemy', because its management of public access to wilderness areas entailed, from our perspective, unacceptable compromises. On at least one occasion I recall the Service being censured for installing pit toilets and concrete barbecues around a camping ground, but our concern to defend nature's purity extended well beyond such blatant intrusions of urban comfort and artifice. During one walk through a rugged, trackless area in the central Blue Mountains, my companions destroyed a number of stone cairns erected by earlier walkers to mark ridge junctions. Though few in number, and consisting only of piles of rocks a foot or so in height, these navigational aids were, we felt, gratuitous; they were required only by persons insufficiently experienced to walk in the area. Perhaps mistaken for a leisure pursuit, bushwalking was as professionalized as many an academic discipline, and its terrain as insistently and jealously defended.

The attachment we felt to the bush was of course wholly unlike that of someone whose life was deeply invested in the land. The specific value that the country possessed was not connected with its centrality for one's subsistence, but founded rather in its absolute dissociation from production. The experience of the bush was the opportunity, as the tourist cliché put it, to get away from it all, to sever oneself from what otherwise constituted one's life; and this severance could only be properly effected if the land was severed not only from one's own, but from everyone else's lives. Though we certainly revisited places, and wove experiences around them into memories, our lives were in no sense dug into and in turn yielded up by the soil; nor were our persons in any sense exemplifications of beings that were animated within the land, ancestors or creators who had left their traces in landforms such as monoliths and waterholes. If one's self was there at all, it shimmered for a moment on the country's surface, a Calabash Creek instant that was all too transient. Attachment depended not an intimate relation with the land but on our radical distance, our alienation.

These interests in the bush led me into one of the best courses I took as an undergraduate, not in a subject that I later specialized in, but in biogeography and geomorphology. This deepened my sense of landscape as a historical effect – as the product of successive phases of global cooling and warming, of changing temperature regimes and sea levels, and simultaneously of more local and recent developments. What was exciting about this was the mutual interaction of longer-term processes and histories that were immediate and tangible, and were taking place within one's own life cycle; as temperatures oscillated, patches of subalpine forest could be seen to expand and die back from year to year. Most importantly, though, in Australia as elsewhere, the longer history was not simply a natural history but also a human one. I learned not only the word anthropogenic, but the fact that the eucalypt forest of the southeast, which I had enjoyed so extensively and thought I knew so intimately, was to some extent the product of millennia of Aboriginal burning. For as long as people had lived in the country, fires had been casually but deliberately lit – presumably to flush out prey, to promote regrowth and new shoots that attracted game, to make signals, to make the bush easier to walk through, and no doubt for other purposes. What we had defined on the basis of the apparent absence of human intention

**16 Engraved human figures on rock,
West Head, Lambert Peninsula, Sydney**

was in fact an artifact – not the product of a calculated effort of management, to be sure, but an environment pervasively altered.[21]

The conservationist attitude – its yearning, its integrity – thus partook of the dispossession I've identified in some of McCahon's work. We always should have known better: the grooves in the exposed sandstone platforms beside creeks were produced by the sharpening of basalt axes (a stone that in many cases could only have been traded in from beyond tribal boundaries), while carvings were faintly outlined on platforms of the same sandstone. Whales, fish, and hybrid creatures that we presumed were totemic, could be discerned; there too were human figures whose explicitly marked sex seemed to attest to prior acts of love in this landscape – or at least were sufficient to embarrass the teachers in charge of teenagers on school excursions.

The understanding of the way in which Aborigines could be seen not only as former and perhaps still rightful owners of the land, but also as its authors, both reinforced and undid an endorsement of indigenous claims. A common attitude that seems to support indigenous peoples is animated by comparisons between white Western modernity and the spiritual authenticity of tribal cultures. Upholding societies closer to nature in order to denigrate technology and overdevelopment has, of course, been a discontented Western rhetoric since Montaigne if not Herodotus. The most conspicuous difference between primitivists today and their antecedents such as Tacitus, Rousseau and Diderot is that the latter understood that they were playing with rhetorical types, while many of the New Age adherents I have met take them absolutely literally. Aboriginal people can therefore be caught out if it is revealed that they too transformed or depleted their environments, even if they did not, like the Polynesian inhabitants of Easter Island, actually impoverish them to a point of crisis. Never mind the fact that the modifications to the fauna, the species lost, were minuscule in comparison with the changes produced in the first couple of decades, let alone the whole history of European pastoral settlement; the problem is that Aborigines and indigenous peoples generally cannot be mystical if they have histories. The look of the bush told us that they did have histories that were eclipsed – concealed *partially* and *temporarily* – by our own, both by the national narratives of white settlers, and by the personal narratives of white individuals; though knowing that those histories were there did not, of course, tell us what their forms or plots were.

Impacts and accommodations

Collins' lament for the disruption of indigenous society was an early articulation of the idea of 'fatal impact'. The notion that indigenous peoples (or colonized peoples in general) were tragic victims of imperialism has a long and varied history. Though sometimes announced triumphally, by those assured that white civilization ought to spread, and that the unfit would die out, the idea is more often associated with a Western critique of colonialism, or an 'imperialist nostalgia' that regrets the passing of the cultures and the peoples it is in the process of invading.[22]

In the Pacific, the fullest account of the colonialist destruction is Alan Moorehead's book, *The Fatal Impact*, that appeared first in 1966 and has been reprinted frequently since, much to the irritation of scholars of the Pacific who have laboured to establish the complexities of processes that Moorehead described in a compelling but broad-brush fashion. While the continuing popularity of the book obviously owes a good deal to the kind of writer Moorehead was, it also suggests that the public are not really interested in a more nuanced view of Pacific history, that would present colonial intrusions as typically hesitant and contentious, and often effectively resisted, accommodated or domesticated,

rather than disrupting a paradise and sweeping all before them. While historians of many regions have sought to qualify exaggerated views of the colonial impact, popular perceptions for North America and other regions seem doggedly attached to a 'fatal impact' scenario.

Moorehead's sense of Tahiti as a primitive, sexually liberated Arcadia destroyed by missionary intervention built upon earlier romanticizations such as that of Pierre Loti and Gauguin, and *The Fatal Impact* made Gauguin's *Nevermore* emblematic of the melancholy situation of the Polynesians:

> she lies inert and naked on her bed, and Gauguin painted her waiting for nothing, hoping for nothing, the petals of the tiare tahiti scattered about her, a dark conspiratorial couple in the background and all around them the mystical shapes and symbols of the tropics. On this canvas the painter has written in English the one word 'Nevermore'.[23]

This conclusion was so fitting and resonant that a more recent writer could not resist reproducing it:

> looking down on her from the walls are all the mystical creatures and symbols of a tropical paradise once familiar but now forever lost. On the back of his canvas Gauguin wrote in English one word – 'Nevermore'.[24]

Gauguin's title was in fact derived from Edgar Allan Poe's poem, *The Raven*, in which 'Nevermore' is the bird's refrain. Like the shrouded figures in the background, it is an obscure portent, or perhaps a direct reference to the recent death of the infant daughter of Gauguin and Pau'ura, the woman depicted. Certainly the painting's singularly sombre tone – which is not characteristic of Gauguin's Polynesian work – may be best explained by this circumstance. *Nevermore* was not a comment on the state of the Polynesian race. Although Gauguin has been represented as a colonialist voyeur, his corpus in fact displays much engagement with the novel forms of syncretic Tahitian culture that had emerged with Christianity and colonization, in the domain of dress, for instance.[25] While many writers have poured scorn on modern Tahitian garments, taking the introduced 'Mother Hubbard' dresses to manifest the stifling effect of missionaries upon indigenous sexual licence, Gauguin recognized that Tahitian women had made these garments their own, and in portraits such as *Vahine no te Tiare*, he presents them wearing them with great dignity.

17 PAUL GAUGUIN
Nevermore, O Taiti, 1897

18 PAUL GAUGUIN
Vahine no te Tiare
(Woman with a Flower), 1891

This is not the place for a reassessment of Gauguin. My point is simply that the 'fatal impact' interpretation of *Nevermore* is hyperbolic and gratuitous, and that its inappropriateness reflects the wider nonsense of the fatal impact thesis. Certainly Polynesian cultures had been affected by disease and had lost their political autonomy. But the suggestion that indigenous life had degenerated into fatalistic lassitude is a myth, and can be refuted by works of indigenous art contemporaneous with Gauguin's Polynesian paintings.

The carvings of Tene Waitere, an important Ngati Tarawhai sculptor from the Rotorua area near the centre of New Zealand's North Island, are the products of a colonial situation but not of a dying culture. Ngati Tarawhai, of the Te Arawa tribe, had long been renowned producers of carvings for canoes and chiefs' houses, working on commission for local and more distant Maori clients. In the latter part of the nineteenth century and during the twentieth, they continued to provide houses and other pieces for Maori communities, including memorials for soldiers killed in the world wars. After the Maori-Pakeha wars of the 1860s, however, they also increasingly supplied tourists and the Rotorua tourist industry.

19 Tene Waitere at work

With Christmas Greetings.

F. T. SERIES. No. 464. A HAKA FOR A PENNY, ROTORUA.   Photo by N. Z. Tourist, Dept.

20 A Haka for a Penny, postcard from Rotorua, New Zealand

Visitors were initially attracted to the area by the hot springs and associated geothermal phenomena, such as the siliceous pink and white terraces at Rotomahana that were destroyed by the eruption of Tarawera in 1886. Maori culture soon featured among the attractions of the place, not least because the manager of the new Geyser Hotel, C.E. Nelson, was something of a Maori folklore and art enthusiast. From 1892 he employed Tene Waitere, already an established carver, to produce large pieces for the hotel and surrounding areas, and smaller articles such as bowls, pipes, walking sticks and replicas for sale to visitors. During this period Waitere also carved the deservedly famous relief panel featuring male and female tattoos on three heads (fig. 9) for the ethnologist Augustus Hamilton, and worked with Anaha Te Rahui and Neke Kapua on the Rauru meeting house, substantially carved over 1897 to 1899. While earlier houses featured the ancestors of the chief or local group who commissioned them, the carvings in the Rauru house were of founding deities of pan-Maori significance, such as Maui, whose exploits were already well-known to interested Pakeha through published anthologies of myth and 'Maori lore'. The ethnologist Roger Neich suggests that the carvings were probably used as points of reference in guides' talks; tourists would also have witnessed dances and chants, and perhaps paid children to do an abbreviated version of the war dance, 'a haka for a penny'.[26]

Rauru, opened in 1900, was sold to the Hamburg Museum in 1904, where it remains. The New Zealand government's failure to purchase the house was lamented as early as 1905, when it was described in an Australian journal as 'one of the most perfect [carved houses] existing' and 'a great example of comparatively modern work.'[27] The figures are indeed remarkable for their naturalistic elements, their experimentation with profile, and their overall vigour. Waitere and others produced many further houses and replicas on commission for Europeans, including a model village for Whakarewarewa (Rotorua) and the Christchurch International Exposition of 1906.

It is the sheer quality and power of much of this work that belies the fatal impact idea. This not to say that Maori had not suffered as a result of colonization (though Ngati Tarawhai fought on the European side during the wars of the 1860s). Many of the carvers had to struggle to establish their land claims during the 1870s, and the scant evidence suggests they received meagre remuneration for their work for Nelson and others. Yet just as Maori remote from colonial development retained autonomy, the business of tourism left a space for the perpetuation and elaboration of Maori culture. It in fact stimulated and required such expression, not only on the part of carvers, but from other performers and guides. No doubt, had these people been expressing themselves exclusively for visitors, or on demand for patronising colonial ethnologists, their creativity would have become routinized and shallow. It did not, because there was also continuing demand from their own communities; what was being produced still had life and salience in the indigenous domain. In this sense, settler colonialism was a contradictory effort: over a period of actual invasion and dispossession, it proceeded through savagery and terrorism; at other times, indigenous culture could be positively invoked, staged and stimulated.

Exchange and antagonism

The preceding cases prefigure strands of an argument that are recurrent and intertwined throughout this book. The chapters that follow are organized roughly chronologically, and do not jump back and forth as this one has. At the risk of reproducing rather than representing the confusions of historical consciousness typical of settler societies, I have tried to evoke the presence of the past in the present, and the recurring character of the settler-indigenous contradiction. The time of this book is not really linear history, but a sort of sorcery-history,[28] marked by dramatic connections between the present and foundational moments in the past. The complex social relations of the modern nation can at times seem to collapse into the simple binary ones of the moment of colonization, which may be celebrated and lamented alternately and even simultaneously.

The discussion of McCahon sketched out an attitude we might adopt in coming to terms with the heroes of white settler art. Not just the intentions of those artists, but the ways in which their works have been appreciated and canonized might be approached with suspicion. To what extent are the multiple claims upon the land presented or obscured in work that overtly aims to provide a new nation with a visual high culture? Suspicion, importantly, is not condemnation. Nothing would be gained if we were to begin by assuming that white art was merely an instrument of domination, a uniform ideological apparatus that sustained colonialism's material appropriations. Art is not an instrument but an arena – one in which art works, critical discourse, institutions and markets are often uncomfortable with each other's claims. The nationalist rhetoric around a body of painting may not be sustained by the work itself. The work of McCahon, and many others, is contradictory on questions that are fundamental for the formation of settler nationality. Is the land new or old? Is it peopled or empty? David Collins' confusions attest to the depth of this fissure in settler consciousness. His account arguably inaugurates a tradition of guilty moralizing that remains alive in the present.

If settler painting often declares attachments to place, what of indigenous people and their claims? The Ngati Tarawhai carvers worked well before most of the indigenous artists I discuss, but the complexities of their situation anticipate those of more recent cultural processes. Settler societies have used native cultures, generally with some awkwardness, to express vicariously their own, colonial attachments to place. They have marketed native cultures to tourists, and constrained and degraded their art forms in various ways. Yet these uses have perforce drawn attention to the presence of indigenous people and stimulated interest in their cultures. That interest has taken many forms, some patronizing, others scientific and objectifying, but it has also led toward a deeper engagement with indigenous perspectives and political claims. That deeper engagement, in turn, can only undermine or compromise settler identities and nationhood. I do not say that colonialism has been a two-way street if that implies a zone of reciprocal flows and equal exchange. But the metaphor is not so bad if we imagine unruly drivers, self-defeating manoeuvres, and energetic collisions. For colonialism has been, above all, a theatre of contradiction; it has been both destructive and fertile, both violent and creative.

21 EUGEN VON GUERARD Aborigines Met on the Road to the Diggings, 1854

In the first few days of February 1995 I was walking through the rooms of colonial painting in the National Gallery of Victoria in Melbourne, and stopped before Nicholas Chevalier's *Buffalo Ranges* (1864) just as a group of chattering teenagers arrived and began to seat themselves awkwardly, cross-legged on the floor. High schools must have just gone back after the Australian summer break, so I imagine that this excursion was some kind of introduction to their whole course. Their teacher, a red-faced, slightly overweight man of about my own age, stood proprietorially next to the painting, waiting for them to stop fidgeting, as teachers must, and then launched into a commentary that was not at all along the lines I was expecting.

'The important thing to ask about art history,' he said, 'is: *who wrote it?* In Australia art has been written about mostly by *white, middle-class men.* They tell it the way they see it – which of course isn't the way other people might see it. If it had been written by women or Aborigines, art history would be very different, wouldn't it?' He proceeded to explain that *The Buffalo Ranges* was one of the most popular paintings in the institution: people loved it because it seemed so true to the rugged grandeur of the southeastern Australian high country, and the romance of early pioneering. Well, if that's how they saw it, they'd been fooled. He attempted, without much success, to elicit his pupils' responses to the work, and went on himself to scornfully itemize misrepresentations at the level of detail: the hut's fence belonged more to an English country cottage than the bush, a cart of that type would never have been drawn by more than two bullocks, the mill had no apparent use, and so on. Having established to his satisfaction that the painting lacked authenticity, insofar as it purported to depict a scene of early settlement in the area, he stepped back, shook his head and observed contemptuously but almost regretfully, 'what a wanker!'

I should not have been as surprised as I was by this performance. Secondary school teachers are as likely to invert as reproduce the 'official' narratives of national history and culture, in which a painting of this kind, and the progress of white settlement in general, are normally celebrated.

What has become official in Australia, in fact, is precisely such ambivalence; everyone from senior government figures to museum curators and teachers will lament the history of colonization at one moment and go back to celebrating the pioneer spirit at the next. I was, however, taken aback. If the teacher was trotting out not only clichés but falsities (Australian art history has not been written mainly by middle-class men), he was also enunciating premises that were, at some general level, not that different from my own. Art histories are never innocent of wider politicized ideas concerning the constitution of society and cultural development. And of course paintings demand scrutiny; landscapes are indeed frequently illuminated by consideration of what they distort or disguise as well as what they reveal of rural development and social relations. Yet I was not sympathetic to the demystification that I'd witnessed. We have become too accustomed to the truism that the perspectives of women, blacks, migrants and others are marginalized, as if they are all somehow devalued in a similar way for similar reasons. We may suppose that something is gained by lambasting expressions of the dominant culture that have for too long been uncritically celebrated, but perhaps such assaults do not so much empower those whose stories have been left out as deprive anyone and everyone of the opportunity to understand the enduring appeal of the works in question.

It was the very antagonism of the commentary that was telling. The speaker was reacting against the popularity of the work, and the vigour of his effort to subtract value from a renowned painting seemed commensurate with the power of canonized artifacts in a public institution. More generally, he responded to the prestige and centrality of landscape in nineteenth-century Australian art, which extends into the present in both New Zealand and Australia. Many major and an enormous number of minor artists have continued to image the mountains, the outback, the pioneers and the sunlight and heat that is taken to be quintessentially antipodean, while earlier work in the genre remains very popular, not least as cards, posters and calendars for living rooms.

Yet this power is as uncertain as it is considerable, in part because Chevalier, his contemporaries and more recent artists can only be said to work within a single genre according to the baldest classification: there are obvious differences between a view of a farm, a rugged panorama and a more intimate image of a river or of coastal scenery. Not only are these subjects essentially unlike, but the immediate intention in one case may be to celebrate the possession of a particular estate, and in others to convey the specific character of the vegetation, or evoke more generalized affinities between people and place. It would, however, be going

22 NICHOLAS CHEVALIER The Buffalo Ranges, 1864

too far to insist that Western landscape art possesses no general values, that there can be no general theory about it. Despite their heterogeneity, European and colonial settler landscape conventions mostly bear claims about property, or about cultural affinities between people of certain nations or classes and tracts or types of countryside. There may be exceptions to this rule, such as the romantic landscapes in which the awesome might of nature seems to belittle any issue of human possession, but landscape painting must be the form of settler visual culture that relates most directly to the practical struggle of colonization, which is, first and foremost, about the occupation of the land and attachment to country.[1]

The interpretation of landscape is moreover vital to any cross-cultural art history, because the assertions concerning attachment and belonging that may be overt or implicit in sketches, paintings and prints are not always simple statements about who owns what. They often also depict or foreshadow change. This may be valued positively as progress, negatively as dispossession or environmental carnage, and perhaps even ambivalently as all of these. Landscape paintings are therefore often also history paintings, in the sense that they imply stories and destinies that are moralized and exemplary. In the colonial world, this is most true in North America, where the primeval vastness of land coalesced with the future prospects of the settler nation. The romantic vision of US landscape artist Thomas Cole, for example, with its fusion of the cyclical growth and decline of civilization with sublime landscape, had no direct counterpart in antipodean painting, but related preoccupations were consistently expressed, if typically in less aggrandized terms.

This chapter is concerned with the ways indigenous presences have been acknowledged and denied in landscape imagery, and with how settlers evoked their own attachment to land, especially in a generalized national sense. What is important is not simply the content of particular works, but those works' careers in collections, reproductions and popular responses. It emerges that while some artists have engaged with the settler-indigenous relation in all its problematic complexity, the images that have been most celebrated either relegate indigenous people to a picturesque folkloric status, or – more commonly – fail to represent them at all.

Tabooed ground: Augustus Earle

Among colonial artists, Augustus Earle (1793–1838) is exceptional for the reflexivity of his work, which often emphasizes the presence of the traveller (the artist himself) and his party, and the contingent awkwardness of travel, as much as the landscapes seen and the people encountered.[2] Earle's art is not well known outside Australia and New Zealand, but is appealing now for the occasional irony of its vision, and the fact that it neither sentimentalizes nor bestializes non-European people. He was not alone in being ethnographically curious, nor in producing a great deal of work that documented indigenous culture, but his visual images and written commentary are unusual in the degree to which they are engaged rather than distancing. George French Angas, who similarly worked in both New Zealand and Australia (as well as in South Africa and elsewhere), depicted Maori carvings and Maori people more extensively and minutely than Earle, but was dismissive of the Maori notions of *tapu* or taboo, that for him merely exemplified the superstition to which one might expect such people to be captive.[3] Earle, on the other hand, did not understate or familiarize the exotic subjects he encountered, but was instead inclined to highlight their strangeness, commenting on their barbarity at one moment, and celebrating or attempting to rationalize them at the next. Taboo, for instance, is barbaric when an unwitting violator is summarily clubbed, yet also a sensible way of ensuring agricultural production when access to the ground upon which plants are growing is forbidden.

In the account he wrote of his nine months with Maori in 1827, Earle expressed his horror of cannibalism and an indigenous system of slavery on a number of occasions, but also frequently alluded to the 'taste and ingenuity' of Maori carving and tattooing: 'it was most gratifying to behold the respect these savages pay to the fine arts.'[4] His qualified but high regard for the people echoes Cook voyagers' responses to some Polynesians, and what was common enough in his own time: classical parallels were not simply invoked at the moment of literary composition, but had allegedly struck writers as they perceived islanders. Encountering a chief and his party on one occasion, Earle reported that the group had 'almost seemed to realize some of the passages of Homer, where he describes the wanderer Ulysses and his gallant band of warriors.'[5] Conventional remarks of this kind assimilate the people mentioned to a generic antique nobility, but Earle was really more interested in the singularity of Maori culture, which at this time was yet to suffer from any significant settler depredations. He was struck, for instance, by the wildness of their dance, in which both men and women participated, and which reached a pitch of frenzy that inspired horror in the viewer.

If Earle was inclined to witness a cultural spectacle and allow himself to be astonished by it, that tendency to acquiesce before circumstances rather than assert some kind of judgmental authority emerges also in his landscapes. In the *Distant View of the Bay of Islands* (1827, fig. 10) he seems to acquiesce in the fact that he is in another people's land. He does not simply present a view, abstracted from the circumstances of travel, nor does he present himself as the discoverer of a previously unknown place, surveying the country from a commanding vantage point. The subject of the work is really not so much the view as the group in the act of viewing. In fact, only Earle must pause to look, because the place that is new to him is not new to his companions, though the man before him also surveys the country as he walks. The artist is central in his watercolour, predictably and yet also paradoxically, since the social distinction between himself, the sole European, and his indigenous fellow-travellers is no more consequential than the hierarchy evident among the Maori. Four are porters, while the man before Earle is clearly a warrior of stature, and the authoritative figure in the party.

Even if this is merely a gesture towards a depiction of the particular relations that constitute Maori society, it does imply (rightly) that indigenous life persists in its complexity and autonomy. Its internal order remains as significant as its relation with foreigners, and at least the moment of European contact made visible here does not so much compromise as exhibit the degree to which Maori remain sovereign in their own land. 'We had travelled all day,' Earle wrote of this journey, 'through a country in which every object we saw was of a character that reminded us forcibly of the savage community we were with…sometimes we beheld an uncouthly carved figure, daubed over with red ochre, and fixed in the ground, to give notice that one side of the road was tabooed.'[6] In all likelihood, such a carving would have represented an individual ancestor, and have conveyed a particular narrative and claim to the land connected with that person's *mana* (or spiritual power) and genealogy, but Earle's simplification, by reducing the object to a sign, heightens rather than diminishes its exotic and mystical power. Maori are not simply the owners of territory which Europeans were just beginning to settle; the geography in general is formed and demarcated according to their religious notions and their art forms, exemplified by this carving that connotes both the law and the violence of *tapu*.[7]

I am not suggesting that Earle is deliberately or polemically asserting the rights of natives; it is rather that in this particular place, in 1827, the question of whose land it was hardly arose. Perhaps the fact that Maori were hosts and the artist was a guest was simply a circumstance of his visit, as it seems in a number of other views;[8] though in retrospect at least it becomes notable that he chose to make the fact so explicit, and it is a fact that might have been contextualized in a number of ways. Immediately after the passage I've quoted, Earle notes that 'An extraordinary contrast was now presented to our view, for we came suddenly in front of a complete little English cottage.'[9] This is a missionary settlement, and anyone familiar with travel writing of the period will anticipate a nice little disquisition on savagism versus civility, strikingly illustrated by the contrast between the grim darkness of the heathen villages and the neat cheerfulness of the Christian gardens and dwellings.

Earle, mindful of the genre and that expectation, taunts his reader by recounting the cold reception provided by the missionaries, and goes so far as to suggest that 'there was no touch of human sympathy' – a fairly radical observation, given that such insensibility was repeatedly cited in commentary on the cruelty of native heathens. He subsequently found other evangelists equally unwelcoming, and noted after one visit that on his party's return to their 'savage friends' the welcome 'formed a strange contrast to that of their Christian teachers, whose inhospitable dwellings we determined never to re-enter.'[10] This may best be regarded as mischief ('sweeping sarcasms on the English missionaries', for one reviewer),[11] but it is significant for its refusal to recognize generalized spiritual reform and progress toward civilization in New Zealand. Despite Earle's emphasis upon the barbaric quality of certain Maori customs, he does not see Maori society as categorically savage, and does not endorse an effort to transform and uplift it. Nor does he regard the missionary activity that had proceeded to that point as even remotely promising. The social conditions depicted in the *Distant View of the Bay of Islands* are the way things are, not the 'before' of the 'before-and-after' story otherwise fundamental in evangelical and colonial historical imaginings, which conflated past and future with darkness and light.

This is not to suggest that Earle was opposed to settlement or change in New Zealand. He was, in fact, keenly interested in the scope for 'improvement', and anticipated a kind of colonization in which Maori would be 'hardy and willing assistants, and very different from the natives of New South Wales.'[12] This was to say a good deal, given the extent to which 'improvement' was a key term in the lexicon of progress of the period, in both Europe and the colonial world.[13] What made the difference between prospective junior partners and the indigenous Australians, who would be unavoidably dispossessed, was no doubt the prior evidence for Maori industriousness, particularly in the field of agriculture. Earle's sense was that in 'every part' of the country 'which the natives have cultivated, the produce has been immense.'[14] If this investment of labour gave Maori some right to continue occupying the land, it is not clear why they would need to become mere 'assistants' in a process of development. But Earle's sense of an appropriate social relationship between future settlers and indigenous people can only be guessed at: at the time of his visit, there were probably fewer than three hundred white people in the whole of New Zealand, and serious colonization was more a hypothetical possibility than a definite prospect. It was only in the decade after his death in 1838 that the numbers of settlers escalated, after the Treaty of Waitangi had been signed (6 February 1840), entailing New Zealand's annexation by the Crown.[15]

What is significant about Earle's *Distant View* is not that it depicts indigenous people as the occupiers of their own land: many paintings and prints from both Australia and New Zealand show Aboriginal people or Maori engaged in subsistence or ceremonial activities. But those images were generally patently romanticized and unhistorical. They evoked an idyllic pre-contact pattern of life, abstracted from the circumstances of contact and intrusion that made European depiction possible. When interactions with Europeans were depicted, natives were shown as belligerent and therefore categorically savage; where native people were presented in colonial contexts, they were often already impoverished and degenerate – which is how Earle showed Aboriginal people in Sydney, emphasizing the corrosive effects of alcohol and dependence.[16] *Distant View* is unusual for the presentation of a peaceful encounter in which Maori figure definitely as masters, not of some limited or immediate area, but of a whole landscape.

The difference between Earle's handling of the indigenous presences near the Bay of Islands and in Sydney reflects the fact that indigenous Australians around the Port Jackson settlement had, by this time, suffered some forty years of invasion. He did not make them look like masters of their land because they no longer were. When Earle was painting indigenous Australians outside this intensively settled area, he did not refrain from presenting them as guides, but made this visual statement less forcefully and less consistently than in his New Zealand works: the kind of guiding and hosting that his Aboriginal figures do is less authoritative than that of the Maori chief in the *Distant View*. The latter's sovereignty is manifest; that of the Australians is not.

A well-known oil by Earle incorporated the Blue Mountains scenery not far inland from Sydney that was to become inexhaustibly popular among subsequent painters. *Bougainville Falls, Prince Regent's Glen* (c. 1838) lacks the solemnity and the imposing presence of the *tapu* 'marker' of the *Distant View*, but reiterates the theme of the dependence of white visitors, who are here in almost comic difficulty, upon indigenous guides. The artist himself seems to be ignoring his companions and the scenery while sketching one of the Aboriginal men, who poses as though in noble isolation. This could be seen to put a frame around the business of indigenous portraiture, implying a mismatch between the artist's idealizing work and the circumstances of the journey, and a further discrepancy between sublime topography and the clumsy business of getting around and over it. If there is self-mockery here it is admittedly restrained, but this remains a more provoking work than any other nineteenth-century Blue Mountains landscape, or indeed virtually any Australian mountain landscape of the period. There are certainly later paintings that are aesthetically more impressive, by Conrad Martens, Chevalier or W.C. Piguenit, but few that display anything like this reflexive intelligence; artists were generally more concerned to reproduce the grandeur of the scenery than describe the social relations among parties of observers.

23 AUGUSTUS EARLE Bougainville Falls, Prince Regent's Glen, c. 1838

The exceptional nature of Earle's treatment of the relations between indigenous peoples and settlers emerges from comparison with better known contemporaries, such as George Catlin in the United States. Catlin, the pre-eminent frontier artist of the period, can be seen to have possessed a committed ethnographic vision, and was moreover a vigorous critic of settler genocide. He produced animated images of native ceremonies, as well as many portraits that are dignifying if also a little rigidifying. Unlike Earle, however, he was preoccupied with the documentation of ways of life and customs that he took to be waning, hence he was concerned with the kind of cultural authenticity that was to become a hallmark of salvage anthropology (and this is also true of Paul Kane, fig. 1, who essentially made it his mission to do for Canada what Catlin had done for the United States).[17] What is striking in Earle and

24 GEORGE CATLIN The Last Race, Part of Okipa Ceremony, 1832

almost wholly absent in Catlin, Kane and most other travel artists of the early to mid-nineteenth century, however, is reflexivity: Earle is present in his work, not simply to provide scale, or to stand in for the spectator, but as party to an encounter. The artist does not provide an authoritative representation of a scene, lifted out of a particular, shared time, but rather exhibits the transactions which enabled the image to be made – that is, the awkwardness of colonial travel. Catlin is represented in some of his own work, notably in the frontispiece to many editions of his *Letters and Notes on the North American Indians*, in which he depicts himself, surrounded by a native audience, in the act of painting a chief.[18] But the point of this illustration is authentication; it in no sense records the contingencies of the artist's observations. Catlin insists that he was there, and that his paintings were executed from life; to reinforce the

25 AUGUSTUS EARLE A Bivouack, Daybreak, on the Illawarra Mountains, 1827

26 AUGUSTUS EARLE A Bivouack of Travellers in Australia in a Cabbage-Tree Forest, Daybreak, c. 1838

point, his introduction is followed by a series of testimonials from government Indian Agents, who certify to the accuracy of his portraits and renderings of costumes and landscapes.

The importance of Catlin's art and his writings emerges from their very considerable circulation. The most remarkable expressions of Earle's vision of antipodean encounters acquired at best a limited presence in the public visual culture of the period. In one watercolour, *A Bivouack, Daybreak on the Illawarra Mountains*, Earle presented a European and an Aboriginal man in a condition of parity. Human sameness is marked in the way the two men face each other and warm their hands before a fire. But Earle rearranged the figures, removing this implication, as the painting was being worked up in oil; and it was, of course, the oil and not the watercolour that was exhibited at the Royal Academy. It's true that three prints out of the set of ten New Zealand lithographs that Earle published in 1838 did illustrate the traveller's reliance upon indigenous hosts and guides, with almost the same emphasis as the *Distant View* and the *Bougainville Falls*, but these probably received rather less circulation than the handful of illustrations in the 1832 *Narrative*. In that book, the description of the walk to the Bay of Islands is not accompanied by a print after the *Distant View*, despite the direct connection between the text and that image, but only by a plate of the carving in isolation. Reduced to a curiosity, the object no longer binds land and indigenous culture, and ceases to impose a prohibition that visitor and native alike are compelled to respect. Like most of the rest of Earle's original work, both the watercolour and *Bougainville Falls* remained with his descendants until the 1920s, and were not exhibited until the 1960s.[19]

The power of the artist's vision appears to have been diluted still further in a *View of the Bay of Islands* taken 'from' Earle's drawings which certainly had many more viewers than any of his original work or published prints. This was painted by Robert Burford's assistants for his popular panorama exhibited in Leicester Square in 1838, and was probably stimulated by the then-recent formation of the New Zealand

27 From Robert Burford, 'Description of a View in the Bay of Islands, New Zealand, now exhibiting at the Panorama, Leicester Square' (London, 1838)

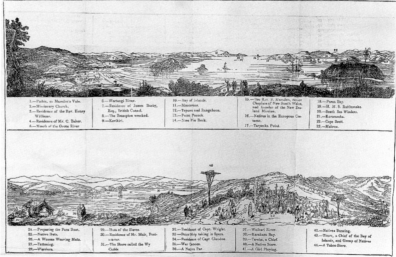

Association, a body dedicated to the promotion of settlement. It is possible that Earle was fully sympathetic with the organization's initially liberal aims, but whether he endorsed, or had any influence over, the panorama based on his work is unclear.[20]

The 360-degree view, also exhibited two years later in New York, is known only through Burford's published guide and fairly crude engraving, which presumably does no justice to a work with a circumference of some 48–52 m (160–70 ft), which surrounded those who paid a shilling to gain access to the viewing platform.[21] The print makes it clear that the intention was to present a broad-brush contrast between a range of exotic Maori practices, and the expanse of the bay, around which European ships and new settlements are visible, surveyed by the missionary Samuel Marsden. Marsden, a key figure in settlement politics in both Australia and New Zealand, was not in the area at the time of Earle's visit, but was connected with the New Zealand Association and identified in Burford's text as the 'best earthly benefactor' of the (native) New Zealanders.[22]

Though the descriptive commentary has a good deal to say about the vicious and degenerate character of most of the whites settled in New Zealand, it contrasts the 'thoroughly savage state' of the Maori, who are said to be 'dirty in their habits, and swarm with vermin', with the natural opulence and future prospects of the place: 'nature seems to have formed it for what it will no doubt shortly become, a rich and populous maritime colony.'[23] Whether Earle would have had any problem with this, I have no way of knowing. But this rhetoric and, apparently, the panorama itself were bleached of the complexities of Earle's vision of settler-indigenous relations. Not only his essentially private watercolours, but some of his prints and published writings refused precisely this sort of simplistic progressive story.

Representations of the complexity of settler-indigenous relations were often diluted in this way as works were reproduced and popularized. This is striking (to turn briefly to a later nineteenth-century example) in Charles Blomfield's paintings of the famous pink and white terraces of Rotomahana, near the central North Island town of Rotorua, in New Zealand. These delicate siliceous formations, created from the mineral deposits of hot springs, were a prime attraction among the geothermal phenomena of the area, which came to be regularly visited by tourists from the 1870s on. Among the artists who painted the terraces was Blomfield, who was fortunate to have done so shortly before they were completely destroyed in the major volcanic eruption of 1886; the cherished landscape features subsequently became the objects of a curious mythologizing and nostalgia, and Blomfield made a successful career

28 CHARLES BLOMFIELD
White Terraces, Rotomahana,
1897

29 CHARLES BLOMFIELD
Panoramic View of the
White Terrace, Rotomahana,
1885 (detail)

out of repeatedly copying his own 1885 paintings.[24] One of the earliest of these works shows a Maori confidently walking along the lake's edge toward the centre of the painting; two visitors rather gingerly pick their way around the bottom of the terrace, well behind him to the right. Though the comic element that is so striking in Earle is absent here, the same dependence of white travellers upon a native guide is manifest. The figures make the picture much more than an image of an unusual natural phenomenon; they make tourism part of its subject-matter, and make indigenous participation in the business of tourism explicit, without implying that participation is at all servile. These suggestively arranged figures are, however, simply omitted from later versions of the painting, such as the mediocre 1897 example in the Auckland Art Gallery, which is unfortunately the one most seen.

Last musters: John Glover

Tim Bonyhady has suggested that nineteenth-century Australian land-scapes work with a number of basic images, including the Aboriginal arcadia, the pastoral arcadia, and the wilderness. Even though the first two (or all three) are frequently represented in the work of one artist, there is an essential incompatibility between the representation of Aboriginal people engaged in subsistence activities or other quotidian pursuits, and the evocation of a promised land available for flocks and white settlement. Bonyhady suggests that the second rather than the first of these images conformed with the interests of settler culture: 'For most colonists, paintings of Australia as an Aboriginal arcadia must have held little appeal because they showed Australia as belonging to the Aborigines'; it is therefore not surprising that such works generally found a market back in England but not within the colonies themselves.[25]

I find Bonyhady's account illuminating and persuasive, but want to argue that the apparent contradiction between the Aboriginal and the pastoral arcadia was resolved through a narrative, namely the imaginary 'fatal impact' account of settlement referred to in the previous chapter (pp. 43–5). This pernicious myth postulated that indigenous populations were vanishing, less from specific causes such as introduced diseases and settler violence, than as a natural and fateful expression of the contact between savagery and civilization. Even when artists were fully aware of settler assaults against indigenous populations, their interest in commemorative and romantic imagery mostly predisposed them to avoid depicting actual conflict, and instead to represent a dehistoricized indigenous population in sombre terms. The important work of the British neoclassical landscape painter John Glover (1767–1849), resident in Tasmania from 1831 to 1840, has already been extensively discussed by Bernard Smith, John McPhee and Ian McLean, as well as by Bonyhady and others, but can usefully be reconsidered in this context.

Glover's presentations of Aboriginal people in arcadian Australian settings do not imply that Australia belonged to them. Certainly he renders landscapes and vegetation as attractive and park-like, but his Aborigines are frequently mysterious and savage. He generally depicts

30 JOHN GLOVER A Corroboree of Natives in Mills Plains, 1832

them in the gloomy middle distance; they therefore appear as a nomadic horde rather than as individuals or as a socially differentiated community. In all but a few of Glover's paintings of Aboriginal groups, there is no human arrangement that suggests kinship, families, the joint collection and consumption of food, or even the most rudimentary form of patriarchal authority. Instead, natives brandish spears and adopt the curious postures associated with corroborees. Their shelters, when depicted at all, are of the simplest kind; the people are shown on the land, but manifestly do nothing to improve it. They are threateningly rather than pleasingly exotic, and commentators have typically found them 'monkey-like' or grotesque.[26] In these views, Aboriginal people are simply too distant to figure as social beings, whose customs incorporated land tenure and inheritable use rights rather than merely bizarre and raucous dances.

This is hardly surprising, since these works were produced immediately after a decade of extraordinarily sustained guerilla warfare on the part of indigenous Tasmanians. Though sporadic fighting was still going on at the time of Glover's arrival in the colony, it was brought to a conclusion soon afterwards by George Augustus Robinson's 'Friendly Mission', a series of journeys aimed at making contact and conciliating the various Aboriginal bands. Motivated by philanthropic and evangelical commitment, and substantially assisted by Aborigines who had already joined government missions and who therefore had their own understanding of the need to bring violence to an end, Robinson was able, over a two-year period to early 1832, to bring virtually all the Tasmanians in. Removed to Flinders Island in Bass Strait, their numbers declined dramatically until 1847, when most of the survivors were repatriated.[27] In this case, therefore, the 'dying race' discourse reflected the facts of depopulation and expulsion, even though it did not result in the disappearance of the Tasmanians, as was long imagined. While Robinson's actions were initially celebrated, this history soon became a difficult one to acknowledge. The awkwardness is manifest in the fate of

31 BENJAMIN DUTERRAU Mr Robinson's First Interview with Timmy, 1840

the painter Benjamin Duterrau's extended project to produce a 'national picture' featuring a meeting between Robinson and a group of Aboriginal people. Though various etchings, related portraits, portrait busts and studies were completed, Duterrau's definitive work was unfinished at the time of his death in 1851, by which time interest had lapsed. His notion that the conciliation marked a foundational moment for the colony's history had clearly lost its resonance.[28]

In the 1830s, there was a spectrum of settler opinion concerning race relations, and Glover appears to have been among those who respected the indigenous people and condemned the wanton violence of some whites; this is implied, at least, by his description (in a private communication) of the settler John Batman as 'a murderer of blacks and the vilest man I have ever known.'[29] He also wrote that he sought to show the 'gay, happy life the Natives led before the White people came here,' and a few paintings indeed do present the arcadian landscape and its inhabitants harmoniously.[30] In most, however, the happiness of the band is not manifest, at least to my eye; as Ian McLean has pointed out, the sinister character of the indigenous presence is suggested by the fact that gum trees proximate to Aboriginal groups are curiously sinuous: the trees that overhang plump cattle in Glover's pastoral scenes lack this distortion.[31] Though he once painted a classical subject, *The Bath of Diana*, in a Tasmanian setting, here again the idea rather than the execution is ennobling.

The sense that Aboriginal people are passing into obscurity is also conspicuous. In *A Corroboree of Natives in Mills Plains* (1832), especially, the dimness of the ground, starkly contrasted with an iridescent (and probably over-cleaned) evening sky, suggests the twilight of the race. A slightly later work, similar in composition though featuring a camp rather than a corroboree, is fatefully titled *The Last Muster of the Tasmanian Aborigines at Risdon* (1836). Though this presumably refers to some assembly of a group of Tasmanians at Risdon before their removal to Flinders Island, Glover refrains from depicting their status as virtual captives and indeed omits any indications of interaction with Europeans. Without the title, it would not be clear that this was anything other than a camp scene, though it shares the foreboding mood of the *Corroboree of Natives*, and it is suggestive that the historical incident and the evocation of pre-European indigenous life are equally subdued and melancholy. What appears to be a Glover sketch for a Tasmanian Adam and Eve (fig. 33) exemplifies these ambiguities. Aborigines are elevated through biblical presentation, but are destined to be expelled from their Arcadia.

32 JOHN GLOVER The Last Muster of the Tasmanian Aborigines at Risdon, 1836

33 JOHN GLOVER Figures in the Landscape, c. 1834

34 BENJAMIN DUTERRAU
Trucanini, Wife of Warreddy

This is significant on two counts. First, it seems that Glover, probably despite his intentions, could be seen to justify the destruction of Tasmanian society by implying that the people's impending doom was a matter of destiny, rather than a result of the violence of the 'Black war' and Robinson's 'friendliness'. It is significant, at any rate, that the confusion of his concerns still tends to be resolved in such terms: a journalist recently summed up the painter's oeuvre: 'his remarkable and poignant images of the doomed Tasmanian Aborigines at their corroborees, innocents in an unspoiled light-filled paradise.'[32] Regarding the Tasmanians as 'innocents' is no doubt better than seeing them as devils. But it is a benevolent and paternalistic attitude that takes us back to the space of David Collins' regrets and confusions.

Secondly, the Adam and Eve sketch, like the *Bath of Diana* and Duterreau's Aboriginal sculptures, exemplifies a larger transfer of Christian and classical imagery to Aboriginal subject-matter. Although there is something of this in Earle's New Zealand work too, we have seen that he acknowledged pre-existing Maori culture and artistic traditions to a considerable degree. From an early moment, then, colonial art in New Zealand was in some sense a creole or hybrid practice. Artists in eastern Australia, in contrast, either declared possession of a Europeanized country, or acknowledged the indigenous presence in Europeanized terms. It must be emphasized that this is a relative contrast, not a categorical one, and that of course some artists in Australia were more attentive to indigenous culture than were some in New Zealand. We will see, however, that the specific character and presence of Maori culture is consistently described and acknowledged in New Zealand art. If, in Australia, Aboriginal people were often depicted, Aboriginal art was barely acknowledged until well into the twentieth century, and then in ways that were often derided.

Australian scenery: Eugen von Guérard

Eugen von Guérard (1811–1901), born in Austria, and trained mainly in Germany, was one of the most successful artists resident in Australia between the 1850s and the 1870s. Though many of his paintings exemplify a scientific romanticism, his work ranges across the several 'images in opposition' that Bonyhady has documented (p. 65). The variety of von Guérard's handling of indigenous and settler presences in the antipodean landscape does not accord with the terms in which his work was celebrated – namely for its elevating depiction of Australian scenery for an Australian nation, a vision that required the exclusion of the indigenous presence. This is conspicuously the case in his most successful work, and in the work that was published in print form.

The early painting *Aborigines Met on the Road to the Diggings* (1854, fig. 21) is exceptional within von Guérard's corpus for depicting a transaction between Aboriginal people and whites, in this case men travelling on foot to the goldfields (where the painter had unsuccessfully tried his luck over 1853 and 1854, before reverting to his profession in Melbourne). Although the work's horizontal format incorporates a wider view, the attention is focused on a tight group of five individuals around a possum-skin cloak, an Aboriginal product that was in considerable demand among settlers. There is nothing comparable to the strong marking of indigenous precedence in the land that I've noted in Earle's *Distant View of the Bay of Islands*, but it is evident that the white men are prospectors on the road, and have paused briefly to make a deal with a local man who is is no sense subordinate to them, and who appears as robust and healthy as his wife, child and kin. If there is any asymmetry, the travellers seem in the dependent situation, the crouching man having adopted an entreating, if not exactly a pleading, manner, while the transaction is being ignored, or witnessed with restrained interest, by the other Aboriginal people present. They are, in other words, neither unduly frightened nor fascinated by Europeans, and have obviously had dealings with them before. *Barter*, the title under which this work was exhibited in the Victoria Jubilee Exhibition in 1884,[33] suggests a shared capacity to haggle, and the degree of sophistication in cross-cultural exchange that is to be expected of a group of people camped adjacent to a well-used track.

This has been aptly described as an 'anecdotal' painting,[34] and it is clearly an image of a particular or a typical encounter, not an effort to represent some larger truth concerning indigenous-settler relations. Had Australian colonial artists been motivated to represent settler-indigenous relations on the model of transactions between near equals, the cultural history I am describing would have been very different. In fact, the condition of near parity represented here was unusual. There were no doubt a variety of situations like this, in which Europeans were passing through country and making limited demands that Aboriginal people could accommodate and take advantage of. But this was hardly the dominant dynamic of contact; that entailed the appropriation of land, inevitable conflict over animals and water, and violence in which the superiority of European weapons and numbers was all too clear.

One body of von Guérard's art does imply a larger celebratory narrative, namely that of growth and prosperity of white civilization in Australia, and particularly the opulence of certain pastoral properties whose owners commissioned paintings. In general, the special effect of an estate view lies not in the fact that it indexes wealth, but that it confers cultural value on property by imbuing it with the dignity of high art. This normally entails some idealization, and often the suggestion that the farm depicted is not merely a particular productive unit, but the bearer of some virtue or exemplary purpose. One squatter, investigating new pasture near the Murray River, wrote that the grass 'was as green and fresh as Eden'.[35] Such promised-land rhetoric is commonplace in descriptions of antipodean landscapes and is often implicit in visual representations of them.

Views frequently emphasized the sheer expansiveness of the land, the brilliance of the sunlight, the rule of property indicated by regular fencing, the abundance of sheep or fine cattle, and the civility of country residences. In works produced earlier in the process of settlement, there is also sometimes a narrative element in the juxtaposition of disorderly 'virgin' bush on the periphery of a property and the cleared pasture or garden that has succeeded it. John Glover had celebrated his own land garden and 'harvest home' in these terms in Tasmania, and with varying emphases subsequent painters such as Conrad Martens, von Guérard, Chevalier and Louis Buvelot in Australia, and Albin Martin in New Zealand, produced work to commission that suggested farming proceeded with a fair degree of divine approval. None of this is especially surprising; the important point in this context is that although the paintings concerned were almost invariably produced for private rather than public display, they cumulatively created an elevating vision of the business and future of the colony which wholly excluded indigenous people. The notion that a pastoral civilization was being created out of a primal wilderness implied that Aborigines had never existed, or at best that they were a feature of the receding wilderness.

Two von Guérard paintings amount to striking exceptions to this rule. The most remarkable, *Panoramic View of Mr Angus McMillan's Station, Bushy Park* (c. 1861), could be seen to prove it in that it was commissioned by a pastoralist perceived to be 'kindly and sympathetic' toward the people whose lands he had settled – though he had been involved in a massacre of Kurnai people (now known as Gunnai) twenty years earlier.[36] In any event, his philanthropy was not disinterested, since, as Tim Bonyhady points out, the gold rush in the 1850s had caused a shortage of white pastoral workers, and the use of Aboriginal labour consequently increased. This implied the presence not only of black employees, but a whole fringe camp population of kin – 'as many… as choose to hang about' – to whom rations were customarily supplied.[37] This is significant insofar as it indicates that a local economy was organized not purely on the model of wage labour, but to some extent on the basis of indigenous principles of generalized reciprocity, which required, for instance, that sexual access to a woman would be reciprocated by a flow of gifts to her relatives. For the most part, this mutual accommodation was not made visible in painting, which emphasized fine prospects rather than labour, but von Guérard does image a compatibility between a benevolently marginalized indigenous population and pastoral activity.

Given the particular interest of pastoralists in the quality of feed, it is notable that he adopts a low point of view which emphasizes the density and greenness of the grass, while the great exaggeration of the horizontal plain suggests the expansiveness and seemingly limitless prospects of the estate.[38] But though *Bushy Park* certainly conveys the

35 EUGEN VON GUERARD Panoramic View of Mr Angus McMillan's Station,
Bushy Park, c. 1861 (pair of canvases)

splendour of the countryside, it is a painting that presents a relationship
rather than just a rural property: the house is in the marginal middle distance, and the emphasis is instead on a simple and forceful juxtaposition
of Aborigines and cattle (fig. 11), which has surely been opted for very
deliberately, given that the artist's initial sketches featured a far more
conventional homestead view.[39] Von Guérard may have been prompted
to produce this very atypical estate portrait because he visited Bushy
Park while travelling with Alfred Howitt, who was to become a significant figure in early Australian anthropology; von Guérard's interest in
Aboriginal matters at the time is attested to by an ethnographically-
minded sketch of a canoe.[40] But it is notable that he was also travelling
with John King, also a participant in the 1840 massacre, and for whom
he produced a similarly unusual estate view, in which a small Aboriginal
group occupies the foreground. These works were not simply expressions of an ethnographic interest: they record the historical fact of one
population supplanting another. We can do no more than speculate
about what was in the minds of King, McMillan and the painter at the
time, but we might presume that the two murderers-turned-benefactors
of the Aborigines whose lands they resided upon were attempting, in
some awkward way, to come to terms with this history, or at any rate
that von Guérard interpreted their interest in this way.

The juxtaposition of two bulls with a small Aboriginal group was
highly charged, since it was well understood that the introduction of
grazing animals dramatically reduced native fauna, and provoked conflict. The beasts trampled and spoiled water supplies frequented by other
game, caused food shortages among Aboriginal people, and prompted

36 EUGEN VON GUERARD Bushy Park, Gippsland, Australia, 1860

them to kill stock, not only to eat, but also deliberately to subvert the basis of the intrusive economy.[41] Even if a settler were well-intentioned, the explorer Edward Eyre asked in 1845, 'what recompense can he make them for injury he has done, by dispossessing them of their lands, by occupying their waters, and by depriving them of their supply of food?

...In the place of the kangaroo, the emu, and the wallabie, they now see only the flocks and herds of the strangers, and nothing is left to them.'[42] A later popular history offered a similarly fair summary of the basic character of frontier conflict: 'We occupied their land, and violated their customs every day.... The growth of squatting westwards irritated them still more, because it meant much new game in their hunting-lands which yet they were ill-treated for killing. How should they comprehend the legal difference between cattle and kangaroos? They speared the cattle and the stockmen shot them.'[43]

The Aboriginal people depicted in von Guérard's *Bushy Park* are not at all the 'children of the woods' who figure in so many evocations of life before contact.[44] This is not an imaginary reconciliation of a pristine way of life with European pastoralism, but is intended as an image of actual coexistence, albeit one that seems deliberately schematic; the woman, if not the Aboriginal men, was not actually resident around Bushy Park, but had been sketched some years earlier in the Grampians, Victoria.[45] The blankets, which were distributed through a paternalistic charity system, denote a situation of dependence on settlers, but the weapons indicate that some form of traditional hunting is sustained, as is some degree of autonomy. Separateness is maintained by the fact that the bulls are on one canvas and the indigenous people on the other, but the symmetry nevertheless insists upon shared occupation. Farm labour is presumably the basis of this cohabitation, but is not made visible here, and this is not necessarily because work was simply too undignified a subject for a painting of this kind. Aboriginal hands were found by pastoralists to be unreliable, not because they would not complete specific tasks, but because they refused to settle on properties permanently. 'In these districts, during the summer months,' wrote the settler Hugh Jamieson in 1853, 'nearly all, from the oldest to the youngest in the various tribes, have the greatest desire to abandon every employment, and indulge in the roving life of naked savages...during these migrations we always experience considerable difficulty in retaining out of the whole tribe the necessary number for shepherding alone.'[46]

For Aboriginal people, therefore, mutual accommodation seems to have cost only intermittent subordination. Though social relations on properties between owners, managers and white hands as well as any Aboriginal employees were, of course, always hierarchical, Jamieson indicates that Aboriginal people were in the habit of entering and withdrawing from station employment as it suited them; an Aboriginal propensity to 'go walkabout' was later to become proverbial, and even to become a sort of emblem for domestic tourism in Australia.[47] Even if it was not von Guérard's intention to refer to this kind of inconvenient mobility, the small group he depicts is plainly on the move – the men seem to have halted only momentarily – and the painting thus reflects the degree of autonomy that Aboriginal people retained. The exercise of this partial and residual independence was, however, fatally telling from the perspective of the writer I've quoted. 'Every year's experience clearly shows that there is a certain limit to their usefulness and general improvement. I use the word limit advisedly...we seem to have no encouragement to look for or to expect any advance.'[48] This pessimism wilfully overlooks indigenous motivations for summer travel: participation in no doubt adapted forms of customary gatherings. To use a term from our time rather than theirs, this was cultural survival.

Even though Hugh Jamieson anticipated that white workers would replace Aborigines as soon as the labour shortage eased, relations of this kind were actually sustained in rural areas over decades, and were to have a much longer history on properties further outback, such as the western Australian station of Katherine Susannah Pritchard's novel *Coonardoo* (1929). Yet von Guérard's *Bushy Park* does not simply describe co-presence as an incidental situation but insists forcefully on co-presence as a historical fact, and on the juxtaposition and contradiction between indigenous life and farming; as such it must be unique. Neither this nor the earlier *Aborigines Met on the Road to the Diggings* were highly visible paintings in the nineteenth century, though I do not suggest that there was any conspiracy to keeps works that presented settler-Aboriginal relations in complex terms out of public view. The first painting would, in fact, have been seen by a considerable number of people when it was exhibited, thirty years after having been painted, at the Victoria Jubilee Exhibition in 1884; it then attracted cursory but favourable comment from one reviewer. It is not surprising that *Bushy Park* should have remained out of the public eye, since although a couple of the artist's homestead views were loaned to public galleries or published in engraved form during the nineteenth century, most remained with the families who commissioned them, frequently until drawn into the market in the 1960s and 1970s, and were neither exhibited, reproduced, nor commented upon in print until then.[49]

The works by von Guérard that, on the other hand, were seen and acclaimed from the mid-1850s on, were his views of wilderness. These were generally romantic or sublime landscapes featuring waterfalls, mountains, and foreground vegetation that was handled with great specificity, along the lines advocated by Alexander von Humboldt and exemplified in the Americas by painters such as Frederic Edwin Church.

It is instructive to examine the terms in which these paintings were celebrated. In 1854 two works, including a *View of the Australian Pyrenees*, were declared to be 'undeniably Australian, the color and shape of the foliage, and the peculiar tint of the herbage, dried up by the summer sun of these latitudes, are essentially characteristic.'[50] In 1857, *Ferntree Gully in the Dandenong Ranges*, which attracted particular notice and was later published as an engraving, was found to be 'equally valuable as a botanical study, as a depiction of one of the most characteristic features in Australian scenery.'[51] Similarly, in *Mount William from Mount Dryden* the critic found that 'Mr Guérard...has caught, in full force, and has succeeded in expressing, the character of the scenery. With him we do not see merely a forest, a mountain, or a plain, but he gives us, unmistakeably, Australian forests, mountains, and plains.'[52] In 1862 it was suggested that while visiting artists were likely to present 'exotic and inappropriate...European interpretations of Australian subjects', von Guérard, though not native born, had 'become acclimatised', and had 'saturated his mind, so to speak, with the characteristics of Australian scenery, until he is enabled to interpret it with unerring fidelity.'[53]

Although cultural nationalism is generally regarded as a phenomenon of the 1880s and 1890s in Australia (as it was in Canada and New Zealand), and though the colonies of New South Wales, Victoria, Queensland, Tasmania, South Australia and Western Australia remained separate until Federation in 1901, this commentary is plainly nationalist in several senses. Reference is made again and again not to vegetation or scenery specific to regions within Australia, but to what is peculiar, characteristic and essential in Australian scenery in general.[54] While subsequent traditions of nationalist criticism in both Australia and New Zealand placed great emphasis upon the supposed distinctiveness of the quality of light,[55] both von Guérard's practice and his critics emphasized the singularity of the vegetation. In fact, sclerophyll forest dominated by eucalypts is perhaps the only environmental feature sufficiently widespread to count as a peculiarly Australian type of scenery – there are surely otherwise pretty basic differences between the sandstone cliffs of the Blue Mountains to the west of Sydney, the volcanic lakes of western Victoria, and the irregular weathered granite of the high country. Yet my protest is perverse, because von Guérard's accomplishment was to create this sense of Australian distinctiveness by painting these diverse regions in a fashion recognizably his own. Though his scientific romanticism, like Chevalier's, engaged with regional peculiarities, it also assimilated diverse examples of Australian scenery to a common painterly idiom, thus making each visible in 'essentially characteristic' terms.

37 EUGEN VON GUERARD Ferntree Gully in the Dandenong Ranges, 1857

This evocation of typical scenery would have been less potent had von Guérard and Chevalier (who were frequently commended together) not also presented the landscape in elevated and inspiring terms. While commentators emphasized the artists' grasp of what was distinctively Australian, the presentation of its magnificence from a perspective grounded in Western art, and in an idiom derived from the particular tradition of romantic landscape, enabled ready comparisons to be made with European topography. These comparisons took the form of chauvinist claims for the quality of Australian scenery; such claims were also to be made of the lakes, falls and mountains of New Zealand. Commenting on von Guérard's 1863 *View from Mount Kosciusko*, a writer in the *Ballarat Miner* asserted that 'This picture alone is a complete rebuttal of the theory, if such a theory now be held by anyone, that Australian scenery possesses no elements of the sublime.'[56] If this strident colonial nationalism is hardly unexpected in a gold-town newspaper, it is notable that the same point is at issue in a more urbane report concerning another painting:

a replica [of the *View of Forest Scenery near Woolongong*, 1860] has been taken to Europe by Major-General Macarthur, who purposes exhibiting it in London, together with other pictures from the same easel, to show our countrymen at home that Australian scenery rivals that of Switzerland and Italy: that we, too, have our Alps and our Apennines, our Lake of Como and our Bay of Naples, our Tyrol and our Westmoreland; not yet hallowed, it is true, by historical associations, nor rendered for ever memorable by modern poem, and by classic song, but with the freshness of the dawn of Creation still clinging to a portion of them, and untrodden solitudes,
'Where no one comes,
Or hath come since the making of the world,'
Surrounding him with awe and mystery.[57]

This competitive attitude toward Europe was to have quite a history, though from at least the early twentieth century, many Australians would assume that their landscapes were not merely as attractive as those in Europe, but considerably more so. The vexed issue was instead whether Australian culture could only ever be more than derivative and inferior in relation to its primarily European sources.

Given the assertion that this art presented both the distinctiveness and the quality of the scenery, it is hardly surprising that its public importance was emphasized. Grand claims were made – that work exhibited could be visited with great profit by the public, or deserved a place in a national collection – as were more utilitarian ones. This was as much the case in New Zealand as in Australia over the period. The two major works executed by von Guérard of dramatic South Island scenery there – one a view of Lake Wakatipu, the other of Milford Sound – attracted wide audiences, and much was similarly expected of Chevalier. Soon after he arrived in the country in 1865, the *Otago Witness* declared that 'the Government ought to treat this expedition as in the nature of a public work, and render to Mr Chevalier all the assistance in their power. His labors will be of great benefit to the Colony, and will no doubt help its attractions as a beautiful and desirable land for settlement.'[58] Chevalier's travel was in fact supported by public money, and when the work was shown some seven months later, it demonstrated, according to the same newspaper, that European alpine scenery was at least equalled in New Zealand, while the fact that the artist had been accompanied by his wife attested to 'the safety with which these lovely spots can be visited.' Given the projected exhibition of the work in Europe, it was 'hardly too much to anticipate that many tourists may be induced to

38 EUGEN VON GUERARD Milford Sound, New Zealand, 1877–9

visit New Zealand, who would otherwise have been content with the knowledge that it was somewhere in the Southern Ocean.'[59]

While estate views were private celebrations of the resources and prospects of the colonies, the romantic and sublime landscapes enabled a population to celebrate a country as its own. Paradoxically, however, they did so by evoking an awesome and largely dehumanized wilderness, which lacked historical or national content. The painting I began this chapter with, Chevalier's *Buffalo Ranges* (1864), was not a 'pure' bush landscape but a hybrid composition incorporating pioneer settlement. The work was created with a view to special public canonization. It was painted for a competitive exhibition organized by the then-new National Gallery of Victoria, and was awarded the prize, despite being found deficient in certain respects.[60] Chevalier set himself a difficult task in reconciling the comfort of the foreground with the grandeur of the ranges, but presumably felt that the introduction of a historical and celebratory reference to settler achievement would enhance the work's appropriateness as an inaugural acquisition for the national collection; and he was apparently right. Although Bernard Smith is not alone among twentieth-century viewers in finding the painting 'rather pompous and dull stuff',[61] the earlier critics were generally enthusiastic, and even applauded precisely the feature that the teacher I mentioned at the beginning of this chapter condemned. 'A very fine, very truthful, and very beautiful picture…. A tumbledown cottage, such as one may meet with in many a Surrey and Hampshire lane, the fragments of a deserted water-mill, a lane wandering between into rich hill-side woods, form a foreground on which the eye rests with a sensation of comfort. Above are the vast forms of the mountains, slightly capped with snow, and glowing under the light of incipient sunset.'[62]

If, for some viewers, there was still a great gap between the kind of essentially European rural scene that could be regarded with positive affection, and the actualities of Australian pastoral estates, some of von Guérard's published views can be seen to combine magnificent scenery with a humanized landscape. But here we must return to the question of the indigenous presence. Von Guérard is one of the artists who worked through Bonyhady's several image-types, depicting Aborigines in pristine circumstances, pastoral arcadias and of course the primeval wildernesses that, as we have seen, were his most celebrated works. Aboriginal people occasionally figure as staffage in the romantic and sublime landscapes, but generally only as individuals who provide some foreground scale, rather than in groups implying a socialized occupation of the land.[63] Aboriginal and European figures are not used together in this way, as they are in Earle's work, and when Europeans instead of indigenous people appear, they play the conventional role of standing in for the spectator. Aboriginal people are never presented as co-viewers of the landscape, but are rather features within it, and elements of its wildness. In *The Weatherboard Falls, NSW* (now Wentworth Falls) in the Blue Mountains, an Aboriginal man is shown just having been startled by a large snake, and hence appears in no sense as a master or even a comfortable occupant of the natural environment.

The terms in which this painting was praised in the *Argus* in 1862 are especially interesting. 'The physical features, the local colour, and the pervading sentiment are entirely Australian. We do not require either the description in the catalogue, or the presence of the aborigine in the landscape, to assure us that the subject is racy of the soil.'[65] In other words, the Aboriginal man is not taken to be of either ethnographic or romantic interest, but instead is considered as a localizing signpost, and one in any case rendered superfluous here by the accomplished specification of Australian scenery. Although this painting was highly celebrated, and was exhibited at the Royal Academy in 1865, it is notable that von Guérard adapted it by removing the Aboriginal figure when it was published with his lithographs of Australian landscapes in 1867. He may

39 EUGEN VON GUERARD The Weatherboard Falls, NSW, 1863

40 EUGEN VON GUERARD Weatherboard Falls, NSW, published in 'Eugen Von Guérard's Australian Landscapes' (Melbourne, 1867)

have been responding to the critic's implication that the native was gratuitous, but probably also took into account the fact that the Falls were becoming increasingly accessible to visitors. In 1867, the railway reached the Weatherboard Inn that had been built nearby some forty years earlier, and the spot was even visited by the Duke of Edinburgh during the first royal tour of Australia shortly afterwards.[66] Although the caption suggests that the lithograph predated both these developments, the accessibility of the place was noted; the inn was '59 miles east [in fact, west] of Sydney, with which there is daily communication by mail.'[67] The savagery and danger implied by both snake and native were no doubt considered inappropriate to a place that would be frequented by tourists.

Von Guérard's album of twenty-four lithographs presents his own corpus selectively, in a fashion more specifically determined by the project of representing a colonial nation in the making. In a generic sense, the publication derived from the albums of travel views which had been popular since the late eighteenth century. But many of these works depicted the non-European world for Europeans; the Daniells' *Oriental Scenery* is a typical example. Von Guérard, by contrast, was producing for an emerging domestic audience. Unlike Glover's paintings and Earle's lithographs, von Guérard's prints were published and sold in Melbourne for colonial consumption. Their ideological effect might have been more like that of those collections of views of England, Scotland and Wales that helped Britons see the country as a totality, and so imagine it as a national entity. Von Guérard's publication appeared well in advance of the moves toward Australian Federation, but was consistent with a colonial nationalism that was nevertheless emerging. Its range of visual statements sustained this nationalism, as well as its necessary exclusions. Although, as we have seen, many of von Guérard's earlier paintings had included Aboriginal people, only one of the prints did, while the texts accompanying them included much hyperbole concerning the colony's opulence: 'No range of hills was ever richer in beautiful varieties of minerals....'[68] *View of Lake Illawarra* comprises both the generalized version of the pastoral arcadia – an encompassing view rather than a celebration of a particular property – and a sublime and typically Australian range of hills.

This set of prints could be seen to consummate the emergence of a sense of place, a landscape for a nation, that had secured a basis in art institutions and the publishing business. If what is printed and canonized of course always fails to reflect the complexity of what is seen and depicted, selectivity in this case had more specific effects: the facts of

41 EUGEN VON GUERARD View of Lake Illawarra, NSW, published in 'Eugen von Guérard's Australian Landscapes' (Melbourne, 1867)

interaction between settlers and indigenous people, and their very cohabitation, were obscured. But an Aboriginal presence was not wholly erased. There evidently remained a demand for romanticized views of pre-contact indigenous life: Charles Troedels' popular and nearly contemporaneous series of chromolithographs included François Cogné's moonlit and definitely classicized Aborigines of Merri Creek (a stream now incorporated into the Melbourne suburbs), and an only slightly less arcadian print after von Guérard's own *View on the Upper Mitta-Mitta.*[69] The messages of colonial visual culture were always mixed. Despite their heterogeneity, however, very few works did justice to the indigenous presence or the complexities of settler-indigenous interaction.

Some settlers took the view that a fuller engagement with traditional indigenous life would provide the basis for a more distinctive Australian art. In the early 1880s, the sometime squatter and ethnologist Edward Curr noted that painters such as von Guérard and Buvelot had rendered effectively the scenery of the seaboard and ranges, while the interior had been neglected. Given the singular importance of sunlight for the Australian impressionists who were about to make an impact,

42 FRANCOIS COGNE Merri Creek, Plenty Ranges, published in 'Souvenir Views of Melbourne and Victorian Scenery' (Melbourne, c. 1865)

it is interesting that he suggested that the desolate plains and hills of the outback had their own appeal, 'bathed as they are in the fierce glare of the sun and wrapped in eternal stillness.'

> Another kindred subject, which seems to me to abound in picturesque and characteristic detail, is the camp life of the Blacks, and I have often been surprised that no artist has taken it up. Possibly their ungainly appearance about towns, where alone the artist is likely to see them, may have had something to do with it. There, certainly, they are neither picturesque nor prepossessing; but it is different when one sees the half-nude, statuesque figure in the native cloak, and the stately carriage of the untamed man amidst the surroundings of camp life, beneath the appropriate gum-trees of the lagoon, or the deep shadows of some luxuriant pine-ridge. Indeed, if Australia possesses a subject out of which a new and characteristic school might come, I should say it was the Aborigines. No doubt, to learn their ways, and depict them, would entail a good deal of time and application, but how novel such paintings would be, and what admirable records of the ways of the race![70]

Neither here nor elsewhere does Curr seem especially chauvinistic or political, but it is notable that he takes a certain cultural nationalism for granted: the value of colonial art would lie in a 'new and characteristic school', 'characteristic' meaning distinctive to the country. He evidently had some familiarity with the typical landscapes of the best-known artists, but was not aware that von Guérard, among others, had produced work of precisely the kind he called for. It is not surprising that someone who wrote extensively on *The Australian Race* should advocate a school of painting depicting Aboriginal people, but significant that this school was seen as necessarily depicting them in pristine conditions. Art – at least high art and national art – required dignity and grandeur, and acculturated indigenous people could only lack those attributes.

Colonial Impressionism

Just a couple of years after Curr's book was published, a 'new and characteristic' school of Australian painting did emerge. Although the impressionist techniques of the painters subsequently grouped together and known as the Heidelberg school met with initial opposition from prominent critics, the principal artists – Arthur Streeton, Tom Roberts, Frederick McCubbin and Charles Conder – were for the most part remarkably successful. Their celebrations of Australian sunlight, of the beach, of pioneer life and of Australian history captured the imagination of the public – as well they might, for the best of this work retains great beauty and immediacy. Although the Heidelberg painters produced diverse work, including portraits and some very fine urban scenes, the most highly acclaimed and enduringly popular work imaged the bush and folkloricized bush life. As Bernard Smith and many other writers have pointed out, the last decades of the nineteenth century saw an essentially urban population engaging with questions of national identity, and increasingly empathizing from a distance with rural lives and attitudes: 'the frontier exercised an enormous influence on the imagination of all Australians.'[71] In some cases their paintings were intended as national icons, or acquired that status, and it has been sustained and reinforced ever since in public perceptions and auction rooms. The Heidelberg artists are always heavily represented in Australian art calendars and popular books of 'great Australian paintings', they are still imitated by many amateur 'Sunday' painters, and their work has never been eclipsed in popularity, despite the great interest in recent years in Aboriginal art.

43 ARTHUR STREETON The Selector's Hut: Whelan on the Log, 1890

44 FREDERICK McCUBBIN The Pioneer, 1904

The school has been written about extensively by many critics and art historians, to whom I am indebted.[72] My intention here is not to attempt a fresh overview, but rather to emphasize two points of special importance for this book's arguments.

The first is that from an early point this Australian impressionism was seen to have a distinctly national character, which was elaborated upon in subsequent commentary. Although it is hardly likely that the aspiration to produce work of national salience was relevant to all the artists, particularly in the movement's early phases, the notion is more powerful in retrospect precisely because it comes to encompass diverse imagery. Some of the work recorded comfortable and accessible countryside – the suburban periphery rather than the wilderness – while both Roberts and McCubbin were to move toward historical paintings, Roberts painting bushranging scenes and McCubbin sentimental evocations of the hardship and loneliness of pioneer life. The mythic subjects and the more familiar ones could be seen to define and affirm each other, the former lending meaning to the latter while partaking of the same naturalistic idiom; even the most deliberately exemplary compositions thus retained authenticity, specificity and reality.

It is symptomatic of the privileged status of this body of work that it has long been celebrated as the *first* Australian art to embrace a local rather than a European vision of the Australian countryside, and this perception persists, despite its rejection long ago by Bernard Smith and others.[73] The terms in which Heidelberg painting has been celebrated, in fact, are highly reminiscent of those quoted above in affirmation of von Guérard's work, but the Heidelberg vision was always better able to play a definitional role in a national visual culture than the sublime landscapes. The preferred subject-matter of von Guérard and Chevalier was magnificent and remote; it elicited the awe-inspired regard of the spectator, but was not exactly country that one lived with or walked through. The bush depicted by Streeton and others was typically near town, and, as Ian Burn has shown, the attitude was that of the city visitor, particularly the upper-middle-class professional men who were at this time interesting themselves in botany, photography, sketching and fishing.[74]

These recreational activities, an early expression of the bushwalking I discussed in the previous chapter (p. 40), were not only taken to be therapeutic and invigorating (as time in the country surely is) but moreover to enable urban Australians to mimic and partake of pioneer experience, by camping, cooking over fires, and drinking billy tea. There was thus not merely an ideological, but a performative and embodied connection between a romanticized frontier experience and the representation of familiar bush. While rural pioneers would not, for the most part, have been especially interested in the characterizations of their lives in art, those who engaged in bush recreations could recognize their own practices in these paintings, understanding them as typifying Australian practicality and adaptation to the bush, the qualities from which the nation's prosperity had been built. It is significant that many lesser imitators have since extended this vision, depicting periurban coast and countryside virtually exhaustively. Hence, while the original and canonical works could be seen in public institutions, reproductions and the works of 'commercial' and amateur artists gave the same representation of national landscape a presence in many homes.

The second point I want to make is that this visual culture almost totally excluded Aboriginal people. No major work by any Heidelberg artist featured any aspect of indigenous life. Roberts appears to have been the only one who represented Aborigines at all, but roughly fifteen sketches and minor paintings depicting indigenous people hardly repre-

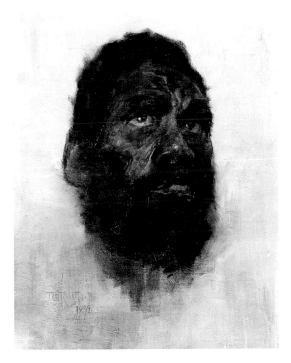

45 TOM ROBERTS Aboriginal Head – Charlie Turner, 1892

sent a major strand in a corpus of over seven hundred documented works. Most are portraits, the best known being the *Aboriginal Head – Charlie Turner* (1892), which apparently depicts a man from Corowa in New South Wales.[75] The dying race theme predictably resurfaces: another Corowa subject, 'Gubbie Wellington', was described in Roberts' own inscription as 'Last of the Murray River tribe(s)', while the *Sydney Morning Herald* found that the value of *Charlie Turner* 'will grow year by year with the gradual disappearance from our midst of the original possessor of the soil.'[76] In fact, however, what was disappearing was not the Aboriginal population, but scope for an art that featured Aboriginal people.

The Aboriginal presence in painting diminished in part simply because of the steady marginalization of Aboriginal people in settled southeastern Australia at a time when prevailing artistic precepts favoured subjects that were actually witnessed, though McCubbin and Roberts were not inhibited from producing essentially imaginative or historical compositions. This is probably less important than a larger sense in which Aborigines had, from the viewpoint of white settlers, become culturally gratuitous. Earlier, they had not been presented in their complexity but used like gum trees to mark Australian distinctiveness. That marking was now more effectively accomplished through the evocation of glorious light, and what was marked was an environment with which Europeans sought unproblematic bonds. If the idea of the Aboriginal arcadia was awkward or objectionable for some mid-nineteenth-century settler audiences, because it reminded them of the facts of prior indigenous occupation, by the 1890s white Australians were making efforts to imagine themselves as 'natives' – the term being widely used to refer to colonial-born people of European descent. Indigenous emblems such as boomerangs might play a part in this effort, but to a substantial extent it was animated by a less vicarious engagement with the bush and the land. It was precisely this manifold experience – ranging from pioneer myth to summer camp and quotidian seaside visit – that the Heidelberg painters imaged so powerfully.

This is not to say that Aboriginal people dropped out of public visual culture altogether. Their exclusion from high art was partly required by the fact that undignified, acculturated and dispossessed indigenous people about town simply did not constitute appropriate subject-matter.

A CURIOSITY IN HER OWN COUNTRY.

**46 PHIL MAY A Curiosity in Her Own Country,
published in 'The Bulletin', 3 March 1888**

47 CHARLES GOLDIE
The Calm Close of Valour's Various Days, 1906

Such figures did appear in cartoons and some genres of commercial art. The New Zealand cartoon *A Curiosity in her Own Country* by Phil May is a remarkably critical and poignant evocation of the dispossessors' enduring interest in indigenous people. However, Maori were to remain consistently visible in New Zealand painting, particularly through the enormously popular portraits of C.F. Goldie, which were imitated by many lesser artists. The circulation of this sort of work was consistent with the degree to which Maori always remained more prominent in New Zealand society than did Aboriginal people in Australia; like Native Americans, though not to quite the same degree, the first Australians became almost invisible in the cities and more densely settled areas. A culture of occasionally self-critical curiosity emerged that enabled white Australians to encounter 'Aboriginality' through images and objects, while rarely engaging with Aborigines in person. Over much of the twentieth century, this curiosity was expressed in artifacts rather than art.

48 ANTON SEUFFERT Secretaire, c. 1870

Today cultural diversity, like ecological diversity, seems to be threatened by technology and travel. New forms of communication, transnational media, migration, tourism, and the spread of consumerism supposedly lead to the blurring of national cultures everywhere. In Europe, on top of this, it is feared that political and economic unification will suppress deeply rooted national identities in favour of some nebulous European-ness. Encroaching homogenization is generally taken to be a recent development, but the potentially corrosive effect of increasing international communication upon national cultures was remarked upon in the antipodes more than a century ago. A writer on *The Australians* found in 1893 that the promising beginnings of colonial literature had 'formed but the brilliant dawn of a cloudy, colourless day. Mail steamer and cable have brought England too close. Her popular literature has swamped all native originality.'[1]

'Native' referred not to Aboriginal but to settler culture, and settler culture appeared to possess a tenuous distinctiveness. If this anxiety anticipated the fear of cultural standardization that has since been regularly refuelled by jet travel, Hollywood, television, and most recently the internet, the colonial predicament was in a more fundamental sense an inversion of the present European one. While the notoriously 'insular' British are now allegedly struggling to understand themselves as citizens of a larger supra-national community, Australians and New Zealanders at the end of the nineteenth century took their membership of the British 'race' for granted; what they found difficult to articulate was their nationality within it. These colonials did not want to secede from the Empire, but they did seek separate nationhood. If the desire for political autonomy was often seen to follow from a sense of distinctiveness, it in turn called distinctiveness into being. National character or something like it had to be made explicit and visible.

This chapter is concerned with one of the ways in which colonial nationality has been evoked and displayed. I examine the chequered histories of the use of indigenous references in design and decoration in Australia and New Zealand, and explore the curious slippage that enabled indigenous figures and motifs to have both native and national connotations. Over the last hundred years, this has been a potent but peculiarly awkward project. Its history adds a distinct perspective to questions discussed very extensively over recent years in critical writing on colonial imaginations. Self-definition through the assimilation or rejection of otherness has often been analysed in generalized psychic terms; my approach, in contrast, is historically specific, and insists on the difference between the broader tradition of Western primitivism and settler interests in local aboriginality.

I also avoid taking the success of these efforts of colonial self-definition for granted. The native/national 'and/or' that underlay them was an unstable conjuncture, not a smooth appropriation. It turns out that nationalist 'applications' of indigenous art were not always found to be compelling, and were notably less so for Australians than New Zealanders, at least until the 1940s. If European attitudes toward 'primitive' cultures always lurched between celebration and denigration, settler primitivism wasn't and isn't simply ambiguous. In fact it appears, in the longer term, to have been uniquely self-subverting.

Marginal nations

In Australia, as we have seen, pioneer life was frequently ennobled by its representation in high art. Locality, however, could also be immediately specified through images of indigenous people and native fauna and flora; and this mode of evoking nationality was conspicuous in domestic craft, as well as in decorative art and design for public and commercial presentation. In both Australia and New Zealand, from the late nineteenth century onward, a settler iconography began to emerge, and images of indigenous artifacts and people, as well as kangaroos and kiwis, subsequently proliferated in official media such as stamps and banknotes, in popular printed material, in ceramics and fabrics, and in a bewildering variety of other forms and contexts.

Taken as an ensemble, these references could be seen to provide a solution to a problem of colonial identity. It was often supposed that settler culture was unavoidably derivative, and could figure only as a displaced and second-rate version of Britishness. There was much anxiety on this point in settler periodicals from the 1880s onward, and the contrasting qualities of culture and life in the colony and at 'home' preoccupy later writers, such as the great Australian novelist Henry Handel Richardson, author of *The Fortunes of Richard Mahony* (1927).

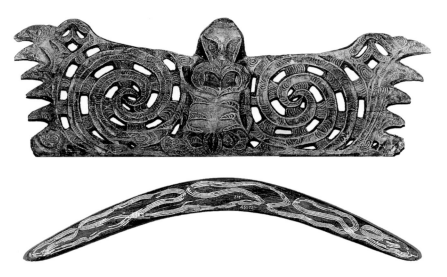

49 Maori carved-wood lintel or 'pare' from the Ngati Whatua (Kiataia region)

50 Aboriginal engraved hunting boomerang from Coopers Creek

The spectre of cultural deprivation and marginality in Australia, and the themes of distance and isolation in New Zealand, remained very much alive in antipodean cultures into the 1960s, and in some respects persisted until more recently.

The responses to this predicament were diverse, but included the effort to inject something singularly local into colonial culture. Aborigines and Maori were characterized by some racist settlers as generic savages and cannibals, but their material culture and art were notably distinctive. Maori tattooing and carving, and Aboriginal boomerangs were absolutely unlike cultural forms from anywhere else. The fact that their stereotypic versions were not actually characteristic of the entire indigenous populations wasn't important: here were emblems that provided settlers with a vicarious native status, and a body of imagery wholly distinct from the visual traditions of European cultures.

Engagement with indigenous subject-matter, both natural and cultural, was certainly advocated in these terms from time to time. As Margaret Preston was to write in 1941, with characteristic urgency, 'The attention of the Australian people must be drawn to the fact that [Aboriginal art] is great art and the foundation of a national culture for this country.'[2] If Preston was well ahead of her time in celebrating the indigenous art for itself, the subsequent proliferation of popular adaptations suggests that signs and styles of aboriginality did appeal to white antipodeans. But it is not clear that the audience's interest stemmed from an unequivocal yearning for local identity. Like people everywhere, white Australians and New Zealanders did not and do not think of themselves exclusively in terms of nationality; they have, at the same time, always attached importance to familial, local, religious and political allegiances, as well as transnational cultural affinities, ranging from the old imperial bonds to the allure of Hollywood and other contemporary popular cultures. As I have already suggested, a preoccupation with local identity among artists and intellectuals cannot be read as a direct reflection of a predicament perceived by a population at large, or one inherent in antipodean 'popular culture'.

New Zealand: kowhaiwhai marginalized

It is striking that indigenous art was drawn into creole design by New Zealanders earlier and far more extensively than by Australians. Although native people and natural subjects have long been imaged prolifically in both nations, the fact that Qantas was to put the kangaroo on the tailfins of its jets while Air New Zealand opted for the *koru* motif, derived from Maori painting, typifies the preponderance of faunal emblems in one case and cultural allusions in the other.

By reason of their blackness and their nomadism, Aboriginal people were generally regarded by Europeans as lower on the scale of human beings than Maori. Exceptional liberals and discursive ambiguities notwithstanding, harsh denigrations and racist generalizations become depressingly familiar to any reader of Australian colonial writings. Early travellers and settlers were not always oblivious to the aesthetic power of local art forms, however: witness the evident interest of the Port Jackson Painter in the forceful body paintings of men from the vicinity of the Sydney settlement (fig. 14). But it is notable that illustrations of this kind were not reproduced in engravings or otherwise rendered familiar to a wide audience. In contrast, early European observers responded positively to Maori bodies, Maori societies and Maori art: they may have found the anthropomorphic sculpture grotesque, but frequently vaunted the ingenuity and power of the involuted curvi-linear designs characteristic of carving, painting and tattooing alike. On Cook's first voyage, Joseph Banks found the 'truth with which the lines were drawn was surprising, but above all their method of connecting several spirals into one piece, which they did inimitably well, intermingling the ends of them in so dexterous a manner that it was next to impossible to trace the

51 Engraving after SYDNEY PARKINSON,
The Head of a New Zealander

connections.' He says this of one of two styles he encountered; 'the other was in a much more wild taste and I may truly say was like nothing but itself.'³ Small wonder then that Sydney Parkinson's depictions of tattooed men and canoes would have to be counted among the most widely reprinted images from the entire visual archive of European exploration; in the 1830s and 1840s artists such as Augustus Earle and George French Angas were marketing subjects with which their audiences had some familiarity, however powerfully exotic they remained.

While Europeans were certainly ambivalent about the attractiveness of Polynesian design, its regularity and evident sophistication enabled them to draw it into a global account of the evolution of art. Maori carvings figured conspicuously in the single most important mid-nineteenth century European text and sourcebook on design, Owen Jones' *The Grammar of Ornament* (1856).⁴ This book was organized in an evolutionary fashion, beginning with 'Savage Ornament', and progressing through Egyptian, Greek and various Asian cultures to the Renaissance and subsequent European styles. It is notable that all the illustrated

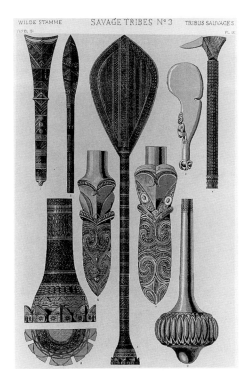

52 'Savage Tribes No 3', published in Owen Jones,
'The Grammar of Ornament' (London, 1856)

designs and styles of 'Savage Ornament' were from the Pacific; Africa, Australia and the Americas were entirely unrepresented. Though the Polynesian examples came first and thus ranked lowest, their inclusion attests to a certain compatibility with Jones' general 'grammar' that may have been the precondition for subsequent quotation in European-settler design.

Maori artifacts were already being extensively collected by settlers, and there are isolated instances of the adaptation of Maori motifs in furniture from the 1860s. The most striking examples are Anton Seuffert's inlaid cabinets (fig. 48), which feature images of Maori warriors and the extinct giant bird, the moa, within a frame composed partly of curvilinear devices based on Maori carving. During the 1880s carvers such as Tene Waitere from the Rotorua area of the North Island began to transpose the sculpture motifs to souvenirs such as small boxes, walking sticks and pipes,[5] but settler-produced creole design only really gained a foundation in the last decade of the century, with the serialized publication of Augustus Hamilton's *Maori Art* between 1896 and 1901. One of a broader wave of ethnological works on Maori prehistory, mythology, customs and tattooing, Hamilton's prolifically illustrated book was ostensibly addressed at anthropologically minded readers; yet it provided commercial artists and designers with a mine of images, and moreover itself exemplified the availability of Maori art to the decoration of printed material. Devices consisting of crossed clubs and masks headed certain chapters, but the most striking feature was the decorated binding (fig. 53). Tightly symmetrical carvings were reproduced on the spine, while a band of curvilinear pattern based on *kowhaiwhai* painting appeared on the front; the lettering itself incorporated the branching and terminal bulbs called *koru* that made this form of painting highly distinctive. The book exemplified a colonial synthesis of Art Nouveau that emphasized naturally inspired curvilinear ornament, decorative serif fonts and Maori design.

Given tribal art enthusiasts' preference for masks, clubs and carvings, it's not surprising that *kowhaiwhai* should since have been discussed less extensively than sculpture. These painted forms, prominent in traditional and neo-traditional Maori art, became extraordinarily visible in creole design, while scarcely figuring in the anthropological and art-historical literature at all.[6] It's as though what came to be *the* Maori and/or New Zealand motif spoke for itself; as though commentary was not simply superfluous but somehow precluded by the irreducible effect of *koru* and *kowhaiwhai* forms themselves. Perhaps textual elaboration was avoided simply because the 'and/or' of settler identity so paradoxically foregrounded and at the same time displaced the indigenous term. If this operation was surely prone to come unstuck in the course of discursive expression, it might retain force and coherence in the form of an image.

In any event, the brief and somewhat rambling account of *kowhaiwhai* in Hamilton's book amounted to the first and, until the 1980s, virtually the last discussion of the art form inadequately characterized as 'rafter painting'. *Kowhaiwhai* are conspicuous on the rafters of tribal meeting houses, but the patterns also appeared on other architectural elements and structures, on canoe paddles and prows, and in some carved and incised forms, such as on decorated gourds. Neither Hamilton nor the missionary Herbert Williams, author of this section of the book, could have avoided encountering a good deal of figurative painting, and rafter paintings that were geometric rather than curvilinear and in colours other than the standard black, red and white, but Hamilton took a certain range of curvilinear patterns to constitute authentic *kowhaiwhai* and left out the rest. Out of the twenty-nine patterns illustrated several became the classic *kowhaiwhai*; these were initially drawn upon by book designers in particular, who in many cases directly imitated the binding of Hamilton's own publication.

It is not surprising that among the many printed works imitating Hamilton closely is *Waiata Maori*, a sheet of songs by Alfred Hill. Though born in Australia and resident there in the latter part of his life, Hill was not only New Zealand's first professional composer, but emphatically a national composer too.[7] His works included the cantata *Hinemoa* (1896), the romantic opera *Tapu* (1902), a 'Maori' lament, a 'Maori' string quartet, a 'Maori' symphony, and a whole series of other works on indigenous themes. The best-known set of songs, *Waiata Poi*, was distributed widely inside and outside New Zealand; at least within the country, the sheet music was frequently reprinted, presumably for performance at home and school. Hill also provided the score for the 1938 film *Rewi's Last Stand* (directed by Rudall Hayward), and a number of other New Zealand 'westerns' that dramatized incidents from the land wars of the 1860s between settlers and Maori; Maori designs, needless to say, were conspicuous in these movies' titles and promotional materials.[8]

The adaptation of *kowhaiwhai* in design was thus not an isolated phenomenon, but an element of a wider engagement with Maori history and folklore. This was not simply spectatorial but to some extent embodied: Maori parts were sung, while individuals with interests in indigenous culture such as Augustus Hamilton, the anthropologists Elsdon Best and Edward Tregear, and Hill himself occasionally adopted Maori dress, either playfully or in the course of exhibitions of Maori culture of one sort or another. This is not to say that the engagement was necessarily sympathetic or more than superficial: while some of the ethnologists had sustained and intimate relations with Maori people, their publications were too often bleached of shared experience, while popular works certainly tended to trot out the same hackneyed plots and characters. The lyrics of *Waiata Maori*, for instance, describe a 'lovely brown-eyed creature/Flax-robed and dark in feature', who was juxtaposed with the stereotypic warrior of 'flashing eye and lolling tongue'. His 'defiant song' appears in the score beneath an instrumental note requiring a 'Wild Barbaric Frenzy'.

Kowhaiwhai frequently provided a frame or border for a pictorial design, especially in printed media, but also in china. A series of Royal Doulton sets, produced between about 1907 and 1955 exclusively for a New Zealand market, could be seen as the most successful instance of this kind of adaptation, mainly because the relatively generous allocation

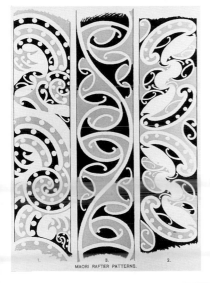

53 AUGUSTUS HAMILTON 'Maori Art' (Wellington, 1901)

54 'Part of the verandah, or porch, of the large house of the Nagati-Porou at Wai-o-Matatini, East Cape', published in Augustus Hamilton, 'Maori Art' (Wellington, 1901)

55 Kowhaiwhai patterns published in Augustus Hamilton, 'Maori Art' (Wellington, 1901)

56 Title-frame from the film 'The Te Kooti Trail', 1927

57 New Zealand
£1 note incorporating
kowhaiwhai, issued
1934–67

58 DOUGLAS ANNAND
designs for Australian
coins from the artist's
sketchbook

of space to the pattern does justice to its dynamism (fig. 67). (Doulton's Australian crockery of the period features not cultural references but native flowers.⁹) The canonical dusky maiden that appeared on some plates recalls the figure evoked in Hill's lyrics, and similar images were used on covers of his published music.¹⁰ Later china tended to model Maori carving in a far more vulgar way, exaggerating the features such as protruding tongues that had initially struck European observers as extraordinarily grotesque.

Maori designs, including *kowhaiwhai* borders, appeared on all the New Zealand banknotes current between 1934 and the introduction of decimal currency in 1967. Australian designers gave some thought to the use of Aboriginal men and artifacts on coins over the same period, but came up only with awkward possibilities that were not pursued; a decidedly elegant kangaroo instead graced the penny. The *kowhaiwhai*

59 New Zealand stamps
incorporating Maori design motifs,
1935–40

60 New Zealand $1 stamp, 1993

on the £1 note was based on Hamilton's pattern number 3, which was widely adapted in other printed media such as postcards, record covers and wrapping paper. Elements drawn from Maori art appear extensively also in fabric design, both in hand-printed craft products and mass-market goods such as tea-towels and cheap shirts. These, like the applications in printed material, have remained ubiquitous up to the present.[11] Postage stamps typically carried reduced and schematic *kowhaiwhai*; in the 1930s and 1940s these often framed members of the royal family, animals unique to New Zealand such as the kiwi and tuatara lizard, folkloric scenes of Maori life, and evocations of a pastoral promised land. Agricultural accomplishments and Maori subjects both continued to be conspicuous, but, with a shift to less cluttered designs, *kowhaiwhai* borders were dropped in the 1950s, to reappear in 1993 around kiwi in a set designed for a world stamp fair.

In no other settler culture have indigenous art forms been mobilized so consistently in nationalist design. While in the United States much use was made of images of Native Americans, indigenous art forms were not themselves adapted and disseminated. The closest parallel to the Maori case is that of Northwest Coast art, which is similarly highly distinctive, and readily adapted in design. Just as Maori carving served in many contexts as shorthand for New Zealand, totem poles became a Canadian emblem, while the associated painting and weaving styles were widely appropriated, and still are highly conspicuous in commercial and tourist imagery in British Columbia. Yet the fact that this iconography came from one region within the country appears to have inhibited its usefulness at the national level. Just as Australians consistently preferred the kangaroo to forms derived from Aboriginal art, it was the maple leaf rather than the mask that featured on the Canadian flag and as the logo for the national airline. The prominence of indigenous reference in New Zealand has been unique.

Good barbarians and bad anthropologists

It's well known that some of the most famous innovations in twentieth-century Western art were inspired by forms derived from tribal art. This could be seen as just one extension of a much deeper primitivist tradition in European culture, which typically contrasted over-refined metropolitan life with the natural simplicity of South Sea islanders or Native Americans. But if modernist primitivism is more about the borrowing of visual forms than the theoretical politics of comparison that we associate with the Enlightenment – with, for instance, Diderot's celebration of Tahitian simplicity – a political and moral dimension is only just below the surface: tribal societies were considered to retain a crude aesthetic vigour, and perhaps mystical propensities, that had long gone stale or been lost in Europe. As we have seen, New Zealand designers appropriated zealously from indigenous art, but it is not surprising that their efforts have been overlooked by the many scholars and curators concerned with modern primitivism. Settler cultures were generally interested neither in the Enlightenment nor in the modernist variants of primitivist rhetoric, but rather in their own localization. Maori design provided national emblems, and Maori myths and tales provided a romantic national prehistory of gods, canoe voyages, warriors, maidens and battles. The content of Hill's operas and the sentimentality of the young Maori mother mark the degree to which these efforts were congruent with late nineteenth-century romanticism rather than part of a modernist battle against academic art and unenlivened illusionism.

The specifically national character of settler primitivism is underlined by the way in which New Zealand writers presented the noble savage as warrior. It has long been something of an axiom in popular perceptions of Australian and New Zealand histories that Maori were generally treated much better than Aboriginal people because they had put up a fight for their land.[12] The notion that there was no violent resistance in Australia is plainly false: as we have seen, writers such as Collins acknowledged that the early Sydney settlers were engaged in 'open war' with Aborigines, but that view of the situation was subsequently forgotten, or obscured.[13] Without going into the question of how frontier conflict in various parts of Australia differed from Maori campaigns against settlers, which were certainly more organized and sustained, it's clear that the positive and negative European responses to Maori and Aborigines respectively are established in Cook voyage commentary, and are reinforced and elaborated in much subsequent travel writing and visual representation well before the New Zealand wars of the 1860s and 1870s – recall Earle's disparaging comments on 'the natives of New South Wales' (p. 57). This, however, makes it all the more illuminating that warriorhood should be seized upon as a Maori attribute that warranted respect. And seized upon it certainly was, not only to affirm Maori worth, but to suggest a special affinity between the British and Maori races.

The ethnologist Edward Tregear introduced his survey of Maori culture – a book bound, needless to say, in native scenes and designs – by cautioning readers not to condemn Maori for past violence and cruelty. Incidents that were indeed horrible were no more than so than some 'similar red blots in English history.' Tregear suggested that many facets of Maori life reminded readers of 'the human in us all'; though common humanity could, it appeared, be recognized in rather particular and gendered ways. 'Brave men looking over crossed weapons and loving women cooing to their babies find their kin all over the world. Very close is this kinship between the restless sea-rover from the Northern isles and his darker brother of the Southern seas.'[14] If maternal affection thus manifested a certain global sameness, the temperament of the warrior, and that of the adventurous voyager, pointed specifically to the mutual recognition of British and Maori men.

Tacitus' celebration of the martial bravery and virtues of the Germans, that so shamed Roman luxury, stands as a paradigm, as well as one of the earliest and most influential expressions of primitivism in

European political thought.[15] If the features of 'simpler' societies selected for approbation have certainly shifted over time, the theme that modern urban life is corrupting is reiterated with remarkable consistency. For those of Tregear's generation, what was upheld was not political liberty or harmony with nature, but the uncultivated manliness of the Maori warrior. This superficially resembles the martial virtue of Tacitus' German, but settler-ethnologists such as Tregear do not exhibit the censorious attitude to civilization that is otherwise so widely a feature of primitivism. Their interest in the type in fact has less in common with the paradigm that could be traced back to Tacitus' *Germania*, than with nineteenth- and twentieth-century German appropriations of that text. For a succession of ideologues seeking to trace Aryan purity and military might back to ancient history, the Latin author became a key authority – the writer, as Simon Schama has put it, of 'the birth certificate of the German race.'[16] This national primitivism is not critical and ironic but tendentious and earnest. It proceeds not by contrast, but rather by conflation: the aim is to assimilate an ancient, or another, society to one's own.

Assimilation had in fact figured more explicitly in an earlier, very earnest book of Tregear's entitled *The Aryan Maori*, which helps account for the intensity of interest in Maori origins over the period of emergent New Zealand nationalism. While late nineteenth-century European ethnologists were frequently concerned with theorizing the global diffusion of culture and the migrations of particular 'races' – in works that are in retrospect distressingly elaborate and ludicrous – these concerns acquired a peculiar twist in New Zealand. Tregear was only one of a number of writers who claimed a Eurasian and specifically Aryan origin for Maori. He believed that this could be attested to by numerous linguistic cognates, though better scholars had already appreciated the basic distinctness of Indo-European and Austronesian (or Malayo-Polynesian) language families. For those less sensible like Tregear, the Latin *taurus* (bull) and Maori *tara* (courage), like *porcus* (pig) and *poke* (dirty) were among words that were surely related.[17]

These philological extravagances suggested a primordial kinship between colonizers and colonized. The supposed high regard of the former for the latter was accounted for by the fact that Maori were, after all, Caucasian. The implications were momentous. As one writer noted, there was therefore no shame in miscegenation, which otherwise amounted to the most public dark secret of settlement. For Tregear, Maori were not 'free-booting Huns or Vandals…but colonists seeking new homes beneath strange stars. We of Europe have set out on the same quest. Encircling Africa, the two vast horns of the Great Migration have touched again, and men whose fathers were brothers on the other side of those gulfs of distance and of time meet each other, when the Aryan of the West greets the Aryan of the Eastern Seas.'[18] As the historian M.P.K. Sorrenson has aptly commented, 'What better myth could there be for a young country struggling for nationhood and for the amalgamation of its races than this reunification of Aryans?'[19] Maori and Pakeha were not only of the same stock, they were engaged in fundamentally the same pioneering endeavour: never mind that one party seemed to be doing it at the expense of the other. The only problem was that Tregear's fanciful linguistic hypotheses were ridiculed so effectively by his peers that he was compelled to drop the line of argument; hence, by the time he published *The Maori Race* in 1904, affinity was imputed in the far more general terms we have already quoted. What might have made a good national myth had not passed as decent anthropology.

Future imperfect

In settler societies, cultural colonization proceeds most energetically not by the 'theft' of motifs or art styles that are reproduced in creole culture, but through forging national narratives that situate indigenous people firmly in the past, or in a process of waning, while settlers are identified with what is new and flourishing and promising. In this way, the potential paradox arising from the use of natives to affirm the native status of settlers is mediated by a narrative of succession: future is to past as settlers are to savages. Crude as it might seem, this temporal construction of the colonial relationship is plainly attested to in a bewildering range of texts and images – not least those of Glover and others, discussed in the previous chapter – that find settler accomplishments blessed, while lamenting the passing of the indigenous way of life.

The sense that native culture was on the wane was continually reinforced by ethnological writers, who emphasized the complexity and interest of ancient aboriginal customs, legends and art, while ignoring or disparaging contemporary indigenous life. Herbert Williams' section on rafter patterns, and many other passages in Hamilton's *Maori Art*, pronounced the indigenous traditions dead by rejecting innovative *kowhaiwhai* as 'too often adulterated', and as bearing 'glaring signs of contact with the *pakeha*.' Though regretting that 'the Maori artist' was generally 'singularly ignorant of his subject', however, Williams undermined his thesis of artistic decay by conceding that the sense of loss was not shared by Maori themselves. 'Accurate information' was difficult to obtain, it seemed, because the 'modern designer, as a rule, thinks himself as good as, or better than, his predecessor.'[20]

A slightly later work suggested a wider context for these efforts to document vanishing cultures. Johannes Andersen's *Maori Life in Ao-tea* – yet another book featuring *kowhaiwhai* and Maori scenes on a decorated binding – carried a dedication 'to the Older Maori People of Ao-tea-roa and to the Younger Poets and Artists of New Zealand, with hopes for the immortality of the one at the hands of the others.' The point was elaborated upon in the preface:

> I would appeal to the artists of New Zealand: do not allow the scenery, entrancing as it is, to constitute the main subject of study; seek inspiration from the ancient indwellers, – to the picture of whose stirring and myth-shadowed life, the scenery is after all no more than the frame. Has no man the magic to picture a Maori defying death, a Tawhaki hurling his lightning?...the poetry to pourtray a love of Tane, or even a Puhi-huia?[21]

Andersen was perhaps less concerned to foster a national culture than to validate his own antiquarian obsession with Maori folklore. But in either case it is significant that it made sense to commend Maori culture to New Zealand readers in these terms. And not only Alfred Hill's compositions, already cited, but many other literary and artistic works make it plain that this sort of advice was being heeded. A creole culture was emerging, featuring Maori, yet almost exclusively authored by and for whites.

This 'almost' marks a loose end in this notion of settler identity. In a logical sense, settler colonialism seems to be a zero-sum contest: either one party or the other holds the land and effective sovereignty. In practice, however, the conflict is never definitively resolved. Settlers do not succeed in eliminating natives, nor do natives expel settlers and reclaim their resources. As Patrick Wolfe has put it, the histories of these societies are therefore characterized by a succession of shifting accommodations.[22] It follows that the artifacts and art forms that settlers appropriate as emblems are likely to retain life and significance within indigenous communities. While settler self-fashioning is energized by an uncertain 'and/or' relation between the native and the national connotations of objects like boomerangs, the merging of these associations is never complete or final. Settler nationalists clearly understood the relation between indigenous reference and emergent national culture as one of incorporation rather than exchange, but creole forms could always be interpreted in other terms, that refused the 'and/or' slippage. Not only indigenous people, but other viewers too could regard boomerangs and *kowhaiwhai* as acknowledgments of indigenous populations, as affirmations of their present as well as past existence. For decades this response may have been theoretically available, or manifest only in marginal or private perceptions, rather than conspicuous in any sphere of public debate. Yet in the longer term the presentation of indigenous references has arguably done more to subvert than reinforce an idea of antipodean nationality.

Be Aboriginal

From the 1880s, Australian designers engaged with local subject-matter, with such quirky results as a work entitled *Adaptation of the Lyre-Bird to Sculptural Purposes*, illustrated in a journal of 1899.[23] By 1907, however, decorative artists such as Eirene Mort felt that everything still remained to be accomplished in the establishment of 'a National School of Australian Ornament.'[24] Her own fabric printing, wood carving and furniture design made gum leaves, waratahs and other native flowers work hard; but given what we've seen of visual culture in New Zealand over the period, it's intriguing that this 'National School' made little use of Aboriginal subjects and none at all of Aboriginal motifs.

61 EIRENE MORT Mirror, c. 1906

Though the trans-Tasman contrast is striking, this is only consistent with the art and literature of the period, which also marginalized indigenous Australians when it did not wholly exclude them.[25] As was noted earlier, the famous nationalist magazine, *The Bulletin*, carried a regular section entitled 'Aboriginalities', but it was devoted to anecdotes relating to outback life and other features of white Australian experience. Settlers, not the black Australians who occasionally provided grist for the page's racist humour, were the bearers of this 'Aboriginality'. There were reasons for borrowing the title – as the settler nationalist organization, the Australian Natives' Association, made plain – that might also be reasons for taking little interest in actual natives or their artifacts.

The general lack of interest may be attributed in part to the tradition of harsh denigration of indigenous Australians that had, by the end of the nineteenth century, a long history indeed. Although there was some debate about Aboriginal racial origins, they were patently not Aryans; hence there was no Australian counterpart to Tregear's fantasy of Aryan reunification. There was little awareness of the complexity of Aboriginal mythology, and – at this time – no effort to fashion any sort of national folklore out of indigenous traditions. Instead the pioneer experience was elaborately and vigorously romanticized, notably, as we have seen, by the Heidelberg painters as well as in literature. Hence it is unsurprising that while Hamilton and others were assiduously documenting the various genres of Maori art, publications on indigenous art in Australia were very sparse indeed. It is revealing, moreover, that some of those who did write on the topic refused to accept that work that impressed them had actually been produced by Aboriginal people. Rock paintings of Wandjina spirits from the Kimberley region of northwestern Australia, in particular, were held to constitute an anomaly. For one A.W. Grieg, writing in 1909,

> Not only is the artistic enthusiasm of these savages beyond all reasonable expectation, but it finds its expression in the delineation of an object which is altogether beyond the range of their every-day experience, and which would appear from its constant repetition to be of a symbolical nature....[26]

Grieg dealt with his invented problem by finding that the art could not have been an 'indigenous development'. It attested rather to Sumatran influence, which he imagined might be detected in Asiatic dress and an apparent inscription.[27] By de-emphasizing the local distinctiveness of the art, these diffusionist speculations perhaps rendered it less appropriate to

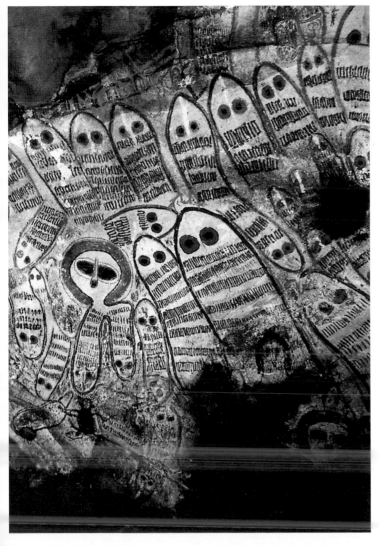

62 Wandjina figures at Mandanggari, Gibb River, Kimberley, Western Australia

63 Aboriginal shield from northeast Queensland rainforest region

64 Aboriginal shield from West Australia

a settler iconography. But this is no doubt less important than the fact that most of the diverse genres of Aboriginal art did not happen to be compatible with European design to the degree that Maori art fortuitously had been – there is no place for carved trees in the grammar of ornament.

Around the turn of the century, there was a still more basic problem: given the paucity of publications, Aboriginal art was comparatively invisible. Even supposing that urban white Australians sought material out, they would have had difficulty encountering much apart from weapons in museum displays, and rock engravings such as those of the Sydney district. The minority of settlers in the north and outback might have witnessed body painting and other ceremonial art forms on ritual occasions, and seen or collected shields, among a wider range of artifacts, but they were pastoralists and prospectors and itinerant workers, not artists or designers. If they had the opportunity to form a diversified sense of Aboriginal life and art, it is not unfair to suggest that for the most part they lacked the will. Before the expansion of domestic tourism, before mission stations began to market Aboriginal crafts in the southern cities, and before photojournalism and film enriched the vision of the vicarious traveller, few who possessed the inclination to study indigenous culture also had the opportunity.

Within the limited range of what might have been seen in the cities, shields in museum collections were possibly the most arresting artifacts. Their seemingly abstract forms, frequently figuring dynamic zig-zags, now seem extraordinarily compelling, but it is not clear that they would have engaged Victorian or Edwardian eyes, nor that they could have been incorporated in the design of the period. Whether perceived to be striking or not, the patterns were, in any case, insufficiently singular to serve as national emblems. This may all be surprising in retrospect, given that a few genres of Aboriginal art are today instantly recognizable and wholly distinctive. Of these, however, central Australian dot painting is an innovation of the 1970s, while only a handful of barks had been collected during the nineteenth century, and these were not widely known. Baldwin Spencer, biologist turned ethnographer, and one of the founding fathers of Australian anthropology, 'virtually rediscovered' the art form of bark painting in 1912. While Special Commissioner and Chief Protector of Aborigines he conducted a brief period of fieldwork in Oenpelli in the Alligator Rivers region, and became interested in the paintings after being presented with one. He proceeded to buy the barks that formed the walls of people's huts, and also commissioned a set; by 1920 over two hundred had been purchased by him or on his behalf for the National Museum of Victoria.[28]

65 Unknown artist, Mimi Spearing a Kangaroo, 1912.
Bark painting from the Baldwin Spencer Collection

Spencer discussed bark painting in two of his major publications, and it was not long before he also advocated its relevance to contemporary white Australian art – or rather craft. In a lecture to the Victorian Arts and Crafts Society, he had expressed reservations about some uses of native flora, apparently regarding the wattle as an awkward basis for pattern. Like Mort and others, he favoured the waratah, and had himself designed a commemorative medal that featured it. But Spencer also encouraged craft workers to visit the museum and 'copy some of the designs of the Australian aborigines or perhaps better still those of New Guinea or the South Sea Islands.'[29] This anticipated by a decade Margaret Preston's oft-cited advocacy of indigenous reference, but it is notable that Spencer's advice was not framed in nationalist terms. The 'better still' those of the South Seas resonates with what seems to have been the established perception that material from Polynesia or New Guinea was more accessible to a European aesthetic. In any event, his proposal seems to have had little immediate impact.[30]

Margaret Preston's arguments, in contrast, were explicitly nationalistic. Although she was aware of Roger Fry's work, and certainly conscious of the widespread interest in 'primitive' forms in Europe, the immediate stimulus to her first articles advocating the application of indigenous art was neither a desire to emulate modernists elsewhere, nor Fry's forceful claim for the merits of what he called 'negro sculpture'. Writing in *The Home*, Preston referred rather to the Australian critic of architecture, Hardy Wilson, who asserted that Australian art and design should emerge from its environment and region. For him, this meant looking to China or Japan. For her, the principle was apt, but a recent trip to New Guinea, and the material in the Australian Museum in Sydney, prompted her to regard Pacific and Aboriginal patterns as an appropriate basis for 'a national decorative art'. Preston apparently regarded these as better sources than the east Asian traditions because the latter had already been drawn upon extensively by many artists elsewhere. 'Hurry then and use our own material in an Australian spirit before other nations step in and we are left without having even tried for a national spirit in applied art.'[31] Hers was not, therefore, a universalizing modernism that stopped at asserting the need for 'fresh stimulus and a return to simple symbols'.[32] It was also, from the beginning, deeply inflected by a Ruskinian localism: art and architecture expressed national life and character, as conversely national vigour, or regrettably national timidity, were apparent in art.

The application of indigenous art was presented not as a complement to the representation of native flora and fauna, but as a preferable, and urgent, alternative to it, at least in the domain of applied art. Given that Preston's most enduringly popular images have been her floral prints (discussed pp. 129–33), it is ironic that she disparaged 'twiddling with' native flowers. It was not the subject itself, however, but a prevailing 'downright realism' that she singled out as an especially deadening feature of 'the South Kensington dullness' that allegedly then pervaded Australian decorative art. The point received further emphasis in a Sunday newspaper piece of 1930, entitled, with characteristic verve, 'Away with pokerworked kookaburras and gumleaves' – that sort of thing was 'degrading the art sense of a young nation.'[33] The 'young nation' comes across, in Preston's writings, as rather a lax class needing periodic scolding, which she delivers with evident relish. Her more positive arguments advocated both the adaptation of form and an emulation

66 ARTHUR PERCY GODBER Rafter Patterns, 1939–47

67 Royal Doulton platter, 1929–55

Cash and carry pockets are a feature of this slack suit in white soleando linen with a pattern of aboriginal motifs in navy. The slacks are high waisted and the jacket designed with a shaped back.

Concentric circles form the most important part of the aboriginal design in this linen dressmaker suit. The jacket has a high buttoned fastening and is finished with tailored revers and collar.

At Last ! — Australian designed fabrics

Neither Picasso nor Dali designed these truly Australian dress materials. Their inspiration is the age-old art of the Australian aborigine; adapted from tribal symbols, they are primitive—yet as new as surrealism is to-day.

"Arunta" they are called, after a well-known Central Australian tribe, and the colours are true to the pigments of the aborigines. Earth red, ochre yellow, and cobalt blue are used to portray native symbols in simple yet enchanting and rhythmic designs.

This season is the first time that these Arunta designs have been used, and their launching marks a step forward for Australian applied art. Emus, kangaroos, boomerangs, the ant eater, the platypus, and abstract designs of a symbolistic nature provide a wealth of material for decorative patterns. They have met with instant success in Australia, and an overseas vogue is also expected. It is an interesting and characteristic variation on the peasant art of European countries. The Arunta fabrics have been launched by David Jones, Sydney.

— For men, too !

The ancient dwellers in Australia painted their bodies with these symbols. Printed in the authentic aborigine colours on Australian-produced fabrics, they make sensational designs for men's fashions. These age-old designs, representing primitive culture, strike a modern and sophisticated note. The savage brandishing his spear, the stylised ant eater, the queer long-legged emu might have been created by followers of contemporary art. These Arunta designs have started something, and their fame is expected to spread overseas, where they will challenge the primitive designs of other lands. *Aboriginal chic!*

Dressing gown in wrap-over style has rows and rows of emus. Cape York geese printed in tan and green on a cream background is a colourful idea in underpants. Natives throwing spears are printed all over the pyjamas. Navy and green are used as accents on a grey background. Reversible shirt in cream with green ducks.

26 AUSTRALIA *National Journal* December 1st, 1940

27 AUSTRALIA *National Journal* December 1st, 1940

28 AUSTRALIA *National Journal* December 1st, 1940

68 'At last! – Australian designed fabrics' and '– For men too!', Arunta-derived fabric design, published in the 'Australia National Journal', 1 December 1940

of a primitive spirit that would lend art simplicity and directness. Given the central role of Owen Jones' *Grammar of Ornament* in the canonization of Maori design, it is symptomatic of shifting times and aesthetics that Preston concluded her first article by noting that 'When one speaks one does not insist on one's knowledge of grammar. Speech is used naturally to convey an idea. Use your art in the same way.'[34]

It is not clear whether all the artists who subsequently began 'talking' with Aboriginal motifs and designs were responding directly to Preston's preaching (those in Melbourne are more likely to have arrived at the same concerns independently). By the late 1930s, however, there were certainly many; and an indigenous style was expressed in graphic design, in fabric and ceramics, and in murals and 'rubber' floors in buildings such as the Australian National Travel Authority's Melbourne offices.[35] What was often unfortunately called 'Abo Art' was quoted in many contexts, ranging from domestic kitsch and architectural ornament to government publications. The Sydney department store, David Jones, consistently marketed 'Aboriginal' material; their summer offerings in 1940 included a range of men's and women's clothes in 'colours true to the pigments of the Aborigines. Earth red, ochre yellow and cobalt blue are used to portray native symbols in simple yet enchanting and rhythmic designs.' The launching of these 'Arunta fabrics' was said to mark 'a step forward for Australian applied art'.[36] And, while Margaret Preston had lamented in 1925, 'Has anyone attempted to make Australian designs for an Australian play?', by 1940 it was possible to point to William Constable's Aboriginal-inspired sets for the ballet *Corroboree*. Aboriginal art did not appear on stamps or banknotes until the 1960s, but earlier applications in printed material were nevertheless important. *This is Australia*, a major book published to mark the 1938 sesquicentenary of settlement, featured generic Aboriginal motifs on the cover and title page, though it's notable that within the text they appeared only in the brief introductory section dealing with Aborigines, and not in the substance that followed, which dealt (as might have been expected) with pastoral and industrial accomplishments and Australia's thriving cities.

Preston published several further articles around 1941, which celebrated indigenous art less apologetically than in her essays of the 1920s and stressed that its quality refuted prevailing characterizations of Aborigines as 'the lowest grade of humanity.' As before, her concluding assertion was generally that the study of Aboriginal art provided 'a chance for Australia to have a national art' but in some cases this seems almost an afterthought.[37] She was moving toward the view that the material was worth looking at for itself, as well as for its usefulness in the fashioning of a national culture.

Preston's endorsement of Aboriginal art thus went hand in hand with the suggestion that it was ripe for appropriation; and it was important that the material was adapted quickly, before the artists of other countries became interested and it ceased to be Australia's own. The instability of the 'and/or' that connected native and national culture made it never clear or predictable whether indigenous art was affirming, or being affirmed by, the applications it inspired. It's no easy matter to measure – the issue being to what extent, and in whose eyes? – but responses to one 1941 exhibition make it plain that the ambiguities were more widely present than in Preston's own writing over the period.

Early in 1941, staff at the Australian Museum began to prepare an exhibition of Aboriginal art, together with material that demonstrated the potential of its applications. What they were doing was not dissimilar to the efforts of Canadian curators almost fifteen years earlier: 'Canadian West Coast Art: Native and Modern' had presented a mix of indigenous pieces and work by settler artists, suggesting that both were grounded in place, with the former providing a decorative heritage ripe

69 'Canadian West Coast Art: Native and Modern', exhibition at the National Gallery of Canada/Galerie National du Canada, Ottawa, 1927

70 'Australian Aboriginal Art and its Application', Australian Museum exhibition at the David Jones department store, Sydney, 1941

for harvest by the latter, whose work promised to establish a genuinely national aesthetic.[38] Essentially the same rhetoric met with an enthusiastic response from Australian arts and crafts practitioners, and around March it became apparent that museum's temporary display areas might prove inadequate to the size of the exhibition. The director at any rate took up an offer from David Jones – an Australian equivalent of Harrods or Macy's – to use their auditorium. (For the department store to host an exhibition was less unusual than it may sound; it had its own art gallery, which carried many significant shows.) Other commercial support, however, was lacking; several major companies declined the museum's requests for sponsorship. One businessman, writing back to the director, directly contradicted the argument that Preston had enunciated earlier against kookaburras and gum leaves: 'Australian native patterns' were 'of very great archaeological interest', he admitted, while doubting that they possessed 'any great artistic value to suit the present times.... Would it not be far better to make more use of our Fauna and Flora as motives for decorative treatment?'[39]

Members of the Arts and Crafts Society evidently thought not, and contributed almost a hundred items, mainly ceramics; these were complemented by photographs of architectural features and specimens of printed material. All this constituted the second section of the exhibition, following a fairly extensive collection of Aboriginal paintings and artifacts, including pieces borrowed from collections in Melbourne and Adelaide. A third section presented works of art (as distinct from commercial applications), mainly loaned by the Art Gallery of New South Wales. Apart from Preston's paintings, these were, however, all depictions of Aboriginal subjects, rather than attempts to emulate an Aboriginal style. The museum was offered Tom Roberts' *Aboriginal Head – Charlie Turner* (fig. 45), but this was not included; the painters represented were instead figures who have since become obscure, such as Benjamin Minns, then a fashionable society figure, and well-known for portraits and cartoons of indigenous subjects. The material was on show for only eleven days in August 1941, but was accompanied by a lecture programme and a competition for art students, and attracted three thousand visitors, according to the museum.[40]

One might have anticipated that the anthropology curator, Frederick McCarthy, who otherwise wrote extensively on Aboriginal art, would have used the designers' interests as a vehicle for the promotion of the indigenous forms in their own right. Though the Aboriginal work itself only constituted one section of the exhibition, Australian Museum staff went to considerable lengths to obtain photographs of rock paintings and engravings, and loans of 'weapons, utensils, sacred objects and orna-

71 Some of the exhibits in the 1941 Australian Museum exhibition 'Australian Aboriginal Art and its Applications'

ments' from collections in Melbourne and Adelaide as well as around Sydney. This must have been just about as substantial and inclusive as any other exhibition that had taken place up to that point, but the claims McCarthy made for Aboriginal art in a press release, and in an article in the museum's magazine, were oddly modest:

> It is not contended that aboriginal art equals the abstract and imaginative qualities, or the richness of design, of the art of many other primitive peoples, nor that it approaches the magnificence of the art of the classical civilizations, but it may be claimed that the variety and simplicity of the wide range of motifs and equally numerous techniques…give it a character sufficiently distinctive to identify it with the people, and for this reason it may be said to represent a definite phase of art in Australia. Adapted with intelligence and taste, aboriginal art can make a unique contribution to modern

Australian craft work.... In addition, the myths and legends, daily life and art motifs, form an inspiration that may give rise to a national decorative element in Australian architecture.[41]

Given the hesitancy of this assessment of Aboriginal art, it's striking that the ambivalence of newspaper reviewers and other critics was about the white 'applications', rather than their indigenous sources:

Best exhibits by far were the aboriginal bark-paintings.... The aboriginal stuff was swell, but all the modern application wasn't. (Glaring examples of the unswell were of the china and glass, and that gay little frieze. All horrible beyond belief....)[42]

And this in a magazine that had featured such 'applications' a good deal in its own pages. Another reviewer was more circumspect, but noted that while the barks showed 'the aboriginal to be a sensitive artist with a true feeling for design' the paintings 'should be compared with the crude

72 Studio Anna hand-painted ashtray in an Aboriginal design, 1956–8

73 Byram Mansell at work on 'Hibiscus and Honey-Ants' Nest' with
a northeastern Queensland shield in the foreground

decoration they have inspired on the glassware on view nearby.'[43] One
craves a fuller range of evidence documenting the reception of this particular show, but the fragments that we do have suggest that indigenous
art was taken to be worthy of attention; a creole culture that attempted,
too deliberately, to ground itself through that art, was not. The response
to this particular exhibition foreshadowed the future of both Aboriginal
art and the new 'Aboriginal' art and design produced by whites. The latter
would proliferate during the 1950s and 1960s, and were even supported
by a published manifesto, Roman Black's *Old and New Aboriginal Art*;
'old' meant Aboriginal art by Aboriginal people, whereas settlers were the
authors of the 'new'. Though this work received wide circulation as
design, none of the attempts in high art genres achieved much repute, let
alone canonical status. In hindsight, it might be observed that Margaret
Preston's work alone rose above the level of kitsch. And even her prints
and paintings, as we shall see, tended to deflect attention from their own
forms toward the indigenous art works themselves.

74 MARGARET PRESTON The Brown Pot, 1940

In the 1860s Eugen von Guérard and Nicholas Chevalier were celebrated for their ability to capture what was distinctively Australian. For some early twentieth-century critics, however, this was precisely what those painters lacked. By 1916, it was not surprising that since they 'hailed from Europe...their Art was essentially alien to its new environment.' And while von Guérard had been accused in 1870 of detailing Australian plants with a botanist's rather than an artist's eye, it had become plain that 'Our flora...was a thing beyond their ken.' So wrote Frederick McCubbin, who proceeded to celebrate Louis Buvelot and more particularly the Heidelberg group, of which he himself was a member. He singled out Streeton's *The Purple Noon's Transparent Might* (1896) as 'almost...a National Symbol' that 'typified the strength, beauty and possibilities of Australia.'[1]

The Heidelberg painters were in turn found wanting by Margaret Preston, whose sustained appeal for national design and national art has already been discussed (pp. 115–19). She acknowledged the interest of Tom Roberts, citing *The Breakaway* as a painting that 'started a fine school', but suggested that the preoccupation with light was fundamentally misdirected. Whilst light was 'fugitive', 'form never changes, and the forms of a country are its own characteristics which the artist must know before he adds his own personality to it.'[2]

Preston was, as always, making both a wider polemical point and a claim for her own work, but the two could be conflated by a particular telling of the evolution of Australian art. Such a story was offered to viewers of the Carnegie Corporation's 'Art of Australia' exhibition, which toured to the United States in 1941. The show began with Aboriginal bark paintings and concluded with Preston's Aboriginal-inspired work. The summary history of Australian art in the catalogue made the message explicit:

> Finally, it has been left for Margaret Preston to strike the one original note in the development of a new outlook for Australian art. Already having made a name for her decorative painting of wild

flowers, she has studied the work of the aboriginal artists all over Australia. She has combined her research and knowledge of their outlook and design with her sophisticated study of European art, and applied it very successfully to the rendering of Australian landscape. In carrying out this idea she has set herself the limitation of using only those colours which are to be found in the particular district which she paints. In this way she enters fully into the outlook of the aboriginal artists, who were limited in their portrayal of colours by the clays and pigments which were found in the various areas.

The inclusion of her painting 'Aboriginal Landscape' completes the cycle of this exhibition, which starts with the work of the aborigines, and ends with the influence of their work as the basis of a new outlook for a national art for Australia.[3]

Some American critics must have been impressed, for this line of argument was reproduced in reviews, and the *Aboriginal Landscape* referred to was the only work from the exhibition that was purchased by an American institution.[4] But the most important feature of the story is that it wasn't at all persuasive so far as Preston's Australian audience was concerned. Her reservations about Heidelberg would not have been widely shared at the time, and nor would they be today, when Roberts' and Streeton's accomplishments are still considered definitive. Moreover, Preston almost certainly wrote the text quoted above herself.[5] Though many critics had good things to say about her work, even those closest to her refrained from defining its historic significance quite so categorically.

Though Preston's arguments for a national art were publicized widely through women's magazines and newspapers as well as through journals such as *Art in Australia*, her views were not generally noticed or endorsed.[6] Her work was celebrated despite rather than because of the engagement with Aboriginal forms that she advocated, and this for the most part remained the case after her death in 1963. Since the 1970s, a few commentators have credited her with being ahead of her time in taking an interest in indigenous art, but the paintings and prints which feature Aboriginal references are now marginal in comparison with the enormously popular flower works and views of Sydney Harbour. Margaret Preston is certainly widely appreciated today for the distinctively Australian qualities of her art, but the national appeal that the work now possesses is not at all the same as the appeal she herself made for it.

Monumental flowers

Preston's work developed rapidly, and followed many particular shifts in direction that it is not my purpose to chart here.[7] Suffice to say that back in Australia during the early 1920s, after seven years in Europe, she became committed to the notion that the way forward lay in a national art – one that was formed by its environment, and that drew something from indigenous traditions. She published a number of essays arguing for the 'application' of Aboriginal art in craft and decorative art, though apparently did not draw from indigenous forms in her own paintings and prints until 1940. Her work from the nineteen-twenties and thirties is in fact diverse, and includes many urban and suburban Sydney views, but is dominated by images of Australian flowers and birds.

The best of her woodblocks, such as the *Western Australian Banksia* (1929, fig. 77) and the *Australian Rock Lily* (c. 1933, fig. 75), are at once singularly beautiful and absolutely controlled. They also possess a kind of self-sufficiency and distance from discourse that is shared by decorative art and still life, among other forms. It's certainly possible to talk about her works in art-historical terms, citing the influence of Japanese printmaking, or their Cézanne-ish shallowness, but such commentary seems at once to say too little and too much. Like any artist, Preston responded to a host of stimuli, but to trace these is to neglect the solid presences that she so consummately evoked.

A newspaper critic suggested in 1927 that Preston's still lifes were 'almost monumental in form'.[8] This comment draws attention to an apparent paradox. For the idea of national art is not easily reconciled with diminutive and decorative works, which have more obvious affiliations with craft and design than with the landscapes and history paintings that were the more conventional vehicles for the expression of national spirit and historic purpose. While the latter were saturated with overt meaning, and were almost measurable in yards rather than inches, Preston's banksias and desert peas seem more attractive and domestic than moralizing and national. This response, however, misses the relation that Preston imagined between the home and the nation. Her claim that 'the beginning should come from the home and domestic arts', and her hope that 'the craftsman will succeed where, until now, the artist has certainly failed', warrant our attention.[9] It's not anachronistic to understand Preston as a feminist, but my interest in her affirmation of domestic cultural expression arises more specifically from the way both her polemic and her practice presumed (following Ruskin and others) that material objects are vital for the formation of personal and

75 MARGARET PRESTON Australian Rock Lily, c. 1933

collective identities. As an intellectual position, this interest in the arti-factual was long marginalized (at least outside the discipline of art history) by the theoretical hegemony of language, ideology and semiotic theory. Over the last decade, however, material culture has re-emerged as a key topic in fields such as anthropology and sociology, and it is argued that people use quotidian objects such as domestic furnishings in an implicitly political way, to define and assert particular identities.[10] In a sense, this is only to make explicit in intellectual debate what has always been obvious in fashion and home decorating magazines, and in the consumption practices those magazines address.

National characters and identities may be endlessly debated in public, and the sense of self that a person possesses does respond to these wider discourses, to be sure; but it is also shaped through practice. The acquisition of ordinary things, modes of dress, and styles of decoration in the home are expressive activities that variously convey attachments to local and cosmopolitan values, religious and political affiliations, and class, ethnic and subcultural solidarities. Further, as Preston asserted, the domestic practice and application of craft and design may anticipate rather than merely express developments in high art, among other cultural domains. If we eschew her preoccupation with the realization of national cultural distinctness, we can nevertheless gain something from exploring the obvious point that 'domestic arts', understood broadly, are arts of self-fashioning.

The *Western Australian Banksia* images the native flower in a fairly severe modernist vase. The accomplishment of the print rests in part on the fact that the solid black cylinder at once echoes the bulk and form of the banksia, while contrasting with its provoking and highly textured irregularities. Yet the vase is not there just for these compositional reasons, nor because Preston happened to own at least a couple of this kind. The container makes it explicit that these flowers are displayed, presumably at home, and thus sets the work apart from a project of botanical illustration. But the domestic aesthetic that is presented is not just any domestic aesthetic. As I mentioned earlier, Preston campaigned again 'South Kensington dullness' and insisted on the need for forms that were shaped by the land and by the environment, understood by her in a national rather than a peculiarly local sense. Her insistence upon the importance of decoration contradicted the enduring idea that it only ever meant mere adornment and feminine prettiness. For this artist, decoration was like architecture; it was culturally expressive, and it needed to be appropriate to epoch and place. Her friend and sometime pupil Gladys Reynell's vase was appropriate to an Australian living room both because it expressed the spirit of its own time, and for its formal correspondence with the weight and substance of the banksia cone.[11]

From this perspective, Preston's flower works are not decorative in any disparaging sense. They could be seen, rather, to possess an argumentative dynamism, deliberately elevating certain subjects through representation in art. What the works described and advocated was the presence of an Australia flora.[12] If, decades later, McCahon could be celebrated for revitalizing the land in New Zealanders' eyes 'by simply pointing to its physical presence' (p. 24), Preston surely gave these flowers new meaning by drawing attention to their presence in the same way. At the risk of making too much of a small picture, I want to suggest that her less grandiose efforts may even have been more effective, if in a diffuse and unmeasurable way. As I noted with respect to von Guérard, the masculine project of national myth-making via the evocation of awesome and remote topography always suffered the paradox of culti-vating human attachment to dehumanized landforms. If the enduring appeal of the Heidelberg school arises in part from the suppression of distance – from those painters' transformation of familiar bush and beach into art – Preston literally brought the bush right into the living room, and into the domestic routine of unheroic self-fashioning. This was not the validation of a pioneer myth, but an affirmation of domestic practices that were true to their antipodean environment.

There appear to be inconsistencies, if not contradictions, between Preston's statements about floral imagery and her extensive use of it. I quoted earlier her disparaging observations on the pervasiveness of gum-leaves, wattle blossoms and kookaburras in design (p. 116). These, she suggested, needed to be repudiated in favour of Aboriginal forms; yet her own art over the years immediately following her most polemical statement along these lines is dominated by Australian wildflowers and birds, including kookaburras. It might be added that earlier designers such as Eirene Mort, whose imitators Preston would primarily have been reacting against, had dignified their twiddling with gum-leaves and wattle by appeal to the importance of a national approach to decorative art. They broadly anticipated, in other words, the terms of Preston's arguments, as well as the subject-matter that she actually used, as opposed to the Aboriginal references that she advocated but herself scarcely employed over the period between 1924 and 1940.

In part, Preston was conflating issues of national authenticity with those of artistic style and modernity. It was presumably not the gum leaves and kookaburras themselves that she objected to, but certain ways of handling them, which seemed traditional and deadeningly realistic. Her work speaks the modernist preoccupation with form more loudly than that of most of her Australian contemporaries. But she did more than replace one approach to representation and decoration with another. By depicting the flowers as forms, rather than as sprays of colour or ornamental motifs, she effectively presented them, as the 1927 critic noted, in a 'monumental' fashion. A monument is a public edifice that marks historical fact, and that encourages quasi-religious contemplation. The connection could easily sound absurd: Preston's woodblocks do not make deliberate or specific historical references, they are not allegorical, and they are not excessively grave – though they are mostly serious rather than simply pretty or cheerful. Yet these works do more than simply connect Australian natural forms with the business of home- and self-making, with mundane aesthetics. A personal response to certain flowers, or the practice of displaying them, has little weight unless the sentiment and the activity are somehow validated and given public meaning – as other activities, such as football or cricket, may be dignified through their connection with patriotic competition. It is not always true that art affirms the subjects and relations that it depicts, but Preston's can certainly be seen to validate and bestow meaning upon the use of nationally distinctive flowers in the arts of the home.

Though she always talked of the urgency of creating an Australian art, Preston avoided turning banksias or black cockatoos into mere emblems of the country. She instead represented the flowers, birds and places alike in a fashion that was and remains compelling for those who know her subjects at first hand. My point is not that she was always truthful (to revive a term that's been banished from the art-critical lexicon) – but that this authenticity made for enduring connections between her art and the lived experience of her audience. The tactility that she imaged – the harsh serrations of those banksia leaves – is known to our fingers, and we have learned to see familiar wildflowers as she presented them. If Preston's enunciations concerning national culture were always too didactic, her art knew better, and worked subtly to encourage a sense of belonging to place and environment.

Fusion or combination?

In the 1930s and 1940s, Preston's arguments at once complemented and differed from those of a number of literary nationalists. They felt generally that Australian culture had been stifled by its British inheritance, and that an engagement with the Australian environment was essential if anything distinctive and vital was to emerge. There were, however, significant variations in emphasis. P.R. Stephenson, in his *Foundations of Culture in Australia*, referred to indigenous people only in passing to note their irrelevance to the emergence of a 'new nation' and 'a new human type' in Australia.[13] In contrast, the Jindyworobak group of poets declared an interest in Aboriginal spirituality, though as Humphrey McQueen has pointed out, the movement's label exaggerated the extent to which indigenous culture, rather than the desert wilderness and related images, was actually exploited in their work.[14]

In 1940 Preston's interest in Aboriginal art became dramatically more evident in her own work. The catalyst may have been a closer relationship with Fred McCarthy, the anthropology curator at the Australian Museum introduced in Chapter Three (p. 122). During the 1940s, in any event, she was to participate in the field trips of the Anthropological

Society of New South Wales to examine the rock engravings around Sydney; she also later travelled through central and northern Australia visiting Aboriginal communities, and especially galleries of rock art.

As had been the case earlier, Preston moved rapidly from one approach to another, possibly manifesting a hesitancy and sensitivity to criticism that belied her public conviction. She drew upon Aboriginal art in a number of quite distinct ways: by working with ochre-like colours, by quoting the patterns of shields and carved trees, by emulating what she took to be indigenous compositional principles, by illustrating Aboriginal legends, by presenting biblical subjects in Aboriginal settings, and by reproducing rock art fairly directly.

Her most successful 'Aboriginal' works surely include the landscapes deriving from the earliest phase of this experiment, such as the *Aboriginal Landscape* (1941). It is worth raising the question of what the 'Aboriginal' adjective here actually refers to. It hardly suggests that the generic tract of country depicted was inhabited or owned by Aboriginal people. Although she made one late work which must be seen as a harsh comment on the Australian government's neglect of the indigenous population, it cannot be said that Preston generally displayed much interest in the prior history of settler-indigenous relations. Her national concerns were forward-looking rather than retrospective, and though by 1941 she certainly celebrated Aboriginal art for itself as well as for its uses in a new Australian culture, she was not concerned to expose the history of dispossession or remind viewers that the country had once been owned by Aborigines. An anachronistic reading of the *Aboriginal Landscape* could take it to affirm the Aboriginality of the country, but Preston's admittedly cursory remarks on colour and related matters point to a more circuitous association. The pigments employed in Aboriginal art reflected those of the land because they were derived directly from it. More generally, theirs was an 'aesthetic form that is of our land', that accordingly pointed the way for a 'modern' artist who wanted to grasp the truth of the environment:[15] the grey and ochre palette furthered that aim. Paintings of this kind may have indirectly acknowledged an Aboriginal presence, but cannot be said to have emphasized one.

Preston was at other times more concerned to display elements of Aboriginal culture: some works, such as the 1940 woodblock print *Fish, Aboriginal Design* and the 1946 monotype of the same title, can be seen essentially as illustrations of Aboriginal art forms, while a later series depicted incidents derived from legends. Where she provided captions or comments on works, it was often made explicit that she took the Aboriginal element to provide a direct route to national distinctness. In

76 MARGARET PRESTON Aboriginal Landscape, 1941

77 MARGARET PRESTON Western Australian Banksia, 1929

78 MARGARET PRESTON Fish, Aboriginal Design, 1940

79 MARGARET PRESTON Aboriginal Design, with Sturt's Pea, 1943

the 1946 *Aboriginal Still Life*, for example, her stated aim was 'to create a still life that would owe its existence to this country, and not to Holland or any other nationality.'[16] This over-riding purpose required little engagement with Aboriginal people or culture, though Preston's appreciation of Aboriginal art did deepen during the 1940s, and she became concerned to challenge widespread misapprehensions, such as the idea that there were essential affinities between 'primitive art' and children's art. Not being really a painter of people, nor a social realist, she never depicted Aboriginal individuals or living conditions. It was left to Communist painters such as Yosl Bergner, Noel Counihan and Marguerite Mahood to depict the marginalization and impoverishment of the Aboriginal people.[17]

Despite the crudity of her own statements, Preston's 'Aboriginal' corpus is too diverse to be dismissed for having merely seized upon indigenous reference as a short-cut to national distinctness. The Aboriginal landscapes of 1941 and 1942 are predated by *The Brown Pot* (fig. 74), a somewhat more radical painting that places the familiar banksias on an essentially abstract background clearly divided into bars and fields of white and ochre browns. The pattern recalls north Queensland shields of the kind Preston would have seen in the Australian Museum, and one in particular that she'd discussed in her 1930 article on the 'application' of Aboriginal designs (pp. 115–16). A similar combination of a bowl of flowers against an indigenous pattern appeared in the 1943 masonite

80 EMILY CARR
A Skidgate Pole, 1942

print *Aboriginal Design, with Sturt's Pea*, which reordered the elements of an Arnhem Land bark. The same general principle, with varying emphases, shaped a number of other works.

There are striking affinities, as well as notable differences, between Preston's project and that of her older contemporary, the Canadian Emily Carr (1871–1945), who for most of her career was a relatively isolated figure in Victoria and Vancouver, British Columbia. After returning from a period of study in France, Carr became increasingly interested in the distinctive sculpture traditions of the native peoples of the Northwest Coast; though she also painted mesmerizing skyscapes and treescapes, totem poles and related carvings became central subjects in many of her paintings. She was not part of the nationalist landscape school, the Group of Seven, but was 'discovered' by members of that circle in the late 1920s, and her work was then celebrated increasingly for its distinctively national qualities. Like Preston, she was highly engaged by local indigenous art traditions and valued them specifically because she saw them as the traditions of her place, but she did not try as Preston did to create new forms on the basis of their colours, elements or design principles. What she did, rather, was to depict them, yet she did this with such emphasis – in many cases the carved form is not a feature within the painting, but rather the object that overwhelms it – that she moved resolutely beyond ethnographic illustration. The fact that the carvings remain part of the landscape also suggests an indigenous presence in the land, as had Earle's *Distant View* (fig. 10); this connection tended to be severed in Preston's adaptations, and rendered at best very tenuous in works such as her *Aboriginal Landscape*. Nonetheless, the values of Carr's work are now as contentious as those of McCahon and Preston.

The really original feature of Preston's *Brown Pot*, and similar works, lies in the presentation of cultural combination as a formal problem. In this respect, they differ from most of the classic modernist appropriations of tribal forms, and this difference is closely linked to a significant contrast between the logic of primitivism in general and the special mission of settler primitivism discussed in the previous chapter (p. 106–9). In the best known works of modernist primitivism, and in the great majority of works reproduced in the Museum of Modern Art's compendious 1983 catalogue *'Primitivism' in 20th Century Art*, tribal forms are assimilated into new compositions, not introduced as separate motifs that are marked off from the rest of the work – Matisse's *Portrait of Madame Matisse* is a case in point. There are, of course, exceptions: the shock value of Picasso's *Demoiselles d'Avignon* (1907) derives in part

81 Fang Mask, Gabon

82 HENRI MATISSE Portrait of Madame Matisse, 1913

from the harsh distinctness of the faces, which are modelled on Dan masks, and Oceanic forms are presented with greater integrity in some of Ernst's paintings, and still more conspicuously by German expressionists such as Nolde and Pechstein, who had both travelled to the Pacific.[18] But even in these cases there is none of Preston's insistent, overbearing, deliberate foregrounding of the Aboriginal element (nor Carr's consistent interest in local native sculpture, as opposed to tribal art in a broader sense). The European modernists generally used whichever Oceanic or African elements interested them, evoking the primitive unspecifically, and usually without specific acknowledgment in their works' titles.[19] Hence viewers of primitivist works might be aware of the general stimulus of tribal art, but would have little idea which aspects of paintings were stimulated by indigenous examples; nor would they know which regions those examples came from, unless they were told. Preston did tell her viewers where to look: as she noted with respect to a 1946 monotype based on the masonite cut *Aboriginal Design, with Sturt's Pea*, 'the flowers are the creation of a twentieth century artist, while the bowl and background belong to a primitive aboriginal art.'[20] What Preston did was explicitly quote, rather than more-or-less surreptitiously incorporate, the tribal source: the Aboriginal form or motif was often distinguished, just as a quoted text is 'marked off'. In a fashion that was essentially without parallel in European modernism, her work thus consistently *pointed toward* Aboriginal art.

Even if the indigenized white Australian culture that Preston so frequently advocated could have been expressed through a synthesis of 'Aboriginal' and 'modern' art, that is not what these works achieve. Their effect is rather to make the fact of difference explicit, and this is surely to lay bare the contrivance of synthesis, and to give the viewer the option of regarding it as awkward or impossible. In juxtaposing genres of Aboriginal art with practices that may have been Asian-influenced, but still belonged firmly to Western art traditions, Preston presented combination rather than fusion, a possibility rather than an accomplishment, a problem rather than a solution.

Stubborn Aboriginal territory

Over the last twenty years Margaret Preston has been praised by a number of writers for her forward-looking appreciation of Aboriginal art. At the same time, however, her Aboriginal-influenced works have received far less exposure than the wildflowers and birds. Certainly there is some embarrassment among those otherwise inclined to celebrate the artist's accomplishment. In 1985, Elizabeth Butel acknowledged that 'Many of her statements about "applying" Aboriginal art come down to us today with an unpleasant clang.'[21] Surprisingly, though, Preston's use of indigenous material has rarely been explicitly criticized; the notable exceptions are a brief but important essay by Ann Stephen, and the more recent critiques in paint of Gordon Bennett (see pp. 208–13). Reacting particularly against Humphrey McQueen's effort to equate Preston's work with a politically progressive Australian modernism, Stephen emphasized the compatibility between Preston's landscapes and conservative affirmations of national strength and nobility. In a section entitled 'Modernism goes hand-in-hand with racism' Stephen drew attention to the breezy crudity of the artist's early writing on the 'application' of indigenous art, but found her later position problematic in a different but perhaps more fundamental way. Preston 'assumed that she was able to transcend cultural differences; and that her values were not in direct opposition to and complicitly involved in the destruction of aboriginal culture.'[22]

We could attempt to theorize the practice of appropriation, and thereby establish whether cross-cultural borrowings are to be construed as legitimate exchange and productive mutual acknowledgment, or rather the rip-off of colonized peoples by exploitative European and settler cultures.[23] But the political meanings of appropriations are not susceptible to this generalized measuring. Although I agree with Stephen that McQueen's presentation of Preston as an oppositional artist is unconvincing, the general statement that she was complicit in ongoing colonization is not adequate either. If appropriations do have a general character, it is surely that of unstable duality. In some proportion, they always combine taking and acknowledgment, appropriation and homage, a critique of colonial exclusions, and collusion in imbalanced exchange. What the problem therefore demands is not an endorsement or rejection of primitivism in principle, but an exploration of how particular works were motivated and assessed. Hence I am concerned with the way Preston's efforts were received in the 1940s.

With a few exceptions, it's notable that the Aboriginal works had a bad press. In 1942, the *Bulletin* set the tone, crediting her with an 'infallible color sense' and finding some of her works 'strikingly beautiful.' But: 'Her latter-day experiments with the Australian abo.'s idiom, however, are more interesting than aesthetically fruitful.'[24] Seven years later, the same magazine featured a more extensive critique of the fairly lavish Ure Smith publication, *Margaret Preston's Monotypes*:

In the aboriginal paintings Margaret Preston is exploring stubborn and dangerous territory. Where…the Aboriginal motives are used purely to make a decorative pattern, the effect is pleasing. But where, as in the crudely symbolic trees of 'Bimbowrie Landscape,' which might have been drawn by a child with its thumb, or in 'Drought, Mirage Country,' with its kangaroos that look like a cross between a fox-terrier and a rockinghorse, the pictures are meant to be something more than decoration, they fail.

It is impossible to respond to them with that instantaneous delight which a work of art evokes, for the interest is focussed on the crudity of the technique; and they are at best curiosities.…

…She is allowing the aboriginals – a people, as she admits herself, too limited in sensibility and technical capacity to have attempted to paint the wildflowers – to debilitate her talent; but what is really required is the opposite process – the enrichment of primitive art by the infinitely greater technical and spiritual resources of the civilized artist.[25]

The writer here not only ignored Preston's insistence that 'primitive' meant neither child-like nor crude, but contradicted her claim that something might be gained from the study of Aboriginal art. Given that Preston's body of Aboriginal-influenced work aspired to exemplify a national culture, but was for the most part greeted with indifference or actual hostility, it was surely more conspicuously at odds with the culture of the period than 'complicit' in that culture's racial assumptions.

As I've already noted, Preston did not explicitly criticize the wider marginalization of the Aboriginal population, though she did positively promote Aboriginal art through her writing and through involvement in a major UNESCO exhibition. What may have been most important, though, was not any political statement she made or failed to make, but the effect of her work. In a general book on Australian art published in the same year as the *Bulletin* review just quoted, the critic and painter Herbert Badham applauded Preston's 'colourful and delightfully fresh flower pieces' but found that her adaptations of Aboriginal motifs amounted to 'derivation *in extremis*'.

There is undeniable refreshment in judicious use of this aspect of primitive culture, but it can, in all reasonable truth, hold but fragments of its pristine intention – fragments which may, through repetition and function moulded by an alien setting, bore to insufferable tears.[26]

Like the *Bulletin*, Badham finds that the work fails. In his judgment, though, this is not because of the crudity of the source material, but because the adaptation that Preston attempts is inherently problematic. He implies that Western and indigenous art systems are incommensurable. Borrowings on the part of Western artists must reduce the 'primitive' culture quoted to fragments which are profoundly distorted in the 'alien setting' that is unavoidably imposed. Yet Badham proceeded to suggest that the art might have unintended value:

> …it is in this connection that Margaret Preston's work is important. Although she has chosen the part of one convention, her pictures themselves draw us irresistibly to an element in art formerly ignored as unworthy of the white man's attentions, an element which embraces the dawning spirit of humankind, and holds it aloof from the soiling touches of modernity.[27]

This is prescient. The effects of Preston's work at once fell short of and exceeded her intentions. If Badham's response is anything to go by, the very awkwardness of some of her Aboriginal compositions drew attention to the indigenous art forms that seemed unsatisfactorily translated. Just as the 1941 Australian Museum exhibition inadvertently revealed the aesthetic strength of indigenous forms that were introduced only to display their potential 'applications', Preston's work deflected viewers' attention, drawing them not toward her grand notion of a national culture, but 'irresistibly' toward the neglected indigenous art traditions themselves. Those traditions pointed in turn toward the indigenous presence, spotlighting a stubborn and enduring obstacle to the idea of settler nationhood.

Recontextualizations

Preston's prints and paintings were never quite comfortable with the rhetoric with which she captioned them. In the case of the New Zealand artist Gordon Walters (1919–95), there is a still more complex succession of tensions between the works and the ways they have been contextualized, more by a series of advocates than by the artist himself. Indeed the history of commentary around Walters provides an intriguing case of art-world myth-making. Though stylistically his hard-edge optical abstract work is wholly unlike Preston's, it raises many parallel issues concerning not only the specific character of artistic primitivism in settler societies, but also the relations between high art, design and national culture.

The hallmark of Walters' work has been a formalized version of the *koru* stem-bulb form, abstracted from the *kowhaiwhai* painting discussed in the previous chapter (pp. 101–5). It is a sign of the times that the artist's use of an indigenous motif should recently have become highly contentious: in 1986 the Maori feminist scholar, Ngahuia Te Awekotuku, condemned the artist's 'repeated and consistent and irrefutable exploitation and *colonizing* of that symbol.' These remarks provoked less reaction than those of a younger curator and commentator, Rangihiroa Panoho. In a 1992 essay in the catalogue of the 'Headlands' exhibition, a major survey of New Zealand art at Sydney's Museum of Contemporary Art, he argued that Walters' work formalized the *koru*, leaving behind its spiritual associations. These comments became central to a broader controversy around the show.[28] Though Panoho's harshest observation – that the *koru* works entailed a 'residual colonialism' – seems more moderate than Te Awekotuku's charges, this criticism provoked an extraordinary backlash, which marked the extent to which an international touring exhibition was understood as an exercise in cultural diplomacy. The show was seen as a context in which New Zealand art ought to have been affirmed, not questioned, least of all in the exhibition catalogue itself. The artist himself reputedly said that he felt as if he had gone out to fight for his country, only to be shot in the back. Though there was much angry correspondence and comment in reviews, the debate gave Walters' work new prominence, and boosted the prices it realized at auction. Subsequently, the Auckland City Art Gallery staged a major retrospective by way of vindication, and one critic, Francis Pound, devoted a whole book, *The Space Between* (1994), to the refutation of Panoho's and Te Awekotuku's cursory remarks.

The Maori critics' stance may look like an effort to proscribe cultural traffic that always has gone on and always will; in an epoch when non-indigenous cultural theorists talk all the time of fluidity and boundary-crossing, native claims about cultural property are often dismissed. The problem is not however a purely theoretical one, consisting of questions such as: 'is culture a thing?'; 'can bits of it be taken and misused?' The indigenous concerns must be seen as a political response to settler culture, and to its extensive and highly visible use of indigenous motifs and styles. Even if a motif is not, strictly speaking, a thing like a piece of land that may be taken and restored, the larger dynamic of colonial history can only suggest resonances between invasions of land and of culture. These identifications in turn suggest that quotations of indigenous art on the part of non-indigenous artists (irrespective of their ambivalence or complexity) are to be censured. The premises of this debate may be

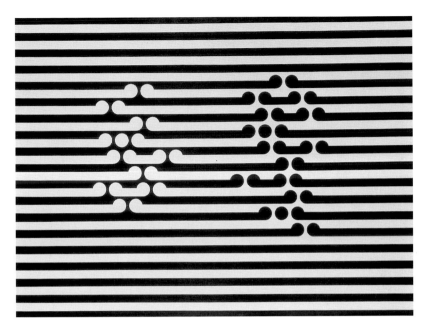

83 GORDON WALTERS Painting No. 1, 1965. © Gordon Walters Estate

unconvincing for some cultural theorists, but their misgivings do not count for much against the moral claims of this indigenous stance.[29]

The arguments in Walters' defence were likewise not reducible to theoretical principles, but emerged from longstanding contentions about New Zealand art and culture. Pound's book in fact elaborated on earlier essays in which he claimed that New Zealand art criticism had been dominated by nationalist thinking and had therefore celebrated landscape painting to the exclusion of modernist abstraction. The most advanced artists – abstractionists such as Milan Mrkusich and Walters – were consequently marginalized. An 'embattled minority of…fully abstract painters [were] condemned during the Nationalist time to relative silence and invisibility, or subjected to pejorative critical remarks.'[30] According to Pound, Walters in particular had rigorously pursued his own vision in isolation, unrewarded by public recognition. Yet during the 1970s and 1980s the attitudes of an enlightened minority gained wider acceptance. A 'post-nationalist' counter-canon emerged, in which Walters and others were finally given their due.

The intensity of the reaction against the 'Headlands' exhibition must have stemmed in part from the fact that it seemed to deny this shift: although the exhibition was eclectic, and though the catalogue included the Pound essay that I've cited, the title itself seemed to reintroduce land-scape and locality as primary points of reference. The appropriation debate, however, raised quite different concerns about Walters' work. What had previously been celebrated for its apparent counter-nationalism now seemed to express a peculiarly national primitivism: the native and/or national instability became explicit, fertile and problematic in a new way. Walters' advocates now emphasized not the rigour and quality of his art, but the productive character of cross-cultural exchange. What some had denounced as appropriation was in fact a moment in a fertile process of taking and sharing. These arguments, exemplified in *The Space Between*, seem to tug Walters' work in two directions at once. Inter-national affinities and local transactions are emphasized simultaneously.

In my view, Walters' painting deserves all the celebration it gets. However, the art-historical tale that has been told is sheer myth. From the time he began to exhibit his mature work in the mid-1960s, Walters was never marginalized or stigmatized to the extent that has been asserted. His isolation has been stressed in order to build an image of a creative figure far ahead of an indifferent and mediocre culture. Whether regarded as a cliché or a marketing device, this myth is pecu-liarly inappropriate in the case of this painter. His work was not antagonistic to wider trends in antipodean settler culture. In fact its indigenous gambit resonated with them, though without ever being quite the same in its intentions or effects.

'What to paint in NZ'

Gordon Walters became interested in European modernism in the 1940s – in Tanguy, Klee and Miro, among others. Over the same period he was encouraged in his interest in Maori art by Theo Schoon, a Dutch-born Indonesian artist then engaged in documenting South Island rock carv-ings, who was later to study and revive the traditional Maori incised gourd. Yet, according to Walters' own later accounts of his development, it was only when he visited Europe in the early 1950s that he gained a sense of what direction his art should take.

> I saw the use that some French abstractionists circa 1950 were making of Pacific Art. The penny dropped. This was one way out of the dilemma of what to paint in NZ. I was elated with this discovery, but between the insight/inspiration and the realization of the idea was a huge gap.... [31]

84 THEO SCHOON rock carving design on the
cover of 'Arts Yearbook 6: Annual Review of the
Arts in New Zealand' (Wellington, 1950)

In the mid- to late fifties Walters produced a number of studies based on Marquesan forms; though he was to go back to these from time to time over the years, it was Maori rather than 'Pacific' art in general that became his most conspicuous point of reference. He began experimenting with the *koru* in 1956, but it was not until the mid-1960s that he was satisfied with the results. The early works retained curvilinear forms, whereas he was to work toward a harder geometric adaptation of the motif, influenced by the Op Art of Vasarely and Bridget Riley. The first fully realized *koru* paintings, such as *Te Whiti* (1964) and *Painting No. 1* (1965), led to several series produced over twenty years, in which the scale, organization and density of the bulb forms were varied. Though Walters also worked with a number of other geometric elements, it was the *koru* that he explored most extensively and the *koru* that became his signature. Some of the paintings, including the very fine *Aranui,* used colours other than black and white, but these seem in retrospect almost departures from the core of Walters' project. That effort centred upon the manipulation of binary relations, relations that were most effectively foregrounded by the formal opposition of black and white.

85 BRIDGET RILEY Fall, 1963

The fact that Walters did not exhibit the *koru* works until 1966 is frequently adduced in accounts of his supposed marginalization, but it is plain that his own rigour, indeed perfectionism, held him back. It is not clear that there was as much hostility to abstract painting as has been maintained, but in any event his work received almost immediate critical acclaim and institutional recognition. He was included in survey exhibitions at the Auckland City Art Gallery in 1966 and 1967, and some work was sent to a group show at a dealer gallery in Sydney in 1968. The paintings attracted generally favourable local reviews, and brief but positive comment in international periodicals.[32] One of the leading critics, Hamish Keith, suggested as early as 1970 that it was time for a retrospective; the artist, apparently concerned about potential damage to the work in the course of a tour, turned down a proposal in the mid-seventies, but the Auckland City Art Gallery eventually mounted a show in 1983. Walters received an Arts Council Fellowship in 1971, and subsequently other government grants; and he was appointed visiting senior lecturer in painting at Auckland's Elam art school in 1972. To be sure, he was by this time in his early fifties, but he had nevertheless moved swiftly and smoothly from the situation of a non-exhibiting artist to that of an established figure. The cultural history of his art needs

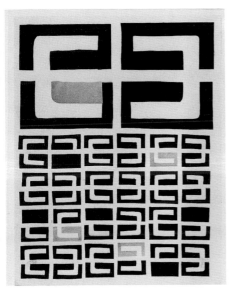

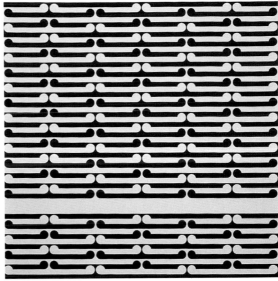

86 GORDON WALTERS Untitled, 1958. © Gordon Walters Estate

87 GORDON WALTERS Genealogy 5, 1971. © Gordon Walters Estate

to work from the fact that these paintings were successful, not from the claim that they were ignored.

Yet they were received in contradictory terms. One of Walters' early advocates, the critic and dealer Petar Vuletic, was vehemently anti-nationalistic. He championed Walters' work for its affinities with hard-edge American abstraction, and Walters' own statements in commentary seemed to sustain this reading. The dealer's brochure for his 1966 and 1968 shows quoted him:

> My work is an investigation of positive/negative relationships within a deliberately limited range of forms. The forms I use have no descriptive value in themselves and are used solely to demon-strate relations.[32]

Some critics initially read the work in these purely formal terms, and in 1968 a Maori woman was prompted to write to the *New Zealand Herald* in response to one such review, pointing out that the stripe ending in a circle was 'the traditional Maori koru motif.'[34] Yet, if in that context attention needed to be drawn to the indigenous reference, Walters had used Maori titles such as *Te Whiti* since 1964. Though many works were also untitled or simply numbered, by the early 1970s the paintings carried Maori words more often than not. In some cases, the works were actually titled by Walters' Wellington dealer, Peter McLeavey; in 1971, he opted for well-known Maori terms such as *Karakia* (prayer) and *Waiata* (lament).[35] These were intended only to 'serve as handles for the current show'. *Karakia*, however, was re-used for a 1977 painting that was acquired by the National Art Gallery (now incorporated into the Museum of New Zealand) and subsequently widely reproduced.

Walters' titles have been extensively debated. Some of his advocates have defended the artist's use of Maori words against suggestions that this is in some sense reprehensible. While Ngahuia Te Awekotuku had pointed out scornfully that there seemed to be no connection between Walters' cool *Mahuika* and the fiery Maori goddess of that name, Pound drew attention to the similarities between the painter's approach to titles and that of the American hard-edge abstractionist Frank Stella. Stella's titles refer to jazz clubs, places in Colorado, and to Islamic cities. They are not intended to evoke specific references but to point, for example, 'in the general direction of the Islamic, in homage to a powerful prede-cessor'. In the same way Walters' 'handles' do not imply that particular gods or historical Maori figures such as Te Whiti are represented, but instead allude to the Maori in a more generalized way.[36]

The further point that has been frequently made in Walters' defence is that many of the Maori names he employs were actually Wellington street names, from the neighbourhood in which he grew up.

> …these names had a strong emotional significance for me. By using them to title my works I was able both to pay tribute to the Maori tradition, which has meant a great deal to me, and to re-interpret it in terms of my own art and my immediate environment.[37]

Pound therefore proposes that Maori concerned about appropriation might take their complaints to the Wellington City Council rather than to Walters. Glib though this suggestion may be, it does point to the extent to which this work is tied up with the cultural geography of New Zealand cities. These are settler places that draw commemorations of empire (Queen Street, Khyber Pass) and indigenous names uneasily together. The significance of this nomenclature in Walters' biography marks the distinctness of his art from the northern hemisphere work that it formally resembles. Unlike Stella, Walters did not use series of titles referring variously to bars, streets, towns and exotic places. He opted either for untitled neutrality or consistently for Maori allusions.

It is the consistency of this reference that is crucial. Along with many European and American modernists, and Margaret Preston, Walters was informed in a variety of indigenous art traditions. Like Preston, however, he foregrounded the indigenous art of his own country and declared its local specificity. Unlike her, of course, he never vaunted such reference as the basis for a national culture, and his personal style was entirely different – he promoted his own work far more discreetly, and didn't seek the stature of a cultural commentator as she did. But his lack of engagement with nationalist rhetoric ought not disguise the fact that his work constituted an answer to the problem of 'what to paint in NZ'. Although the trend to interpret his work in national terms developed over the seventies, he had put it in these terms himself in a 1968 interview:

> It was during this period [while living overseas] that I was able to see myself for the first time as a New Zealander and begin to come to terms with the implications of this. I never much liked the idea of being a New Zealand painter, I just wanted to be a good painter and the more I saw of European and American painting the more the provincial nature of most New Zealand painting became clear to me. At the same time it was only by coming to terms with my being a New Zealander that I could go on to paint.[38]

Here the artist defers reluctantly to nationality. Not nationalism: one may be unenthusiastic about patriotism or preoccupations with building a national culture, but it seems that one must nevertheless acknowledge the formative significance of place, or particular background, upon one's creative expression. And it is strangely axiomatic that this means nationality. Walters might conceivably have aimed to ground his art in forms derived from his local environment, or from the antipodean Pacific in a wider sense. Indeed, in some ways he does both these things, by referring often to Wellington street names, and by drawing upon non-Maori Pacific art forms. Yet what was foregrounded is consistent with 'being a New Zealander', a generalized and encompassing native and/or national reference.

Walters' account of his work in these terms would be less important had it not been taken up by his audience. Though journalists initially stressed the work's Op Art interest, its national distinctiveness was increasingly cited, most significantly perhaps by those outside the art world, who were less concerned to commend Walters' internationalism. There is some irony in the comparison with Preston. While Australians were generally unconvinced that her indigenous works laid the foundation for a national culture, Walters was said to have succeeded in doing exactly that, though he had 'never much liked the idea of being a New Zealand painter'. 'I believe that you have essentially solved the problem of representing New Zealand's identity', a corporate designer wrote to the painter in 1983.[39] By this time the observation that Walters had successfully fused the country's Polynesian and European cultures was becoming commonplace, though it had been noted as early as 1969 that his *koru* imagery seemed 'completely natural to New Zealand painting'.[40]

'High' art and commercial appropriation

New Zealand art historians have generally dissociated Walters' art from the widespread use of indigenous motifs in settler design, often by ignoring the latter altogether, or by asserting that commercial adaptation of the *koru* only became widespread during the 1980s. It is true that its use in logos proliferated in that period, but, as we have seen, *kowhaiwhai* were extensively drawn upon earlier, and in particular were ubiquitous through their presence on New Zealand banknotes prior to the introduction of decimal currency in 1967. Leonard Bell raises the question of whether this kind of quotation amounts to 'pernicious neo-colonization' but proceeds only to say that 'No doubt sometimes it is, other times not.'[41] Even if we are to find in the end that indigenous references are diverse and typically contradictory in their effects, this is surely to stop at the point where we need to start.

It has been quite fairly pointed out that Walters drew attention to Maori art, and treated it as art, as Preston had done for Aboriginal work, in a period when attitudes to indigenous culture were generally disparaging. As also in the case of Preston, this can equally be read negatively as entailing the assimilation of indigenous culture to settler nationalism. If Walters was claiming a right to define antipodean nationality on the basis of an indigenized modernism, however, he was doing so only implicitly, and it would seem unfair to find him culpable on the grounds of his own technical brilliance. And the fact that his art is so visually authoritative permits the wider conclusion that these works (and not those of any Maori) 'solve the problem' of New Zealand's identity.

This reading of the work – a result of its canonization, not the painter's own practice – is not too remote from the assumptions of those advocating the 'application' of Aboriginal designs in Australia in the 1940s. They too imagined that national culture, though drawing on

88 GORDON WALTERS banner design for the New Zealand Film Commission

89 'Mobil New Zealand Travel Guide, South Island' (Auckland, 1990)

Aboriginal art, would be produced by and for whites. Their rhetoric failed because the work itself was weak, and deflected attention onto the indigenous source materials themselves. The case of Walters' art is, like that of Preston, more complicated. This is so in part because there were multiple connections between his art and the business of signifying the nation. The paintings were bought by the Foreign Affairs department for display in New Zealand embassies, and used in New Zealand corporate collections in a similar way; they have been reproduced on book covers, and were central to an education department teaching kit, *Emblems of Identity* (1987). More importantly, Walters himself worked in commercial design, producing at one time a logo for the National Library with what he called 'a discreetly New Zealand emphasis', at another devices for the New Zealand Film Commission that were based more directly on the *koru* paintings.[42] The widespread commercial use of *koru*-based designs from the 1980s itself owes a good deal to Walters. One of the most visible logos, that of Air New Zealand, features a straightened, simplified version of the motif, and it is hard to believe that this was not stimulated directly by Walters' work. And ironically, given the appropriation debate, the most popular travel guide to New Zealand has, in every reprint since first publication in 1973, used a cover clearly indebted to Walters, without acknowledgment of any kind.

In this context, the assumption that abstract art was 'ultra-modernist' and hence estranged from popular culture is misleading. Over the decades, landscape has probably always been the most widely appreciated style of painting in New Zealand, but Walters' abstraction was, like Bridget Riley's, quite unlike most avant-garde art in that its optical play appealed to a wider audience, while the flatness and hard edges were peculiarly adapted to commercial applications. Just as Riley was almost immediately plagiarized by fabric designers,[43] Walters was reproduced in print and in other media.

Francis Pound is surely right, however, to insist that Walters' *koru* works relate to the larger history of Pakeha uses of Maori motifs 'as at once a continuation and a difference.'[44] They are a continuation in the sense that they are inescapably part of the wider cultural effort of a nation of settlers to symbolize local identity through indigenous reference. Yet they are also not the same, because the domain in which the effort takes place is different. The adaptation of indigenous art in design may give Maori or Aboriginal signs public visibility, but it cannot give them dignity, because commercial design, like craft activity, is not in itself a dignified or prestigious practice. These hierarchies of cultural creativity and genre have, of course, been endlessly contested, but even now they are only discredited in theory, because too much is invested in their maintenance.

If the incorporation of indigenous references in 'low' genres could not elevate the forms quoted, the high-art status of painting might ideally work conversely to celebrate them. In European modernism, this cannot be seen to have proceeded in any consistent way, because work from different regions was drawn upon eclectically, and, as we have seen in the case of Matisse, often almost surreptitiously. Tribal art in general may have been affirmed, but not in a way that made much difference to the indigenous people in any particular place.

Where, on the other hand, modernist artists in settler societies drew upon local native traditions, the proximity and specificity of their interest was potentially more consequential. This may have been true of Preston's work in the longer term, though its initial reception reminds us that wider racist attitudes could hardly be changed overnight: for the *Bulletin* critic quoted earlier, her art was 'debilitated' by the Aboriginal element. Walters was working later, with different material, in a different style, and probably in a more sympathetic environment; his incorporation of a Maori form did not attract criticism of this kind. In the 1960s the emerging group of modernist Maori artists seem generally to have welcomed Walters' work: they took it as an affirmation of the *koru* rather than any cheapening of it.

There is also a formal sense in which adaptations of indigenous art vary in the respect they accord their sources. In some cases the most obvious devices are abstracted and converted into trademarks. We saw earlier that *kowhaiwhai* were frequently standardized and literally

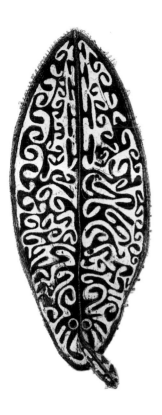

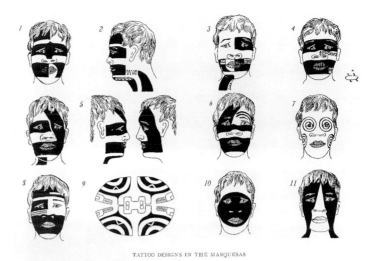

TATTOO DESIGNS IN THE MARQUESAS

90 Namau mask, Gulf Province, Papua New Guinea, painted bark cloth and cane

91 Tattoo designs, published in W.C. Handy, 'Tattooing in the Marquesas' (Bishop Museum Bulletin, no. 1, 1922)

marginalized through being rendered as borders for one pictorial subject or another. What made Walters' art successful was precisely its distance from this reduction of indigenous forms to decorative emblems.

In many statements over the years, Walters acknowledged Maori and other Oceanic works of art that he saw in New Zealand museums as important formative influences. The pre-eminence of the *koru* among his forms has, I think, misled many viewers and commentators. It was not the motif as such but something deeper that Walters gained from the study of Oceanic traditions. The figure-ground ambiguity so conspicuous in the extraordinary masks of the Papuan gulf may well have informed the optical play of the *koru* paintings; the disrupted symmetry that is striking in a remarkable range of indigenous Pacific art practices certainly did. (Among the examples that might be mentioned are Marquesan face tattoos, published in a museum bulletin from which Walters kept photocopies.) It was precisely this technology of visual dynamism that the artist recognized and elaborated upon in his own idiom. Though the *koru* is in no sense accidental or unimportant, almost

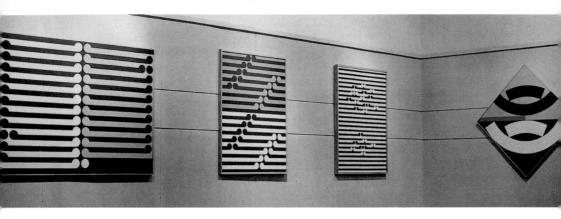

92 GORDON WALTERS Kahukura, 1968. First from the left, on display with other works by Walters in the New Vision Gallery, Auckland

93 GORDON WALTERS Untitled Painting, 1952–3. © Gordon Walters Estate

94 GORDON WALTERS Transparency 7, 1991. © Gordon Walters Estate

Walters' entire corpus could be seen as a tribute to the logic of Oceanic aesthetics, which scholars in the anthropology of art were much slower to recognize and understand.

If not present in every single Walters painting, disrupted symmetry is consistently important from the 1950s onward. This is true both of works featuring the *koru* motif and of those otherwise apparently devoid of Polynesian references, such as *Untitled Painting* (1952–3) and the late *Transparency* series. As the painter noted with respect to *Kahukura* (1968), the work was 'based on the binary principle: a vertical division with two sides differing slightly but maintaining a balance; my basic approach to picture-making, which owes a lot to primitive art in general and Maori art (traditional) in particular.'[45] In another context, defensively stressing his own originality, Walters emphasized the distance between his geometrical approach and the 'rhythmical form' of the Maori *koru*, but he overstated the issue when he asserted that 'the motif is used to establish a system of relationships that follows a logic quite foreign to Maori art.' To the contrary, the dynamism of partial but not complete symmetry is pervasive and fundamental. Flat painting certainly enabled these relations to be handled with a decontextualized intensity in Walters' work, whereas the exploration of doubleness in Pacific art was never simply a logical project, but one engaged with the

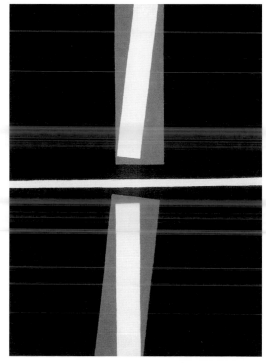

embodiment of power, with twins and Janus figures, and with practices such as fighting and dancing. But it remains the case that Walters' work is highly singular within the whole field of modernist art for its engagement with the generative principles, as opposed to forms, colours or motifs, of indigenous work.

Critics such as Leonard Bell, at pains to emphasize the diversity of Walters' sources and stimuli, have, I think, understated both his debt to Oceanic art and his achievement in synthesizing its logic with a particular Euro-American idiom. On the one hand, the extent to which Maori and Pacific traditions in fact invigorated all his work, and not just the *koru* paintings, was greater than has generally been acknowledged; on the other, his understanding of the indigenous genres has been underestimated. He might therefore be faulted for having taken more rather than less, but might equally be credited for the depth of his respect and engagement. It is silly to attempt to work this through as though it were a problem in arithmetic in which particular terms possessed definite values. The heat of the debate arises from the fact that what is a laudable interest in indigenous art from one point of view is unsanctioned borrowing, an act of theft, from another. Appreciation and appropriation have been intimately connected, and are essentially double-sided processes. By definition, their values are unstable; although some appropriations may evidently be more pernicious than others, and the effects of appropriations in different domains (commercial and high artistic) certainly vary, it has to be said that definite adjudications, positive or negative, will almost inevitably be half right and half wrong.

What may be noted, however, is that without the Maori gambit Walters could not have been prominent. His status would have been like that of the Australian abstractionist Ralph Balson, who produced Constructivist works in the fifties that were not dissimilar to some of Walters' contemporaneous but independent efforts. Balson never achieved the formal power that Walters gained from Oceanic asymmetry; he never gave his work the national reference that the latter made of the *koru*. There are comparably fine New Zealand abstractionists, such as Milan Mrkusich, who have produced strong paintings of limited relevance to New Zealand's public culture.

Walters may ultimately be interesting not for what he exemplifies, but for the very peculiarity of his accomplishment. Australian artists in the 1960s and 1970s were occasionally interested in depicting Aboriginal people, but in very few cases did they attempt to adapt from Aboriginal art in any modernist idiom. This is all the more significant because some of the preconditions that had been important in New

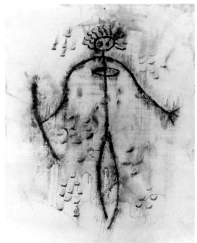

95 RALPH BALSON Constructive Painting, 1951

96 JAMES CANT Mimi-Figure Variation, 1949

Zealand were also present in Australia. Rock-art sites were known and could be visited; and they were visited by as well-known a painter as Russell Drysdale, who wrote about them in the journal *Art and Australia* in the 1960s. Drysdale became increasingly interested in Aboriginal subjects and art forms in his late work, especially painting which featured *pukumani* poles produced by the Tiwi people of Bathurst and Melville Islands in northern Australia.[46] Almost twenty years earlier, James Cant, notable among Australian surrealists, had produced a few prints after rock paintings, not unlike those of Schoon. Yet somehow the indigenous presence was not sufficiently compelling to encourage any artist to build upon it as Walters was to build on Maori reference; a 1969 publication featuring over a hundred painters, *Present Day Art in Australia*, was virtually devoid of Aboriginal reference. Some of Tony Tuckson's Abstract Expressionist works reflect the influence of Aboriginal art – which Tuckson promoted vigorously, as assistant director of the Art Gallery of New South Wales – but this was loose inspiration, rather than the mobilization of a native or national sign.[47] Tuckson did not point to Aboriginal culture through titles, as Walters did; nor did he pursue such indigenous references consistently or make a signature of them; and so there was never any possibility that his paintings would be understood as 'Aboriginal' works that attempted a special synthesis of

97 TONY TUCKSON
White on Black with Paper, 1970–3

98 JOHN COBURN
Western Desert Dreaming, 1987

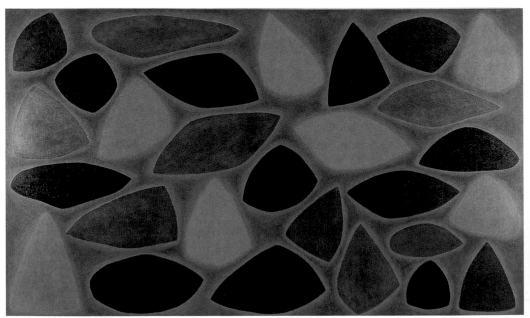

99 Cover of 'DYN', nos 4–5 'Amerindian Number' (December 1943), with drawing of a killer whale by Kwakiutl artist James Speck

100 WILL BARNET Janus and the White Vertebra, 1955

the international and the autochthonous. Some of John Coburn's works from the 1980s refer to Aboriginal dreamings, but reflect an effort to bring abstraction to the Australian environment through the use of desert colours, rather than an interest in exploiting or exploring indigenous art. The tendency, at least in 'high' art, was to engage with place through landscape painting, in conformity with the trend established in the nineteenth century.

A number of artists in the United States, from Marsden Hartley early in the twentieth century through to abstractionists in the 1950s, were interested in Native American art, which featured in art publications, as it did in Australia and New Zealand. Some painters, such as Will Barnet, imaged indigenous subjects, and like Walters modelled their compositions upon indigenous aesthetic principles, in Barnet's case deriving from the 'split representation' which is such a famous feature of Northwest Coast art. This painter, among others, understood his efforts in part nationalistically – he saw these subjects and styles as routes to a truly American art – but the significance of this kind of reference was waning. A number of prominent postwar American artists were said to be influenced by Native American culture, but they did not generally make this explicit through direct reference. One can, for example, look at any number of Barnett Newman's paintings without having any idea that he wrote on and curated exhibitions on Native American art.

It is often noted that connections with Native Americans were formative influences in Jackson Pollock's childhood, and early works such as *Totem Lesson 2* (1945) appear to incorporate figures from Navajo myth. Yet the suggestion, frequently made, that Navajo sand paintings were important to his art is only true in the most generalized terms. There is no formal affinity at all between the fairly rigid schematizations of the sand painters and Pollock's mature drip style, though Pollock certainly believed that there were affinities between his 'methods' and those of the native painters, mainly in that he worked not at an easel but on the floor, and often within the painting, and believed that his painting animated unconscious forces in a ritualistic process.[48] The terms of reference are more specific than those of European modernists, but not much more so. There is nothing comparable to McCahon's use of the indigenous language, nothing like Walters' exhaustive reworking of an indigenous motif, and nothing as awkwardly deliberate as Preston's indigenous sign. Certainly, Pollock could have been canonized not simply as a great painter but as one who produced a peculiarly American art because he drew from Native American traditions. But if the particular basis of his primitivism in the American southwest might have supported such a claim, Pollock himself forestalled such valuation by suggesting that the idea of American painting made no more sense than the idea of American mathematics. My point is not that a nationalist account of this artist would necessarily do justice to the play of motivations and influences that informed his work; it is rather that the United States is different from New Zealand, in the sense that indigenous reference was, in the longer term, not a focus of particular interest.

Hence, although some painters made Preston-like statements concerning the need to make an American art on the basis of Indian inspiration, postwar abstraction was defined to a much greater degree by formalist than nationalist criticism. Insofar as nationality did enter into the appreciation of New York painting, it is not clear that a counter-cultural nationalism that celebrated native spirituality was the most influential attitude. Serge Guilbaut's provocative claim was rather that a Cold War political patriotism in effect identified the artistic freedom and energy of the Abstract Expressionists with American liberty and strength.[49] Whether this Marxist argument is accepted or not, there is not much doubt that many people see the American-ness of this art in its sheer modernity, scale and audacity; Pop Art, similarly, was distinctively American by virtue of its brash mobilization of contemporary mass culture, not because it possessed any connection with native culture. Nationality did not need to be defined in indigenous terms.

Abstract Expressionism, Minimalism and Pop Art were to have their adherents in both Australia and New Zealand. But because these styles so emphatically expressed American-ness in America, they could hardly express Australian-ness in Australia, the insertion of local content notwithstanding. Nationality in art thus continued to be defined essentially via landscape in Australia, and via Maori culture in New Zealand. If the nexus between nationalism and landscape was broken, or at least submerged, in American art, it has remained alive in Australia, New Zealand and Canada. The resort to indigenous reference in the United States similarly waned, in part for the specifically artistic reasons that have been referred to, but also as a result of the sheer marginality of Native Americans, and the much greater visibility of civil rights issues, among other questions of race and cultural difference. If the United States began as a settler-colonial society, the significance of the settler-indigenous relation was clearly pushed aside by the scale and heterogeneity of later phases of immigration. Similarly, native issues have often been eclipsed by wider debate concerning multiculturalism in Australia and Quebec separatism in Canada. In New Zealand, as we've seen, the indigenous presence was more conspicuous, and in recent decades indigenous issues have steadily assumed greater centrality. So it is not surprising that New Zealand's postwar settler art is so singular. Nowhere else, it seems, did so many white artists find an engagement with indigenous culture unavoidable. If, in many cases, their mobilizations of form and motif can be seen as mistranslations, as reductions, the depth of their engagement is nevertheless unique.

101 OTTO PAREROULTJA Totemic Rhythm, 1963

Colonial relations can resemble the whirl and confusion of waters at those points where seas, or seas and great rivers meet: in the conflicting flows it is difficult to pinpoint the moment the tide turns. The uncertain manifestations of a changing balance of power are exemplified in a 1938 publication by Frederick McCarthy of the Australian Museum. His booklet, *Australian Aboriginal Decorative Art*, anticipated the 1941 exhibition of Aboriginal art and its 'applications' discussed in Chapter Three. In his preface, the museum's director alluded to the business of application, noting that 'Designs based on Australian Aboriginal art motifs have been widely used by architects, interior decorators, and commercial artists, and the Museum display of collections illustrating this primitive art is of service in this direction.'[1] It is notable, however, that in his foreword the anthropologist A.P. Elkin, then a pre-eminent figure in Aboriginal studies, made no reference to this 'service'. He saw the value of publishing and displaying Aboriginal art in entirely different terms:

> ...the growing interest in and appreciation of primitive art in general and of aboriginal art in particular has a very important human, as distinct from scientific, implication. It is gradually causing persons who otherwise would either ignore or despise the aborigines to realize that a people possessing an art which is full of traditional meaning as well as expressive of many interesting motifs is much higher in the human scale than had been previously thought. The average white person is not impressed by totemism, kinship and sociological studies of aboriginal life, but a simple presentation of a native people's art is something which he can appreciate. I am hoping that this introduction to the decorative art of the Australian aboriginal...will contribute materially to the appreciation of the Australian aborigines both as a people possessed of artistic powers, and as human personalities. Moreover, in so far as we let the aborigines – the civilized ones in particular – know our appreciation, we shall help them to get rid of that feeling of inferiority for which contact with us has been responsible.[2]

Elkin's language may be dated, but his argument is extraordinarily prescient. In both Australia and Aotearoa New Zealand, as well as in other settler societies such as Canada, the following that indigenous art eventually gained among the majority white settler populations did provide a platform for indigenous people and their causes. Tribal arts in general were increasingly of interest to wider audiences, including those in North America and Europe. For white Australians and New Zealanders, however, indigenous art was especially attractive because it belonged distinctively and uniquely to their countries: as we have seen, antipodean settler modernism and primitivism were unlike the European movements in the extent to which they were energized by location and nation.

Between the 1940s and 1960s this mainstream interest in indigenous art blurred the native and the national, and sustained paternalistic notions – there was much talk of 'our Aborigines' and 'our Maoris' – but it did put indigenous art, and subsequently indigenous artists, into the limelight. Walters and Preston had celebrated indigenous culture, or imagined they were doing so, by incorporating Maori and Aboriginal motifs, without particularly pointing to or affirming individual Maori or Aboriginal artists. In the 1970s and 1980s this vicarious appearance of indigenous signs through the work of white artists came increasingly to be displaced by indigenous art works themselves. Moreover, artists and communities came to claim exhibitions, rather than simply be included in them. As a consequence of these developments, the art that became publicly visible was not determined by a nationalist primitivism, but was acknowledged to have emerged from cultural traditions of great spiritual depth and, in the case of Australia, of great antiquity. Indigenous art was also recognized as reflecting political concerns of the moment: it expressed the tragedy of colonization and the urgency of its redress. Most fundamentally, the mere fact of its presence contradicted the heroic myths of settler nation-building. But the variety of indigenous art works and practices also included critiques of exhibitions, of art worlds and of the insensitivities of white modernist and postmodernist artists alike to indigenous values and histories. Whether or not the tide had definitively turned, it seemed that nothing would be the same again.

Aboriginal Landscapes

A good deal of attention has been paid to the growth of Western interest in 'primitive' art, and the shift – in fits and starts – of classic Aboriginal and Maori material from ethnographic museums into art galleries and the art market. This is indeed a fundamentally important history. It is notable, for instance, that in 1949 the gallery within David Jones' department store – one of the more important, and certainly one of the most publicly visible, Sydney commercial outlets over the postwar decades – hosted an exhibition of bark paintings from Yirrkala and Oenpelli in northern Australia. The 1941 show supported by the same store had privileged the white 'applications', and relegated the black art to the status of their source-materials (p. 124). To follow this up with a presentation of indigenous work from which settler craft was excluded was to contradict the message of the earlier exhibition. In no subsequent display was it to be suggested that the future of 'Aboriginal art' lay in white designers' adaptations.

There had been significant earlier exhibitions in 1929 and 1943, but it was not until the late 1950s that a state gallery (the Art Gallery of New South Wales) bought any traditional Aboriginal art, and not until the 1960s that a few entrepreneurs began buying and distributing work. Government support became significant after the election of the zealously reformist Whitlam Labor government in 1972, and the popularity of Aboriginal art was subsequently fostered by official initiatives.[3]

It is vital to note, however, that simultaneous with developments of this kind was the early appearance of individual indigenous artists working mainly in non-indigenous media.[4] This was not a parallel history, since the emergence of these figures around the edges of the mainstream art market did not in any sense neatly complement the slow growth of interest in traditional art forms. Indigenous art has always been unexpectedly various. Though Australian art critics and curators applied fairly rigid primitivist criteria, and tended to reject pieces that were apparently acculturated, hence denying Aboriginal cultures' adaptability and dynamism, the range of art that interested a wider public was never defined quite so narrowly. This was also true in New Zealand, where the classic material acquired unambiguous 'art' status only at a late point, but then quite suddenly and dramatically. A number of modernist artists of Maori descent, however, had acquired significant reputations by the early 1960s. Their following, like that of most of their white counterparts, was essentially limited to the small New Zealand art world, but it was nevertheless the case that the range of artistic expressions that might be identified with 'Maori' exceeded a stereotypic primitivism.

In Australia, a number of nineteenth-century Aboriginal artists produced work on paper of great interest and vitality, but my aim is not to review the whole history of indigenous experimentation with non-indigenous media (which ought not, in any case, be seen as a separate topic to innovation in traditional or neo-traditional genres). It is rather to point to mid-century developments that provide a background to the indigenous renaissances that gained momentum during the 1970s. In this context, the key figure is the Arrernte (Aranda) watercolourist Albert Namatjira (1902–59). He grew up around the Lutheran mission station at Hermannsburg in central Australia, where the sale of artifacts and handicrafts was being fostered in response to early tourism in the 1920s. He was prompted to take up painting by a number of visiting white artists, most notably Rex Battarbee, from whom he received some training in the mid-1930s. Within a few years Namatjira held solo exhibitions in Melbourne and Adelaide, and became a widely known figure by the mid-1940s. In 1944 a monograph on his work was published and he became the first Aboriginal person to be listed in the Australian *Who's Who*; in 1946 he was visited by the Governor-General; and in 1947 the first of a number of films on him was released. He is thought to have executed some two thousand paintings, but his work reached many more Australian homes than that, since an extraordinary number of reproductions were published. It is moreover significant that Namatjira was the founder of a whole school, which included many of his family members and descendants, and certain other highly talented artists, such as Otto Pareroultja (1914–73). Their work received greater recognition with *The Heritage of Namatjira*, a major reappraisal and touring exhibition of the early 1990s. Given that many of these painters were as prolific as Namatjira, and that they continued to produce over the period that the well-known central Australian dot painting traditions developed, and still do so today, the sheer numerical contribution of the original works, let alone reproductions, to Australian visual culture is remarkable.

From one perspective, the popularity of these paintings is unsurprising. For mass audiences uninterested in, or alienated by, the modernist art of the period, the landscape watercolours were attractively conventional. Their viewers' taste already responded to artists such as the tremendously popular Hans Heysen (1877–1968), who had inherited the Heidelberg School's preoccupation with the gum tree. Heysen, who was to have innumerable imitators, was moreover a key figure for having moved beyond the comfortable rural scenery around his home in the Adelaide hills to paint the harsh irregularity of the desert landscapes. In so doing he contributed to a shift away from a national aesthetic that had centred upon the accomplishments of domestication and displayed the hard-won fruits of pioneer labour, to one that instead imaged the land where white men's tracks petered out. Arid landscapes were to become increasingly significant in postwar Australian art in the works

102 HANS HEYSEN The Land of the Oratunga, 1932

of such major painters as Sydney Nolan, Russell Drysdale and Fred Williams, among many others. The daunting vastness of outback scrub-plains and deserts might epitomize Australia's expansiveness, but could seem also a perilous object around which to form a national attachment. There was no direct representation in Heysen's work of the Aboriginal presence among these dehumanized landforms, but they hardly seemed like regions that might be absorbed by a white settler society either, beyond the extent that a handful of visitors might camp around their fringes to appreciate the very alienation of this wilderness. Perhaps, however, culture was anticipating economics, since in the 1960s huge mining ventures were to promise the nation a transformation of outback rock into urban and suburban prosperity.

It has been suggested that Namatjira and the Hermannsburg school as a whole owed their popularity among whites to the apparently imitative and assimilated character of their art. The same might be said of Ronald Bull, another seemingly conventional watercolourist who grew up in the more densely colonized southeast, and was also a prolific producer of landscapes.[5] The practice of these painters could be taken to confirm the colonization of their culture; their popularity similarly appeared to reflect the dominant society's commitment to the assimilation of Aboriginal people. Certainly, assimilationism was the reigning idea: Aborigines who acquired skills associated with the white world might be approved of, but this attitude presumed that eventually the indigenous population would be absorbed. In effect, frontier killing was supplanted by cultural geno-cide, most particularly through the practice of forcibly adopting out 'half caste' children who were brought up with whites and deprived of connec-tions with tradition and country. All this was certainly appalling, especially in its longer term effect of creating a generation of indigenous Australians who were obliged to 'pass', subjected to racial discrimination, while disconnected from Aboriginal communities.

It is unlikely, however, that these views really encompassed the appreciation of Hermannsburg works. The question of how the paintings actually were received by the wider consuming public, rather than by critics and others whose responses were recorded, is almost unresearch-able, but the notion that the work exemplified assimilation in its imitative character must essentially have been an art-world view, of little wider salience. The public generally has never been troubled by the extent to which paintings of wide commercial appeal conform to long-established conventions, or are 'derivative'. To the contrary, it is this conformity and familiarity that gives much non-avant-garde art its ready intelligibility and appeal. In any case, the Hermannsburg work was in fact quite distinct from the output of the well-known landscape painters. Heysen, for instance, painted the mountains of the interior as though they were pervaded by a savage monotony of tone, as if he was blinded by their barrenness. This is not the vision that comes across in the work of Namatjira and others. The extent to which an Aboriginal understanding of country as sacred and spiritually constituted was implicitly present in their watercolours has been extensively debated. If it is conceded that this is true only to a limited extent – scenes appear to be selected not because they are significant ancestral sites but rather simply for their pictorial suitability – the images nevertheless come across as the works of people intimately familiar with a region and immediately engaged by its depth, nuances and textures, rather than by the stark features that overwhelm an outsider.

No doubt these works were regarded in diverse ways by diverse viewers. It is hard, however, to rule out the possibility that their celebra-tion entailed some acknowledgment of the depth of Aboriginal associations with land. So far from it being pervasively assumed that Namatjira was a 'civilized' or Europeanized Aboriginal, for example, some popular writing explicitly credited the sense in which his art expressed a culture mysteriously tied to place:

This heritage of his comes at his call.
The land that held the wommera and thin spear
Curls to the brush; when conjured by him all
He looks upon is mirrored in such clear
And true reflection that you dream you stand
Beside a pool and see surrounding land
Flawless in structure reproduced therein.
In wonderment you probe his work and swear
He dips his brush in earth and sky and air;
You smell the ghost gums of his tribal ground
And find the flying ants, his totem, drawn
On rock and sheets of bark...[6]

This is not great poetry, but it is of interest for the way it grounds the power of Namatjira's illusionism in his origins and totemic connections with the place. The text's appearance amid a collection of affectionately racist cartoons indicates, however, that the high esteem in which the artist was held was one of few islands of affirmation in a sea of pretty nasty denigration. Yet it also points to an emerging fissure in Australian national imaginings. The raw heart of the continent fired the imagination, but it was not a place in which white Australians could readily live and belong. The prominence of Aboriginal craft souvenirs, and of Aboriginal imagery in the culture of domestic tourism – signalled by the title as well as the content of the magazine *Walkabout* from 1934 – indicated unavoidably that this was, or at least had been, another people's land.

Those dismissive of the Hermannsburg paintings felt that too much 'fuss' was made simply because the artists were Aborigines. There is no doubt that this fact was a significant ingredient in the works' success. Landscape, for so long the pre-eminent artistic vehicle for sentimental appropriation on the part of settlers, was now the more popular for being produced by the first Australians. The aesthetic attachment to the arid centre that was emerging among white Australians generally was therefore not an unmediated response to the stark topography of a *terra nullius*. It was not the response of a McCahon to the spare forms of ridgelines and hills, but an interest provoked also by indigenous life and art; it perforce acknowledged the Aboriginal presence. Even though the earlier generations of Hermannsburg artists rarely depicted Aboriginal people in their landscapes, the interest in the work and specifically in its authorship marks a radical shift from the Heidelberg period, when a transcendent vision of Australia could be conveyed with absolute authority by white artists.[7]

103 FRED WILLIAMS
Landscape with Goose,
1974

I do not suggest that the authorship of the Hermannsburg paintings automatically and explicitly established the prior indigenous ownership of Australian land, or even specifically the interior, as a public fact. Nor was it the case that there was a linear evolution from the unquestioned authority of settler vision to some understanding that Aboriginal people were specially entitled to paint their country, or capable of doing so with a particular authenticity that derived from their long and deep association with it. Some writers took the view, to the contrary, that the Arrernte painters produced work of interest that necessarily reflected 'the limits in both craft and vision, of what these people have yet had opportunity to learn.' The region hence awaited definitive representation on the part of a 'new-day Streeton'.[8]

After all, landscape by white artists – by successive generations of imitators of Heidelberg painters, among others, as well as breathtakingly innovative artists such as Fred Williams (1927–82) – has retained enormous appeal. In Australia, bush landscape still has great presence at all levels of the market, but most especially in the non-elite and subcanonical domains ignored by curators and art critics – the art galleries found in shopping malls, and in the work of amateur 'Sunday' painters sold outside the market. This accumulation of imagery might be read as a white reaffirmation of a right to appreciate and possess the country. The proof is in the practice, but there was also a contradictory proof in Namatjira's presence and his painting. It is characteristic of settler-colonies that neither colonized nor colonizers ever definitively supplant each other. Hence the co-presence of claims that seem to cancel each other out, and hence the difficulty of recognizing the turn of the tide.

Maori modernists

As we have seen, Maori designs and carving styles acquired a public following in New Zealand several decades before there was much interest in indigenous Australian art. Augustus Hamilton's turn-of-the-century book had even been titled *Maori Art*,[9] though it would be unwise to assume that even enthusiasts held the work to be on a par with European painting and sculpture. Many writers affirmed the fineness and ingenuity of design, but they were often making comparisons relative to other 'primitive' arts, chauvinistically asserting the higher development reached by Maori with respect to native peoples elsewhere. The canonical carvings were probably widely regarded as amusingly grotesque, and valued primarily for their uniqueness to New Zealand. The enduring character of this sort of 'appreciation' is typified by advertisements for the national airline published in Australian magazines in the early 1960s.

104 'Take a good look at New Zealand', Teal Airlines advertisement, published in 'Walkabout', January 1961

At the same time, however, a significant body of modernist Maori art was emerging. Many of the key figures – Paratene Matchitt, Cliff Whiting, Arnold Wilson and others – had been involved in the 1950s effort to give Maori arts and crafts new life through educational programmes directed at both Pakeha and Maori schoolchildren. These efforts contradicted the idea that indigenous arts were gradually dying out, or that they were essentially irrelevant to the future development of New Zealand culture. Their own work was not, however, channelled into the reproduction of traditional forms, although these certainly provided stimuli.

Paratene Matchitt (b. 1933) was initially mainly a painter, conspicuously influenced by Picasso, but also increasingly a producer of distinctive sculpture. In the 1960s his work was criticized by one reviewer who clearly had reservations about efforts to synthesize Maori 'decoration' with 'recent trends in European art'. It was, however, generally positively received, and described by journalists as manifesting a new synthesis of Maori and Western cultures.[10] Today this sounds like a deadeningly bland observation, but at the time was important for affirming that indigenous culture might possess contemporaneity. It was not purely of folkloric or traditional significance but rather an expressive resource for the present and future. This was certainly the case of works such as *Taunga Waka* (1971, fig. 113), which presented a central notion of Maori tradition – the collectivity of ancestors in the

105 CLIFFORD WHITING Te Wehenga o Rangi Raua ko Papa, 1969–76

106 ARNOLD WILSON He Tangata, he tangata, 1956

canoe – formally and elegantly. This, incidentally, was one of a number of Matchitt's works displayed in relatively visible public or corporate situations; if the artist never quite made it into the elite in collectors' eyes, he has the advantage that his work has been widely seen.

Matchitt's own creativity was eclipsed by his commitments to teaching and to Maori organizations from the mid-seventies to the mid-eighties, but re-emerged with strength in new timber and metal works from that time onward. These returned to the historical reference of some of his 1960s paintings. The nineteenth-century prophet and military leader Te Kooti (p. 31) established in the last decades of the century the Ringatu faith, the most important of the independent Maori churches to synthesize messianic and political ideas.[11] He is remembered as a fighter who attempted to hold fast to the land over a period of Maori losses, and was certainly also one of a number of leaders who seized upon icons of colonial authority, creating new symbols of Maori power and sovereignty. The proliferation of oppositional flags in this period is particularly extraordinary; though from much earlier in the nineteenth century, the Maori propensity to seize and use these icons of European power, not least in the theatre of ceremony and battle, is arresting. Many of the flags and pennants are extraordinarily large; some are modelled directly on the Union Jack; others feature portraits, scripts and esoteric symbols. The best-preserved of Te Kooti's flags is eloquently spare, bearing a crescent moon, considered a portent of a new world, and a fighting cross, among other motifs. Neither this prophet nor successors such as Rua Kenana were backward-looking mystics, but rather religious activists who exploited novel signs and media that became available to them. It is this dimension of Te Kooti's practice in particular that is commemorated in Matchitt's large-scale works. The motifs are empowered; this might be no more than homage, or it might be a suggestion that his history of revolutionary experimentation can empower the present in turn.

One of the most interesting of these artists may not properly be described as a 'Maori artist' at all. Ralph Hotere is a Maori; he emerged as a significant figure in the early 1960s, studied and exhibited in London before returning to New Zealand, and his career trajectory has been like that of many other 'art world' artists. He has not defined his art around links with a tribal background or a special affinity with traditions, and he has long rejected the label 'Maori artist'. In so doing he anticipated the stance of many postcolonial artists of the 1980s and 1990s, who were concerned to avoid ethnic pigeon-holing, and insisted that they were simply artists, not bearers of cultural identity cards. And Hotere's stance can be seen to be consistent with his work, despite the prominence of Maori references and concerns in it.

Like many of his contemporaries, he was initially influenced profoundly by American painting, and particularly by the Minimalism of artists such as Ad Reinhardt. His works from the 1960s and 1970s are often primarily black and highly finished, sometimes bearing crosses, fine radial constructions rather like the grooves on a vinyl record, or narrow vertical bands reminiscent of Barnett Newman. At an early stage, however, he began to add words to the works, which was surely radically to qualify, if not contradict, the purism of that sort of formalist art. In some cases, his words carried no particular geographic or historical referent: a series of works feature the text 'Malady', sometimes transmuted through substitutions of individual letters into 'Melody' or 'My Lady'. These were, in effect, painted versions of poems by his friend Bill Manhire and others; like McCahon, Hotere often incorporated evocatively inscribed lines of verse into his work. This is perhaps to do no more than literalize the emotion and mood that the canvases of a painter like Rothko seem to breathe, but Hotere's isolated words, texts and numbers often preclude precisely that universalism of spirit. Or rather, where they convey universal emotions, those feelings of anger and pain arise from peculiarly local battles. And this is consistent with a paradoxical quality in his work. It is fine art, but it is also of the world;

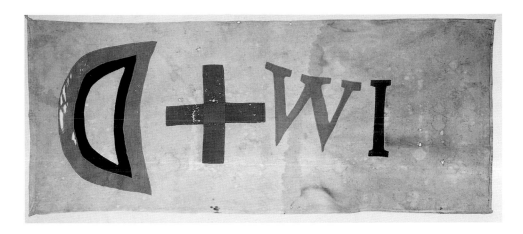

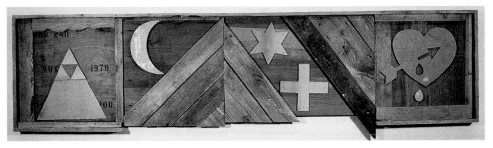

107 Flag of the Maori leader Te Kooti from Te Porere, 1869

108 PARATENE MATCHITT Flag, 1984

and not only of the world in principle, but of an ordinary, tangible and rather particular world.

Hotere's battles include those that have engaged many in the Pacific and New Zealand, such as the campaigns against the Mururoa nuclear tests and apartheid. The 1981 tour of the South African rugby team prompted an extraordinary wave of protest within New Zealand, and the very divisiveness of the issue led New Zealanders to look more critically at the issue of racism in their own society. The French bombing of the Greenpeace protest vessel the *Rainbow Warrior* led Hotere to engage with the notion of the 'black rainbow', which became connected with the 'black window' that already featured in his work. These motifs seemed to grow beyond their specific origins – whatever they really were – into tragic paradoxes or grand enigmas of wide suggestiveness. But Hotere has also consistently painted from very immediate struggles to preserve the environment in southern New Zealand, fighting through his art against an aluminium smelter at Aramoana, and to defend the peninsula upon which his own house and studio were built: Observation Point in the Otago Harbour, the site of a bitter, protracted and ultimately unsuccessful campaign against port developments.

His work ranged from these conflicts at his doorstep to those on the opposite side of the world, such as Watergate and the Gulf War. But it was never restricted to the register of protest. During time in Europe, he visited the Italian cemetery at Sangro where his brother was buried during the war, and the word 'Sangro' becomes a metonym in a succession of elegiac works, some of which incorporate numbers – the ages of men who died – or lines from a poem that his then wife, Cilla McQueen, composed about the site:

> Beneath a familiar sky
> A landscape of windswept manuka
> On the hill
> A rosary of olive trees

Though it has generally foregrounded themes that, like this, are at once universal and personal, Hotere's work has not been devoid of specifically Maori content. Like Matchitt he has commemorated the nineteenth-century warriors and prophets, dedicating one series to Te Whiti. In a number of works he used a text from Ezekiel (30:28):

> and you shall dwell
> in the LAND
> I gave your Fathers
> and ye shall be my
> people
> and I will be your
> God.

Given the centrality of land in the struggle for Maori justice, and the prominence of attachments to Papatuanuku – the Earth Mother – in the work of many Maori artists, it is difficult to read this without registering some injunction to hold on to ancestral lands, and some resonance with the voice of the nineteenth-century prophets. But it is typical of Hotere that the implications remain more open, and it also needs to be acknowledged that the prophetic spirituality of Colin McCahon – itself marked by Maori history – is almost certainly another influence, or a mediating influence.

Hotere's use of forms such as hearts and crosses can similarly be traced either to Te Kooti's flags, or to the more immediate precedents in McCahon, or both. Given Hotere's own sense of himself as an artist rather

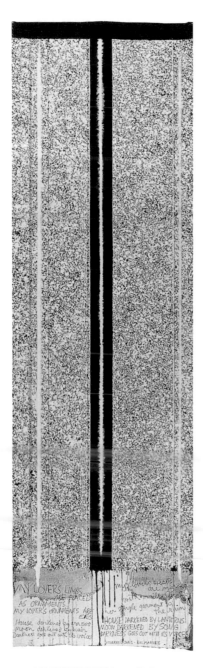

109 RALPH HOTERE Vidyapati's Song –
a poem by Bill Manhire, 1979

than a Maori artist, it would be perverse to insist that his sources were Maori sources rather than those of contemporary New Zealand artistic milieux. Yet his work has consistently been explicitly political, and activist in its accent, in a manner that McCahon's never was. Hence, for example, Hotere takes the prophets' project of subverting the flag further by painting the Maori poet Hone Tuwhare's anti-apartheid poem onto a South African flag (fig. 114). He also produced a series of decidedly sinister adaptations of an official flag developed for the Commonwealth Games in New Zealand in 1974. By the late 1980s, race, sporting boycotts and the British Empire were hot issues. The official device made the initials 'NZ' visible within a Union Jack; Hotere's representation made these look like swastikas and posed the question, 'Is this a Black Union Jack?'

One of the most vital features of this artist's work is one that is only obscured by the distinction between abstraction and figuration. His later work does not become representational in any conventional sense – though phenomena such as rain and rainbows, and the framing window, may be gesturally sketched – but it also ceases to be wholly abstract. Specific reference and meaning is introduced through allusive text, often simply through individual words such as 'Polaris'. More importantly, however, it is manifest through performance, or rather through the residue of expressive action upon materials such as iron and wood. Hotere has tended to work less with canvas and increasingly with timber frames, recycled window frames, glass, stainless steel and corrugated iron. He often alters these surfaces with abrasive tools or heat that become indices of the strife of a particular situation; though by no means all his work suggests pain or violence. In the more political works, such as the Aramoana series protesting the development of an aluminium smelter, he used iron like that found around building sites and fences in any city, and his in particular: it is battered, time-worn and, most importantly, marked with spray-painted slogans. Anger from the streets is empowered and rendered beautiful through transformation into a singular kind of high art that commands price and gallery space yet retains a material connection with the burning issues of the day, and with quotidian artifacts and realities. In another poem, 'Hotere', Cilla McQueen reflected on the *Baby Iron* works:

> & the
> baby iron is a conservator's nightmare, so what, so
> is our roof. everybody's roof is. all subject to such
> change as the rain & rust so let them in, live with
> rust in the heart, how queerly beautiful.

110 RALPH HOTERE A Black Union Jack, 1989–90

111 RALPH HOTERE A Black Union Jack, 1989–90 (detail)

The *Black Union Jack* is indeed 'queerly beautiful' for the irregularity and texture of its frame and material, but it is also a politically potent work, and would be less potent were it not scarred, seared and seemingly running with tears.

This could be seen as a kind of expressionism, and it has gentler manifestations in works such as *Rain*, after another Manhire poem, where the long lines and drips, and the leak of the script, seem to exemplify rather than signify the fall of water. But none of this work has much in common with the more psychological and inward-looking forms of expressionism. Hotere has, in general, scrupulously avoided making statements about his work, which helps explain why it has received little critical analysis, despite the fact that he has long been regarded as a major figure by New Zealand critics and collectors. This silence is understandable and perhaps even appropriate, given the essentially visual, non-discursive and enigmatic character of much of his art, but it does mean that the question of what it adds up to as a project has never been addressed in a sustained way.

An answer might begin with an affinity between Walters and Hotere. Both were strongly influenced by abstraction and Minimalism but were to reject the most basic premises of formalism – and those of modernism in general – by injecting something peculiarly local into their art. In Walters' case, what is inserted is a recognizably national motif that is pursued over a number of decades with the greatest rigour so as to elaborate and reinforce a peculiarly specific artistic statement. Hotere's work lacks both this consistency and the preoccupation with cultural reference. The sign of the local is neither a strategy nor a necessity; no indigenous motif is appealed to as a solution to the problem of 'what to paint in NZ'. That problem is not Hotere's. Apart from his *Black Union Jacks*, he has scarcely referred to the New Zealand nation, or used motifs that had or could have strong national reference, as Walter's *koru* did. His work is instead about questions and conflicts that engage him, that are both global and relatively immediate. In some cases, as I noted, he records a personal loss that binds him to a site on the other side of the world. The connection between a world war and a brother's life marks the sense in which 'global issues' are not abstractions in political discourse but tangible moments in a biography.

Much of Hotere's work preceded the emergence of the contemporary Maori art movement, a movement that has been compelled to address a different question of 'what to paint', or what to carve. Maori artists have had to consider how to express an identity that draws on particular traditions and historical experiences, yet sustains salience for the present. Hotere offered an answer to this that has been hard to recognize, because his statement has accumulated gradually through the various preoccupations of his work; it has not been present in any one of them, but is manifest rather through their combination. It is, moreover, a statement that is difficult to recognize because it lies outside the conventions of discussion about 'identity' that solidified only after his art found its directions. In this language, which has become almost natural to us, identity is a sense of self one carries like a possession. It is a matter of cultural heritage, of origins and the effort to make a heritage live in the present. Though 'identities' are often fashioned against nationalities – and particularly against their colonial imposition – the idea of identity is modelled on that of nationality. On this model, one has a unitary selfhood; one bears a collective cultural identity; one is an Australian or a Maori or a Samoan, and it is somehow axiomatic that this identification defines one's expression and one's art. Indigenous Pacific socialities might have suggested different ideas of personhood – in which the self is divisible, and defined by debts of substance and flows of gifts. But this relational idea has been eclipsed in much rhetoric, if not always in indigenous Pacific practice.

Hotere's work points in a different direction, though not toward a shallow cosmopolitanism. The unmarked 'citizen of the world' has no more presence in his work than the false universality of New York formalism. His range of subjects, titles and practices conveys, instead, a sense of location and engagement that is neither as particular nor as general as the nation. One's being amounts both to more and less than the 'identity' such models of selfhood and collective selfhood permit. His work acknowledges moods and sentiments that afflict us all, and to that extent is humanist, implicitly rejecting national or cultural specification. On the other hand, it often arises from particular sites, their associations in memory, and the battles that are proceeding around them. An icon may be indissociable from a threatened peninsula in the middle of Otago.

Contexts

To put the art of the Hermannsburg school together with that of the Maori modernists – a loose group into which Hotere does and does not fit – is to draw a comparison between apples and oranges. The stylistic differences are striking, but they are less fundamental than the differences between the milieux in which the work was produced and circulated. One might relate the difference simply to a geographic contrast. Australia, like Canada, is a much larger country than Aotearoa New Zealand, incorporating a great deal of land that was of marginal significance to the invaders. There were accordingly substantial regions that were never colonized with the intensity of areas overtaken by urban and rural development. Central Australia, the Northern Territory and other outback regions continued to have strong Aboriginal presences, and were the locations of arresting scenery and national icons such as Uluru (Ayers Rock). The art from these regions had an appeal that originated beyond the art scenes of the Australian cities, and was sustained by domestic tourism, and more widely by the popular culture of vicarious tourism to the outback. Namatjira received some qualified validation through the art world, but was successful and until recently visible through popular reproduction rather than representation in public galleries.

The connections between domestic tourism and the staging of indigenous culture manifest in the Hermannsburg school have affinities with earlier developments in Maori culture around Rotorua. There, from the late nineteenth century on, Maori carvers had taken advantage of the opportunity to adapt their work in souvenir form, and hotel owners commissioned meeting houses or model houses from carvers such as Tene Waitere. Just as the interest in the stark grandeur of the centre gave

Aboriginal people a market for artifacts and art works that acquired a presence in many Australian homes, the unusual geothermal environment around Rotorua much earlier gave Maori souvenirs, and postcards and photographs featuring both Maori and the thermal features, wide circulation in New Zealand's domestic and popular culture. The Maori pieces were, however, objects rather than paintings. They were consequently not described or responded to as art; they did not arouse the kind of debate that the work of Namatjira did; they acquired presence rather than prestige.

Though there is a basic affinity between the process of colonization in the two countries – in each case a settler population struggled to displace natives – the colonial engagement with Maori and Aboriginal populations differed markedly. The origins of the difference might be traced back to the broad-brush contrast in European perceptions between the hierarchical and settled form of Maori society, and the egalitarian nomadism of Aboriginal people. At a crude level, these societies can indeed be contrasted in this way, but this is less important than the fact that these differences were those obvious to outsiders and so broadly informed conduct toward the colonized. Europeans were far more ready to acknowledge Maori property in land, and native forms of social structure and government. In contrast, the tendency was to emphasize the absolute savagery of Aboriginal society, and its intractability in the face of civilizing processes. There was thus a greater willingness to negotiate with Maori landowners and with Maori chiefs than with Aboriginal people that left Maori in a stronger position despite the widespread losses and setbacks of the nineteenth-century wars. Although many Maori leaders resisted colonization, it remained possible for a Maori elite to be accommodated within colonial society in a fashion that had no parallel in Australia. Maori were members of parliament from the 1890s; from an early date, a small but steady stream became teachers, doctors and lawyers, in part specifically because schools for Maori were established on the model of British so-called 'public' schools. Even if Maori people in general have certainly been disadvantaged, and like most indigenous peoples are at the bottom in terms of most social and economic indicators, there has long been a relatively substantial Maori middle class.

Although recent research has drawn attention to many ways in which Aboriginal people worked with white society, from the comparative perspective it is their consistent exclusion, particularly from education and from white-collar occupations, that is striking. No Aboriginal person graduated from a university until about 1960, and to date

112 ALBERT NAMATJIRA The Western MacDonnell Range, Central Australia, c. 1957

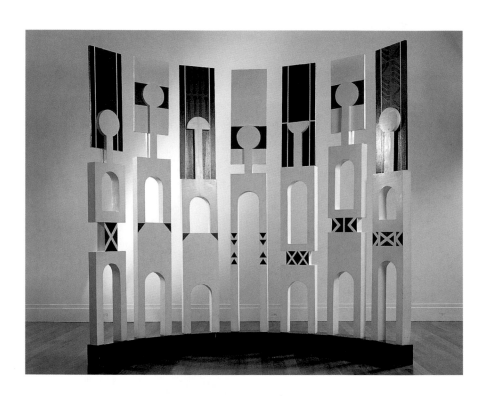

113 PARATENE MATCHITT
Taunga Waka, 1971

114 RALPH HOTERE O Africa, 1981

there has only ever been one Aboriginal member of the federal parliament. (Senator Neville Bonner, who represented the Liberal Party in
Queensland from 1971 to 1985.) Ultimately this is why, in the fifties and
sixties, there is no group like the Maori modernists in Australia. Aboriginal people had no access to teachers' colleges and art schools until
much later.

Exhibitions

Art is curiously dispersed within public culture. The idea that painting
and sculpture are essentially elite genres relative to popular media such
as television is inadequate, because much so-called 'high art' receives
extraordinarily wide circulation through printed reproduction. This is
true not only of old masters and popular modernist art, but also of genres
such as landscape which are endlessly imitated by those described as
'commercial' painters. 'High art' is also a form of popular culture that
has a real presence in many domestic situations, as well as in corporate
and institutional environments outside the obvious museums and art
galleries. The appeal of contemporary art is more restricted, to be sure,
though some work is validated through acquisition and display by the
art institutions.

Some of the indigenous art that I have discussed has reached wide
audiences but lacked particular prestige or legitimation. This was most
obviously the case for Maori carving. Prior to the 'Te Maori' exhibition
that toured the United States and then New Zealand over 1984–7, the
material was widely known, and widely circulated and vulgarized, yet
not appreciated as high art. The work of the Maori modernist artists, on
the other hand, was acknowledged by a limited group of artists, curators
and collectors, but received little wider recognition. It was also, appropri-
ately enough, regarded as the work of a group of individual artists rather
than a collective cultural expression. In so far as it possessed prestige at
all, it tended not to reflect that value back upon the Maori collectivity, or
at least it did not do so in the eyes of a white New Zealand public.

In the art domain, the key nexus between high status and popularity
is the blockbuster exhibition. Bodies of art are marketed on the basis of
their exceptional quality, and increasingly with reference to the curatorial flair that informs a particular selection. High levels of corporate
sponsorship, extensive and lavish advertising, and orchestrated publicity
build up a sense that a particular exhibition is an exceptional cultural
experience, a once-in-a-lifetime opportunity to encounter the corpus of

a master, or the classic pieces from a period or great civilization. Such shows may attract hundreds of thousands of visitors, most of whom will not be regular gallery visitors. Though the crowds are hardly conducive to optimal viewing conditions, the press and the throng are very much part of the intensity and ambience of the event. If the work displayed is that of Rembrandt or Picasso, the artist's status is, of course, reinforced and realized in the eyes of particular viewers, rather than created; but if the work is that of an indigenous population, a new regard may come into being that alters the status of that population in a definite and distinctive way.

This is arguably what was accomplished by the 'Te Maori' exhibition. Had it taken place ten or fifteen years earlier, the show would in all likelihood have been the product of negotiation among a few museum directors and curators, with minimal Maori involvement. The decade of its gestation, however, happened to be a decade of Maori activism. There was a major land march in 1975, a sustained occupation of Bastion Point in Auckland in 1977–8, and annual demonstrations at celebrations on Waitangi Day (the anniversary of the Treaty of Waitangi), among other events and campaigns mounted by Maori parties and activist groups. Although there was no direct link between these radical actions and the exhibition, Maori claims were in the ascendancy. Given that Sidney (Hirini) Mead, at that time one of the few authorities on traditional Maori art, was in any case himself Maori, it is not surprising that he was drawn into the consultative process, and that in due course it was recognized that a wide group of elders and communities needed to be involved in the process of presenting the exhibition.

From the perspective of more recent debates around indigenous art traditions and their curatorial presentation, 'Te Maori' would appear to have been a conservative exhibition, even one that catered to a primitivist appetite for the alien, the archaic and the mystical. The show consisted of sculpture in wood, bone and nephrite, was limited to classic pieces before 1860, and all but excluded pieces produced before that date that manifested European influence or the experimental use of new material. The emphasis was on the awesome object rather than its context, and the exclusion of neo-traditional pieces could easily have suggested that the art traditions belonged essentially to the past – that Maori culture had diminished in the fact of colonization. Certainly, there were misgivings among Maori concerning various aspects of the exhibition, and some tribes did not allow their *taonga* to travel. But, from the perspective of political effect, the traditionalist orientation of 'Te Maori' was far less important than the connection that was continually asserted

115 Maori protesters at Bastion Point, Auckland, May 1978

between the people and the treasures. Maori groups travelled with the exhibition for openings at each of the American venues. They staged dawn rituals, greetings, dances, speeches and blessings.

The apparent primitivism no doubt helped ensure the success of the show, but the Maori presence augmented its appeal, and insisted that the works on display were 'not deceased relics…but living spiritual objects.'[12] A more 'contextual' treatment of the work, of the kind that had been successfully presented for the arts of Amazonia and Madagascar at London's Museum of Mankind in the 1980s, could paradoxically have diminished the exhibition's political efficacy. As it was, carvings spot-lit and isolated in cases and on walls were empowered in a manner that echoed their awe-inspiring presentation in traditional Maori situations, in houses, on canoe prows or palisades, confronting visitors and hosts. While ancestors embodied in wood once impressed or defied those from allied or enemy tribes, they now expressed the *mana* or spiritual power of the Maori collectivity to another group of outsiders. Ironically, this decontextualization insisted on by the art institution was perhaps truer to the original functioning of these objects than any better-informed contextualization in indigenous life and quotidian activity by a museum anthropologist could have been.

In any event, the reviews in New York and elsewhere were good, and the attendances high. The specific effect that the exhibition's American success had upon the domestic audience needs to be seen in the context

116 Uenuku, wood carving from the Waikato area

117 Advertisement for the 'Te Maori' exhibition, New Zealand Herald, 26 June 1987

118 'Te Maori' feature page from the Auckland Star, 22 June 1987

of white New Zealand's longstanding cultural cringe. As in Australia, but to a greater degree, the smallness and isolation of the country had long meant that writers and artists were assumed to be second rate relative to those from the mother country, initially, and subsequently from Europe, the United States and elsewhere. Local accomplishments never counted for much unless a person had an 'overseas' or later an 'international' reputation. Although these anxieties were to some extent shrugged off in Australia by the 1970s, they remained more keenly felt in New Zealand, and international exposure is in fact still crucial for artists, writers and academics in both countries. Consequently, in the 1980s a success for Maori art in the United States, especially in New York, notionally the centre of the international art world, was a triumph of extraordinary significance. It meant that Maori art and culture possessed far greater value and authenticity than Pakeha New Zealanders, and for that matter most Maori, had acknowledged. If any art from New Zealand ranked among the great traditions of the world, it was emphatically that produced by Maori. And the material's neglect was a source of

This will not happen again in our lifetime.

TE MAORI
Te hokinga mai. The return home.

It is the first time in 1000 years such a gathering of ancestral treasures has occurred. It is also likely to be the last time such an event takes place.

What makes Te Maori special is not only the uniqueness of the occasion or the sheer artistry of pieces which range from exquisite pendants to massive gateway structures. It is also the fact that these taonga continue to live as objects of ancestral power and love.

Whatever way you choose to view Te Maori, Mobil urges you to see it.

This cultural landmark has provided fresh insights into an important part of our heritage and has attracted record attendances in Wellington, Dunedin and Christchurch. Admission by koha (donation).

Nau mai. Haere mai. haere mai.

Made possible by a grant from

Mobil

OPEN DAILY 10am-4.30pm
AUCKLAND CITY ART GALLERY — JUNE 28 - SEPTEMBER 10

embarrassment if not shame. A typical report noted that the remarkable carving Uenuku had been 'a favourite among the 750,000 Americans who had visited *Te Maori*...yet in its homeland, most people had never seen or heard of Uenuku.'[13]

The American tour was followed by 'Te Maori: Te Hokinga Mai' (The Return Home), a tour of seven New Zealand venues, culminating in the Auckland City Art Gallery. 'This will not happen again in our lifetime' advised the advertisements. The sense that the exhibition was indeed very special secured an extraordinary attendance within New Zealand of over 750,000, or around 25 per cent of the entire population; about 3,000 had attended the dawn opening in Auckland alone.

As in the United States, the effect of the exhibition arose not merely from the pieces themselves, or from their mode of display, but also from the ritual openings of the show in each venue, and an emphasis in publications, educational material and commentaries by Maori guides upon the *tapu* character of the work. This demanded continuing regard to protocol, and recognition that the gallery became a *marae*, a ceremonial meeting ground, for the duration of the exhibition.[14] The point was not that it was regarded as the *marae* of any particular tribe, but unambiguously as a Maori space, which others were privileged to visit. Not only did the exhibition display a living culture rather than a set of objects, but it appeared to be under indigenous control (notwithstanding the many debates behind the scenes). 'Te Maori' thus vaunted Maori tradition, and insisted that its *mana* required national recognition. As one commentator was to write, the exhibition 'fuelled the expectation that these values and forms will be recognized and accepted by the rest of society. That is one of the important challenges *Te Maori* has set for Pakeha New Zealanders.'[15]

The exhibition could not have had this effect had the debate about 'race relations' in Aotearoa New Zealand not focused increasingly, during the 1980s, on the meanings and significance of the 1840 Treaty of Waitangi. The Treaty, which effected an ambiguous cession of sovereignty on the part of Maori in return for rights and guarantees that were subsequently violated (plainly in some cases and arguably in others), acquired new centrality through the work of the Waitangi Tribunal. The Tribunal had been established in 1975 to hear Maori grievances against the Crown that related to the Treaty, and initially had only limited advisory powers, but became steadily more consequential from the mid-1980s, after it acquired the capacity to bind the government to implement decisions concerning the restitution of resources to Maori, and as its jurisdiction was radically expanded to make admissible retrospective claims over the whole period since 1840.[16] This inaugurated a highly publicized, wide-ranging and open-ended legal process that has proved a crucial instrument for the redistribution of resources in areas such as education as well as more obviously in relation to land and extractable resources. Maori do not dismiss the Treaty – which is now, significantly, also referred to as Te Tiriti – as a tactic of dispossession, but insist rather that it possesses continuing salience and should not only be honoured in the legal domain, but must be regarded as a foundation or charter for bicultural practice in general. Hence curatorial activities, among others, should acknowledge the basic parity between Maori and Pakeha values.

In Australia, there was no treaty, and no single exhibition like 'Te Maori' that had such a dramatic impact. There was instead a gradual shift, in fits and starts, that began with the much earlier albeit only occasional exhibitions of Aboriginal art as art. In a similar way, however, 'Dreamings', curated from the South Australian Museum for New York's Asia Society in 1988, was a great success, not least because New York audiences found the presences and performances of Aboriginal artists profoundly moving.[17] The strong impression it made in the United States certainly paved the way for large audiences at Australian venues, but the effect was less decisive, if only because Aboriginal art was by this time already highly regarded, at least by more liberal sectors of the population. Even so, the popularity of that exhibition was perhaps gained at the cost of exclusions comparable to those of 'Te Maori'. The success of its range of material in New York was in large part because it was radically different from any art previously encountered in major exhibitions there. Hence there was no place for work that manifested contact and exchange with European traditions, nor for the politically deliberate work of so-called 'urban Aboriginal artists', and certainly not for the seemingly naive landscapes of the Hermannsburg school. By the early 1990s, in Australia, it would be possible to present these diverse cultural expressions in one frame, suggesting that they were valid statements alike that displayed the diversity of Aboriginal experience and culture, but it would continue to be difficult to communicate that message to northern hemisphere audiences, who wanted indigenous art to be tribal and cosmological rather than historical or political.

It is extraordinary how, over a decade later, 'Te Maori' is still frequently cited as a key moment. It was a defining exhibition for protocols concerning consultation and cultural sensitivity, but it had a much wider effect, not only in challenging an audience to acknowledge the prestige of Maori culture, but in carrying that audience with it. Questions were raised at the time about the exhibition's exclusion both of traditional women's art forms and of contemporary art. It was asserted that *taonga* such as feather cloaks had been omitted because they were too fragile to travel. Although this was widely repeated, it was in fact no more than a retrospective rationalization. The curators appear to have carried the conventional biases of tribal art connoisseurship and identified art with figure sculpture, which was perforce to neglect women's material, and moreover the significance of various forms of non-figurative design in traditional art. This omission was, however, to be soon redressed in the 1988 exhibition 'Te Aho Tapu' (The Sacred Thread), and in subsequent touring shows such as 'Taonga Maori', a 'Te Maori' style show that toured to Australia in 1989–90.

The exclusion of the experimental tradition in Maori art (figurative painting, for example), may have had longer-term ramifications. It reinforced not only a canon of Maori carving, but the canonical view that indigenous art was governed by tradition and resistant to innovation. In fact it is clear that Maori art can only have been continually innovative, since it differs in fundamental ways from the art styles of the tropical Polynesian island cultures to which Maori are closely related. The distinct and various regional traditions of Maori art that can be identified in the array of pre-contact and early contact material can only have emerged through experiment and rapid adaptation. So far from being a defining aspect of indigenous practice, traditionalism in tribal art tends to be a consequence of colonization. Local artists may replicate past forms to affirm the continuity of their culture, or in response to outsiders' interests in traditional art, or both.

The most obvious casualties of this suppression of dynamism were the contemporary Maori artists. They were completely unrepresented in the United States; during the 'return home' tour there were efforts to mount complementary exhibitions, but these were too hastily prepared to attract anything like the level of attention received by 'Te Maori' itself. This marginalization meant that the Maori culture that was most publicly visible was perhaps awe-inspiring in its spirituality, but lay at some remove from the politics of the present. The prominent Maori academic and activist, Ranginui Walker, was reported to have said at the exhibition's Auckland opening that 'Te Maori' 'creates a nice happy glow but does not help to solve today's problems'.[18] Some debate focused on the fact that the major sponsor was the Mobil oil company, which at the same time was engaged in developments that threatened to pollute the New Zealand coast and were being opposed by Maori groups. Anger on the part of contemporary artists was expressed particularly in Selwyn Muru's *Te Maaoorii*, a parodic sculpture marked by the tattoos of urban Maori youth and other signs of acculturation. A metal oil tap in lieu of the figure's penis referred to Mobil's sponsorship, and the long vowels of the piece's title presumably made mockery of Pakeha efforts to emulate correct Maori pronunciation, and the well-intentioned but limited cross-cultural genuflection that that signified.[19]

The work of Muru, Matchitt, Arnold Wilson, Cliff Whiting and others existed and was undergoing development over the life of 'Te Maori', but existed in a different milieu, for a different audience. The work of an artist such as Hotere, who was not struggling for the recognition of contemporary Maori art, but was instead sidestepping that label, has an even more tenuous relation to such a prominent exhibition. There has been much talk of indigenous political and cultural renaissances: the gap between the affirmation of traditional art and contemporary culture reminds us that the renaissance was no smooth progression, but a set of disparate shifts and gains, that were in tension as much as they were mutually supportive.

In retrospect few would condemn exhibitions such as 'Te Maori' and 'Dreamings' categorically: whatever their limitations, their powerful traditionalism clearly helped create a climate of wider understanding and receptivity. If their appeal built upon romantic and primitivist sentiments, the temporal idea central to primitivism was contradicted. Maori and Aboriginal arts might be spiritual and even mystical, but were not dead. If they were indeed rooted in ancient traditions, if marketing efforts came perilously close to affirming their archaism, these cultures continued to live and grow, and have a contemporary presence. In Australia, the extraordinary antiquity of human art forms on the continent meant that associations with deep prehistory, human origins, and primitivism would always remain alive, however visible living Aboriginal artists became. In the case of 'Te Maori', the presence of Maori people around the pieces – which had to be recognized as *taonga* rather than mere objects – was proof of their present significance. The continuing life of works such as Uenuku indeed suggested an entirely different notion of time and history from the conventional linear conceptions that organize European academic disciplines such as art history. Work from the past was not succeeded by more recent approaches and styles; rather it sustained life in the present, not merely in the metaphoric sense that it retained visual appeal, but in the stronger idea that ancestors were incarnated in, not merely represented by, objects of the kind exhibited. Whether or not such subtleties were grasped by a wide audience, the presence of Maori was undeniable. More importantly, perhaps, the axiom of settler colonialism's linear time, which relegated native peoples to a prior stage in national history, was undermined.

As A.P. Elkin had imagined, so many decades before, and on the other side of the Tasman, indigenous art would indeed establish respect for indigenous culture among a wider public that otherwise tended to be indifferent to the specifics of indigenous society, and one might add to the injustices of colonization. Elkin also foresaw that the prestige the art acquired would bolster indigenous pride, but he imagined this taking place in a fairly paternalistic way: it would be something that 'we' could do for 'them'. He did not anticipate the extent to which self-affirmation would be empowered by indigenous communities' own acts. What Maori did through 'Te Maori', and many subsequent exhibitions, was to claim the space of the museum. Not only the protocols around openings, but gallery management structures and curatorial practices were to be redefined. Whether this terrain of negotiation was a microcosm of the settler colony, or merely a theatre in which a struggle over sovereignty could be mimicked, it was a publicly visible space, and a prestigious one too.

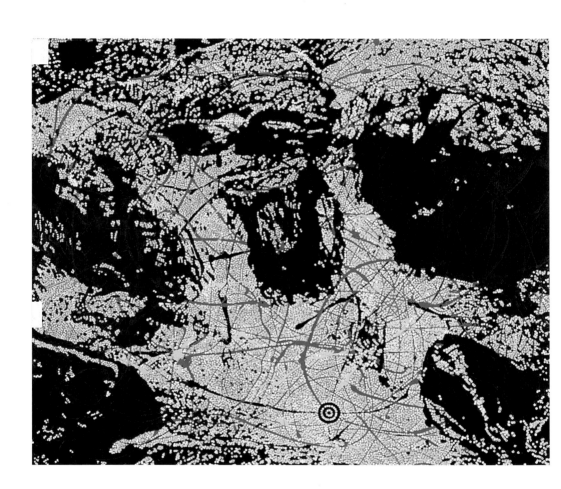

119 GORDON BENNETT Panorama: Cascade (with Floating Point of Identification), 1993

Curators of what was once called 'primitive' art and anthropologists have become notorious for fetishizing traditional cultures, to the exclusion of those cultures' historically adapted and innovative expressions. The criticism of anthropology became most vigorous only after the discipline had largely shifted away from an emphasis on tribal societies, and ceased to be blind to the ramifications of colonial histories, even if a more deep-seated attachment to the exotic undoubtedly still persists in some quarters. However, a preoccupation with 'authenticity' certainly remains powerful in the tribal art market: early, ideally pre-contact pieces are the ones that command the highest prices. But at the same time, curators of contemporary art have embraced the postcolonial movement, and particularly works by indigenous artists who have, in one sense or another, turned away from canonized ancestral styles. These artists are frequently concerned with questions of identity, yet reject restrictive affirmations of tradition, and critically reframe representations of indigenous people. Their works often reproduce colonial images and elements of indigenous culture through the practice of overt quotation that is something of a hallmark of international postmodernism.

The older preference for traditionalist work remains alive among wide audiences, for whom indigenous art styles have a freshness and distinctiveness that much postmodernist art lacks. In fact it may be the work's distinctiveness, rather than viewers' traditionalism, that makes much indigenous art appealing. One renowned example, the central Australian dot paintings from Papunya and elsewhere (fig. 123), is not in any case a traditional genre in any meaningful sense. As is well known, this style emerged in the early 1970s through the transfer of sand drawing motifs and body paintings to murals, batiks, boards and canvases. But this process entailed dramatic transformations of scale, form and context. The marketing of this type of art has consistently emphasized the images' grounding in myth and ancestral spirituality, and this is fair enough, given that in general these paintings are indeed vehicles for narratives that remain central to ritual, landholding, and other aspects of lived culture past and present. Yet it is the very innovation of this art that is its most extraordinary feature. It is hard to think of examples from the art histories of any part of the world where wholly new media were adapted so rapidly to produce work of such palpable strength.

The enduring popularity of more 'authentic' styles of Aboriginal art runs against the contemporary curatorial preference for deliberately postcolonial work. There are thus two, or at least two, hierarchies defining value in the cross-cultural art field at present. One could be seen as an updated version of the old primitivist preference for mysterious and archaic pieces. Now it is those works that are unambiguously grounded in tribal spirituality that are most favoured. Yet this is not to be dismissed as merely an extension of an imperialist cult of primitivist authenticity, because spirituality really does define these works, and it is certainly something that indigenous artists and communities themselves have a stake in. The second hierarchy embraces the critique of 'essentialist' national, ethnic or native identities that has become a reigning cliché of cultural theory. It disparages work that exhibits distinctive tribal identity, and instead advocates hybridity. Yet the labels used to market art are frequently misleading, neither encompassing nor exhausting the interest of works that they inadequately frame. Much postcolonial art may have more to say than academic postcolonialism.

Both of these ways of ranking indigenous art are, at any rate, invidious. Indigenous art that is grounded in tradition – albeit in transformed traditions – can possess great aesthetic vigour and spiritual power. Much

120 ANGKUNA GRAHAM Untitled, 1984

that is challenging is also emerging from artists whose training has taken place in contemporary art schools, and whose styles and references are more obviously affiliated with those of twentieth-century international modernism and postmodernism. There are certainly good works and bad works in many styles and modes, but we cannot suggest that one tendency alone is more intellectually, aesthetically or visually compelling than others. In this chapter, I want to make the simple point that a range of current work holds value and interest. We cannot pin indigenous art down to one mode or movement; the incorporation of indigenous art practices within such art-historical terms, within a periodization in the making, would arguably ignore the most challenging and interesting dimensions of these practices. I am concerned, above all, to go beyond an obvious relativism, which would say that all of these expressions are 'valid'. The significance and effects of indigenous art can only be misunderstood if we insist on celebrating *either* the so-called 'traditionalist' expressions *or* the 'contemporary' ones, instead of acknowledging both. It is when we acknowledge both, I would claim, that the cultural relations of settler-colonialism that I have been describing in this book cease to be simply insecure and instead come unstuck. To grasp this is also to appreciate why a continuum between 'traditional' and 'contemporary' cannot adequately describe the range of artistic expressions that have emerged. This is what this chapter tries to reveal, through discussion of two major contemporary artists, both in this case from Australia.

Gordon Bennett: Nations, histories, bodies

Much debate in cultural theory juxtaposes essentialist and hybrid constructions of identity, and tends to denounce the former for their nationalist exclusivism or their backward-looking nativism. The art of Gordon Bennett (b. 1955) avoids affirming an objectified Aboriginal culture in opposition to colonial ideologies, and instead proceeds by disrupting colonial representations themselves, by recasting them in various ways, and by insisting on the presence of racism and violence within them. This could be seen as a strategy in cultural politics that works through hybrid expression, and that rejects any notion of an integrated self authenticated by a particular tradition.

This is true of Bennett's art, but is not sufficient as an account of it. The more powerful opposition in his work is that between the universal or pan-human aesthetic statement, and the inescapably local character of history and experience. Bennett draws from Minimalism, De Stijl and Abstract Expressionism, forcing features of these movements into a context of human relations that is at once global and national. Motivated by postcolonial theory, he retraces the evolution implicit in Ralph Hotere's work, which, as we have seen, took Minimalist forms out of a universalizing, formalist art and insisted on the particularities of places, events and struggles. For both artists, this has often meant drawing a seemingly neutral form such as Malevich's cross, subsequently used by Reinhardt and many others, into a relation with language, which is to say with content, with the world, and with particular worlds.

While Hotere's contexts were often political and biographic, Bennett has been more consistently oriented toward critical engagements with national narrative. In several series he has worked from the canonical images of Captain Cook and explorers' ships, the foundational moments of possession and the myths of exploration.[1] Importantly, the sources are for the most part not the works of the period, or the original sketches associated with these events, but rather the overtly moralized historical reconstructions produced generations later, such as the engraving after Gilfillan's painting of Cook's declaration of British sovereignty in Australia, and the much cruder figures in primary school social studies texts from the 1950s and 1960s. These images may be subcanonical works from the perspective of art history, but are monumental in the sense that they are vehicles of Australian history and devices of civic education. They present exemplary stories intended to elicit a devotional attitude, not toward the facts of the past, but rather toward History in principle, and the nation that we imagine having been forged through it.

Bennett has something in common with the vandal who defaces the monument, but he goes beyond mere decapitation or graffiti to suggest a reconstitution of national narrative, albeit one inescapably defined by pain, violence and contradiction. This vision, developed through many works, is expressed especially powerfully in *Myth of the Western Man (White Man's Burden)* (1992, fig. 124), in the Art Gallery of New South Wales. The central figure is that of a generic pioneer engaged in planting a post or flagpole, the foundational act in the establishment of a colonial rule of property and sovereignty. Yet the settler figure is seemingly thrown sideways – as David Collins' narrative was, as I suggested at the outset, thrown into confusion by the moral contradictions of a well-meaning invasion, a civilizing mission of soldiers and criminals (pp. 34–8). The pioneer is, from the very outset, caught up in an extraordinary circular storm, a maelstrom of historical events which race like scraps of paper around the tenuously fixed pole. The central date at the

121 SAMUEL CALVERT Captain Cook Taking Possession of the Australian Continent on Behalf of the British Crown AD 1770, engraving after Gilfillan

122 GORDON BENNETT Possession Island, 1991

bottom is 1788. This is enough to signal familiar moments in Australian history, though the artist has also provided a list detailing the events cited: 1795, for instance, refers to the '1st legally sanctioned massacre of Aboriginal people' at the Hawkesbury River; 1799 to the trial of five whites for the killing of Aboriginal boys; and 1802 to the killing and decapitation of the Eora warrior Pemulwuy.

The dates are not disposed arbitrarily, but in ways that suggest oppositions and continuities, and perhaps also a reversal: 1788, marking the establishment of the colony, is linked by the pole itself with 1992 in the top centre. That year is defined in Bennett's notes by the winning of the Mabo case in the High Court and the overturning of the doctrine of *terra nullius*, which had for so long obviated the need to negotiate about the land, or even to acknowledge the dispossession of the indigenous people. The rejection of this axiom of the Australian settler-colonial regime suggested the prospect of resolution, and inspired an optimism that cannot have been vindicated by subsequent events. The future of post-Mabo native title legislation remains uncertain under the conservative Howard Government, elected in 1996 after thirteen years of Labor's generally cautious but nevertheless progressive reform. In any event, the painting as a whole refrained from imagining any narrative closure. Its tempestuous structure implies rather the persistence of conflict, imbalance and damage.

One of the most obvious features of this work is its adaptation of Jackson Pollock's dripping and throwing technique. Bennett has experimented with this in a number of paintings, including the *Panorama* series of landscapes, in which the drip patterns, painted over with black, assume the appearance of a plethora of scars caused by repeated whipping. One of the most conspicuous strands in his art is the identification between canvas and skin: paintings do not represent the body, but instead index the violence of global slavery, and the indigenous ritual violence of scarification, in a direct and highly tangible way. In a number of works, verbal violence is incised onto the canvas, the words literally cut into the paint with a scalpel. The physicality of these techniques and associations takes Bennett's art out of anything like a sterile circuit of postmodern repetitions, enabling his concerns to elicit twitches of pain, fear and empathy in the viewer's own body. These responses would not be so highly charged were they not engendered by the grandiose tragic wildness of Australian history. Yet a critique of the racist monuments to that history might easily be no more than an academic exercise, were it not mediated by, and exhibited through, searing cuts to human bodies and psyches.

123 CLIFFORD POSSUM TJAPALTJARRI Yingalingi (Honey Ant Dreaming Story), 1983

124 GORDON BENNETT Myth of the Western Man (White Man's Burden), 1992

The identification between skin and violence is in the background in the *Myth of the Western Man*, but the expressiveness is not. The painting takes Pollock's technique out of the register in which it has been conventionally understood – as the expression of a creative individual's tortured psyche – and renders it a vehicle for expressing the repressed in the Australian national psyche. The involuted tracery, large and desperate enough to occupy a huge canvas, but still agonizingly confined within it, ceases to be a monument to the angst of a genius's inner world, and instead assumes a geographic location in a fatally contested territory. The chaotic interplay of dripped lines of different colours comes to index not a conflict of emotions or psychic principles, but a confusion produced by the violence of specific events, by an antagonism between contradictory attachments to place that bears fruit in sanctioned and unsanctioned killing.

There are notable parallels with the work of First Nations artists in Canada, such as Lawrence Paul Yuxweluptun (fig. 2). Like Bennett, Yuxweluptun appropriates particular modernist styles, in his case Dali's surrealism, to image a native land in which bodies, spirits and topographies are merged – and upon which colonial violence has been inflicted: Yuxweluptun's 'clear-cut' recalls the pioneer forest clearances that were also the prerequisite for McCahon's evacuated landscape (p. 22). Like Bennett, Yuxweluptun tries to make the colonial nation confront the injuries it has inflicted. Yet there are of course differences. Bennett's work is less preoccupied with the settler impact on the environment (though it would not be difficult to point to other indigenous artists in Australia and New Zealand who share Yuxweluptun's emphasis upon these issues). His arguments are specific to Australia, and his reference is not to Pollock's art in general but to one painting in particular, *Blue Poles*, which can be seen as Pollock's only Australian painting.

The remarks I've made on the tortured character of Pollock's work are not in fact true of many of the drip-painted works, some of which, such as *Number 20*, seem expansive and optimistic. I am describing *Blue Poles* an Australian painting because it has acquired a hybrid, transcultural identity that animates Bennett's painting in a vital way. There is much to be said for the view distilled by Paul Gilroy with a line borrowed from rap lyrics: 'it ain't where you're from, it's where you're at.' Many cultural phenomena are to be understood not through reference to their original meanings, but through the situation of their recontextualization. Hence Kurosawa demonstrates that the Western is a Japanese genre, Pacific Islanders take it for granted that Christianity is a Pacific religion, and modernity and capitalism are indigenized in many ways in many places. There is a limit to this, however. Simply because paintings by Motherwell and Rothko are in the same space as *Blue Poles* in the National Gallery of Australia, I do not suggest that they too must be understood as works defined by their diasporic situation as Austral-American paintings. The identity of *Blue Poles*, however, *is* defined by where it's at, not by where it's from. This is so because of the special circumstances of the painting's acquisition.

Early in the years of the progressive and exciting but always rash and troubled Whitlam Labor Government (1972–5), the painting's purchase for over a million dollars, then seen as an extraordinary sum for a comparatively recent work of art, was widely lambasted in the media, and the quality of the painting vigorously debated. 'Drunks did it!' declared the *Daily Mirror* headline. It was a topic about which almost everyone had a strong view, and many of these views were negative, perhaps not surprisingly, given that the work was being judged on the basis of fairly small black and white newsprint reproductions. For detractors of the Whitlam government, the decision exemplified profligacy and irresponsibility, an engagement with trendy issues such as culture and the environment to the detriment of fiscal responsibility. For supporters the work symbolized a sudden expansiveness in the Australian outlook, reflected not only in the generous allocation to the National Gallery, but in a determination to make that a world class institution in which contemporary culture, including American culture, was represented, not just a narrower Australian and British tradition. The attribution of value to an abstract work moreover signalled a counter-populism, part of an affirmation of literature, theatre and other forms of 'high' culture that would be increasingly supported by the Australia Council, redressing all at once the supposed philistinism of the football-supporting colonial anglophilia that had been so marked among Whitlam's predecessors, the conservative governments of the 1950s and 1960s. This was to insist on a sophistication that the middle-class left revelled in, but which was never quite shared by enough of those who had voted Labor in, and who would subsequently vote Labor out.

This history was to stay with the painting to an extraordinary degree, and is certainly something that most Australian if not international visitors to the gallery are aware of, even today. Gordon Bennett's note to the year 1972 reads 'Aboriginal Tent Embassy set up in Canberra. Gough Whitlam elected and Blue Poles by Jackson Pollock purchased for Australia – (public outraged).'

If the hybrid *Blue Poles* stands for the cultured internationalism that some white Australians felt was suddenly within their grasp in the

125 JACKSON POLLOCK Blue Poles, 1952

1970s, Bennett's *Myth of the Western Man* at once reduces and aug-
ments the work in a fashion that precludes such confidence. There are
not many poles but one, and that one is not simply a form that energizes
a field, but a representation of a post or flagpole. Even without the
whirlwind of dates – that is, dates of massacres and legal findings – this
figuration opens a flood of historical content that can only sweep aside
the universal significances that might be imputed to gestures and forms,
as it harnesses their energy. The Australian who measures his or her
citizenship of the world by appreciation of Pollock's radically abstract
work, which exemplifies a relatively uncomplicated international-local
hybridity, becomes a slightly absurd figure if we accept Bennett's revi-
sion of the national history painting.

The arguments of Bennett's work in the Art Gallery of New South
Wales do not, however, stop with the redefinition of Australian history.
They surely also write something back into the way we imagine the
adventurousness of postwar American art. Pollock was inspired by
various elements of Native American culture signalled by primitivist titles
in early works such as *Guardians of the Secret* (1943) and *Totem Lesson 2*
(1945), though the supposed influence of Navajo sand drawing appears to
have been limited to the conception of art as a healing practice that mobilized primordial and sacred energies (p. 162).

Formalist critical discourse has marginalized these inspirations, or at
least suggested that Pollock lifted them to the level of a universal statement. Gordon Bennett's art is relatively unconcerned with questions of
cultural property and does not suggest that there is an unacknowledged
debt in Pollock – that we need to redress a silence by giving greater credit
to the indigenous cultures as in some way formative contributors to these

very remarkable painterly statements. Questions of the relative significance of one influence against another, and debts to predecessors against individual originality remain essentially on art-historical turf. The implication of Bennett's work is rather that in the kind of world we live in, no cultural expression can be dissociated from histories of colonialism and conflict. The notion that Native American culture might offer a model of spiritual healing relevant to artistic practice is not therefore an innocent idea, but, Bennett contends, the affirmative side of the primitivistic discourse that also licensed dispossession. This assessment may seem harsh to those who continue to regard the primitive reference as an enlightened gesture; it no doubt appears contentious to art historians accustomed to reading Abstract Expressionist works in terms that they do not consider racialized. Bennett's statement, however, emerges from a different experience, an experience marked by the pain of racial abuse.

I have already suggested that Pollock could conceivably have been read in the terms in which Margaret Preston wanted to be understood: as an artist who produced an authentically national art by fusing a vigorous modernism with local indigenous references (p. 62). I am concerned neither really with the reasons why this would be inadequate as an account of Pollock, nor with the aspects of American modernity and modernism that meant that this type of rhetoric was unlikely to be resorted to in the 1950s (though, as I noted, other American artists, such as Barnet, did seek to frame their painting in terms closer to Preston's). Given the degree to which indigenous reference is marginal in Pollock's own work, and tends to be invoked so perfunctorily in the associated critical discourse, it is not surprising that Bennett implies a comment more than he mounts a sustained critique. In a subsequent series of works he does, however, engage with the 'Aboriginal' works of Margaret Preston, already discussed in Chapter Four. Although he quotes some of the indigenous figures and motifs that Preston herself quoted from various sources, this is not a project of reappropriation so much as one that helps us dispose of the idea of appropriation, and of the language of cultural property that goes with it. Bennett's new work locates the violence of settler culture in a new way, which is highly suggestive for the future as well as the history of settler-indigenous relations in Australia and elsewhere.

The abstraction of Aboriginality

The series of paintings and prints that Gordon Bennett produced in the mid-1990s exhibits the preoccupations with racism, identity and colonial conflict that have been manifest in all of his art. But these works also make radical departures. Bennett has stepped away from the interest in embodiment, pain and expression. The more recent works are distinctive for their flatness and impersonality, features which perhaps reinforce the cultural and historical generality of their statements. The key points of reference are De Stijl and Margaret Preston. Bennett's interest in Mondrian, and in related Dutch artists and designers, arises specifically from their aspiration to arrive at some transcendence and unity through the transformation of the figurative into the abstract. While other purveyors of universalized or pure forms have been relevant to Bennett's work, the De Stijl painters are acutely salient. In their earlier work they did not typically start with purely abstract elements but instead produced highly schematized renderings of figurative forms. The central question, then, is not that of abstraction itself, but of the movement between figuration and abstraction. Although Bennett empathizes with Mondrian's aspiration to resolve antitheses, he dislodges the quest from the level of vague theosophy and insists on its historical situation and implications. (I was delighted to find, in his annotations to a Mondrian essay, the words 'Uh Oh! Danger Danger!' next to the sentence, 'The elite rises from the mass; is it not therefore its highest expression?').[2]

History quickly tarnishes the idea of purity, which Bennett identifies with racial purity and a host of associated exclusions. This must seem shocking and irreverent from the viewpoint of conventional art history, or from a discourse which insists that Mondrian's writings and art be seen in his own terms. Bennett's question, though, could be phrased: 'What does purity actually mean, in the world, and in Australia?' His answer is influenced by the language of racial abuse that he mobilizes in his art. Epithets such as 'coon', 'darkie' and 'abo' are the shadowy others of 'purity'.

The 'hybridity' that Bennett advocates is not only the ethnic and cultural hybridity that postcolonial theory has sought to privilege. It is also a deeper philosophical condition: not an unambiguous state that stands as one pole or the other on a continuum, but the zone between, and the process of flow and transition. For better or worse, he suggests, we have to live with the dynamic interplay between the contradictory terms that make up the world: black and white, male and female, good and evil, inclusion and exclusion.

If Bennett has long regarded universality with suspicion, the interplay between figuration and abstraction enables him to turn this critique in a different direction. The juxtaposition of reductive human figures based on Vilmos Huszár's *Skaters* and Preston's decidedly crude

Aborigines implies a link between the abstract and the stereotypic, and this connection is repeatedly made in his works of the mid-1990s. De Stijl's schematization, in other words, enables the artist to draw attention to the abstraction involved in all perception, and particularly the racist abstraction present in settler-colonial imaginations and art. From this point of view, the unschematized figure is as unattainable an ideal as the purified abstraction. All perceptions are caught in some middle ground of imperfect, interpreted thought and representation.

A number of preliminary works for this series were much simpler compositions reproducing particular 'Aboriginal' elements that Preston had featured in her art. If Bennett doubted that reappropriation could be effected simply by reproducing the motif, he also moved away from the absolute simplicity of the De Stijl plane. Although these works remain flat, their grids create several layers; on examination, the disposition of motifs below, within and above the cage-like grids is bewilderingly complex. The message is that elements do not subsist in isolation, as they do in Preston's studies, and indeed in Bennett's own preliminary works in this series. They are instead caught in networks of figures and abstractions; our identities, like these paintings, are composed of included and excluded forms at multiple levels.

The argument of these works that is most salient to this book, however, is pitched at a far less general level. The titles have been variations on *Home Decor (Preston + De Stijl = Citizen)*. They refer to the sense in which Aboriginality has been introduced into the Australian home as decor. There remains something positive in Preston's stylistic utilitarianism – in her project to subvert the art/craft hierarchy and surround us with objects that are appropriate, that are more than non-functional elite art objects. Yet the simultaneous affirmation of craft and Aboriginality also has a grotesque side, since it underlines the extent to which white Australian interest in Aboriginality was limited to art and ornament. Forms and motifs were affirmed, while the people themselves were distanced and marginalized. Natives were called upon to be present on the walls through their artifacts, but required to be absent in their persons. The Aboriginal painting was desired; the Aboriginal neighbour was not.

This is much more than an assault on the kind of liberal hypocrisy that is interested in marginalized or oppressed people in charitable principle, but repulsed by them in practice. It goes to the heart of the issue addressed earlier in this book. The popularity of 'Aboriginal' china, fabric, souvenirs and art forms in Australia roughly coincided with an interest in domestic black kitsch in North America and elsewhere,

126 GORDON BENNETT Home Decor (Preston + De Stijl = Citizen), Dance the Boogieman Blues, 1997

and Bennett draws attention to this parallel by the play between Aboriginal figures and negro minstrels in these works. But, as we have seen, the Australian appetite for specifically Aboriginal material was more powerfully motivated, not only by a racialized exoticism, but also by its Australian distinctiveness. The creation of domestic Aboriginal art and kitsch was the invention of a local modernity, which was at once linked to and distinguished from the modernity of modernism. The paradox of this, as I have emphasized, was that white Australians were simultaneously provided with a native identity and deprived of one, since they were in the process reminded, at least occasionally, that Aborigines and not themselves were the natives. The key issue that Aboriginal 'home decor' raises, then, is not necessarily that sacred forms are appropriated and reduced to domestic ornament, though where it does occur this may certainly be considered offensive. It is rather that

127 MARGARET PRESTON The Terrible Story, c. 1959

this process of adaptation, which always had an affirmative dimension, however aesthetically reductive its particular expression, was consistently accompanied by the rejection or the stigmatization of the indigenous people.

This stigmatization is manifest in Preston's own work in the disparity between the sympathetically presented motifs and the crude figures, a disparity that Bennett's paintings draw attention to. While Preston's images could be explained away on the grounds that she tended to handle the human figure sketchily and schematically in all her middle and late works, that does not alter the works that come down to us, which are the more disturbing as we focus upon the figurative element that may have been unimportant to her.

Bennett's artistic analysis of the issue of indigenous reference is far more productive than the debate about appropriation that surrounded Walters' work in New Zealand. Of course, an artist as engaged in quotation as Bennett could not honestly take the line that such borrowing is somehow improper or unacceptable in principle. Yet his response is not the qualified adjudication that such debate usually gives rise to, namely that appropriations are sometimes pernicious and sometimes not. If this is true, and we accept that the significance of reference and quotation is indeed invariably unstable, it still sidesteps the most politically charged aspect of mid-century Australian appropriations. This is the sorry fact that appropriation was only one side, only the appreciative side, of a grotesque combination of affirmation and rejection. Moreover, this settler schizophrenia was not an anomaly in the history of colonization; the business of simultaneously exhibiting and exterminating the native is consistent with the enduring, invasive logic of a settler-colonial nation. On the one hand, a self-conscious national culture that seemed permanently in the making required Aboriginality for its localizing effect; on the other, Aboriginal sovereignty and autonomy diminished the authority and coherence of the settler nation, and were persistently suppressed. It is not a question of cultural property that defines the politics of the issue, but this strangely fundamental union of adoption and antipathy. In Aotearoa New Zealand the antipathy has mostly been more compromised; there has perhaps there been a continuum connecting celebration and denigration, rather than a grotesque antithesis, yet one generated by the same underlying relations of possession and dispossession.

Rover Thomas: the Land and the Cyclone

Yet there is a space outside all of this, in which neither Margaret Preston's borrowings nor the wider anxieties of white settlers possess any salience. The space and time of *The Home* magazine, of museum ethnologists, of the Sydney art scene, of arguments about Jackson Pollock, were not and are not the space and time of Rover Thomas. The policies and agencies of the Australian state certainly made themselves felt in remote Australia, but the changing times of the Whitlam epoch there were not about a new cosmopolitanism or a new sense of larger horizons, even though horizons had not stopped changing. The Great Sandy Desert was never defined by provincialism or dependent anglophilia, hence it was not a place in which that dependence needed to be unmade. It was and is somewhere else altogether.

Rover Thomas was born in 1926 in the Great Sandy Desert in northern Western Australia; he moved as a child to the East Kimberley region to the northeast, and worked there for many years as a stockman. In 1975, after moving further north to Turkey Creek, he acquired knowledge of the Krill Krill ceremony through visitations from the spirit of a recently deceased kinswoman, who died as she flew over the country in a Flying Doctor aircraft after a motor vehicle accident at Turkey Creek.[3] The Krill Krill ceremonies involve public dances in which painted boards are carried bearing motifs associated with the journeys of ancestral beings around the region. In the early 1980s Mary Macha, a field officer for the Perth-based arm of Aboriginal Arts and Crafts Pty Ltd, commissioned a set of paintings based on these boards, which were initially executed by Paddy Jaminji, a senior kinsman of Thomas. The transformation of the work from ritually specific to marketable forms was thus encouraged by the localized workings of federal government policy, which since the 1970s has been broadly supportive of the development of an Aboriginal arts and crafts industry.

So what? Cultural expressions that are triggered by the activities of the state do not necessarily share the vision or the preoccupations of the state. Thomas subsequently produced a major body of painting himself, and a group of artists around Turkey Creek came to work in a recognizable style, using ochres rather than the acrylics adopted by western

128 Krill Krill ceremony, Turkey Creek, November 1979

129 ROVER THOMAS The Burning Site, 1990

desert artists, and preferring large fields of colour to dense and brilliant dot patterns. This work became well known to collectors of Aboriginal art, and Thomas's received special exposure. His status was fostered particularly by the National Gallery of Australia; he was one the first indigenous artists to whom a major retrospective was devoted; with the 'urban' Aboriginal painter, Trevor Nickolls, he was also selected to represent Australia at the 1990 Venice Biennale.

Unlike the antecedent boards, Thomas's paintings often image landscapes and narratives rather than single icons; these sites and contexts were formerly explicated by the song and movement accompanying the display of the boards, which were never presented in isolation as the paintings are. The extension of content is a significant innovation, but proceeds from the elaboration of one indigenous genre to incorporate the content of others. Though the stimuli that prompted this change were external, the novel form nevertheless expresses local conceptions of place and history.

One group of Thomas's paintings consists of several related sets that narrate massacres of Aboriginal people by pastoralists in the early twentieth century; like the earlier conflicts in southeastern Australia hinted at in von Guérard's *Bushy Park* (fig. 35), the violence followed from the environmental destruction occasioned by the introduction of stock. Waterholes were ruined and plants and game rendered scarce. Cattle were accordingly killed, whether because they were nuisances, by way of reprisal, or because they were one of few remaining·food sources. These assaults on stock provided the pretext for savage reprisals. Three paintings concern the poisoning of a group near Bedford Downs station, who were given beef, bread and ham laced with strychnine. *The Burning Site* images the station, the surrounding hills (into which a single man escaped) and the place where the bodies were burnt. These paintings, which initially strike a Western viewer as powerful abstract works, become intelligible first for their cartographic content and secondly for their historical burden. They are intimately connected with narratives that epitomize frontier conflict, but they do not present action or fateful contacts in a fashion readily comprehensible to non-Aboriginal viewers. Though certain of the most renowned European history paintings, such as West's *Death of General Wolfe*, also depicted death on the colonial periphery, that bare fact is the extent of the similarity. Thomas's history painting conveys the powerful presence of certain sites and the awful force of associated events. It does not aggrandize or moralize that violence.

Not all Thomas's work consists of this kind of coded landscape. Some paintings are more figurative; some are simply and whimsically concerned to image sites or objects that interested the artist; others represent topographic features in profile rather than in the more cartographic fashion of the several *Killing Times* series. Thomas's Krill Krill songs incorporate a major event that is depicted in one of his best-known paintings: at the end of the cycle the 'Devil Devil' or spirit Manginta and the old woman stop at Kununurra bridge and witness the destruction of the city of Darwin by the Rainbow Serpent – Cyclone Tracy. *Cyclone Tracy* (1991, fig. 132) depicts not the devastation of the city that occurred on Christmas Day 1974, but (according to the artist's exegesis) the constitution of the wind: the black column on the left marks the start of the cyclone, the conical area in the centre its full force, while the yellow and brown channels above and below image 'winds feeding the cyclone' and those 'filled with red dust' respectively.

The fact that these paintings are produced for sale and were first painted in their present form because they were commissioned by an outsider – these considerations in no sense diminish their 'authenticity'. Paintings such as *Cyclone Tracy* provide us with a particular opportunity to think beyond the evolutionary language that ranges indigenous art forms along a continuum from traditional to contemporary. There would have been no reason to produce works of this kind, with this appearance, in these media, in the societies of the Kimberleys before contact, before the ruptures associated with pastoral expansion, and before certain non-indigenous individuals and a government-driven indigenous art market recognized that something extraordinary was present in the art of this region. Yet what emerged cannot be reduced to these contradictory effects of settler colonialism, to some belated effort to do the right thing. These works are in no sense simply a reflex of the projects of the market or the state. Though they are not 'traditional' paintings, they are painted from the perspective of a particular Aboriginal man who has rights in certain ceremonies and certain narratives. And yet they are replete with innovations of form, style and subject-matter.

Thomas's paintings are of the present, but they do not constitute 'contemporary art' as it is usually understood; they are in no sense engaged in a critique of modernism, or the cross-referring dialogues and mutual influences of late abstraction and postmodernism. The avant garde has always been defined by a radicalism – variously aesthetic, conceptual or political – yet this radicalism has very rarely questioned a progressive notion of time and of cultural history. In some cases that progressive idea has been more revolutionary than evolutionary, or more pessimistic than optimistic, yet it has always been linear. Rover Thomas's work is outside this history; it has no place in the succession of movements which define twentieth-century art, though it certainly has a historical situation of its own. One does not read his massacre paintings without recognizing that.

At this point a certain reversal becomes imaginable: rather than extending a global art history (from Europe, from international art, or from white Australian art) to encompass these paintings, we might consider whether their landscapes of cyclones and burning sites in fact encompass us – especially, but not exclusively, us white Australians. If so, what space and time do we occupy? I pose this question not simply to underline again the extent to which Australian culture is shadowed by histories of dispossession of the kind Thomas evokes, but to raise a wider question about the space and time of contemporary art.

At one level, this space is extraordinarily dispersed in an epoch in which there are many more competing centres of cultural value. The biennales that an artist wants to be represented in may be those in Korea, Johannesburg, Havana and Taipei as well as Venice and New York; and multicultural art is increasingly visible in all of these places. The conversations, moreover, seem global, or are at least virtual, proceeding as often via e-mail as face to face. Yet despite all this, the 'contemporary' art world possesses a certain coherence. Like academia, diplomacy, tourism and certain spheres of business, it constitutes a transnational milieu in which there seem to be shared understandings of value and exchange. The transnational contemporary art scene is a space of dialogue framed by curators, critics and artists, most of whom are conscious of certain theoretical debates, of shifting practices in performance and installation. There is a currency in artistic practice that makes very different art works recognizable as expressions of contemporary art; there is also a theoretical currency that enables critics and curators to talk about very different works via categories such as identity and hybridity.

How are these conversations to be reconciled with Thomas's burdened sites? I suggest that those sites reveal that the space and time of 'the contemporary' is acutely paradoxical. Things that are and remain radically different are placed together in a frame such as that provided by the Venice Biennale. Thomas's paintings are 'works of art' like others exhibited, but the values and traditions of the art world do not thereby become salient to his work. The fact that *The Burning Site* is a sort of history painting indexes differences between imaginings of history that are nigh incommensurable.

An anecdote: I visited the Rover Thomas exhibition at the National Gallery in Canberra again, for the second or third time, a few days before it closed, mid-morning, during the week. The galleries were quiet; I had the space almost to myself. In the cool and the silence, I felt more capable than before of standing before Thomas's paintings, which struck me as more compelling on every viewing. The calm solidity of their fields of pigment was at once authoritative and impossible to reconcile with either the savagery of the histories the massacre paintings related, or the abrupt dance movements that I knew the antecedent boards were taken through. I was forcibly impressed, too, by the differences between the earlier works on plyboard (up to the mid-1980s) and those on canvas. It seemed that in adopting canvas, Thomas discovered a kind of depth that had dramatically reinforced the sheer presence of his paintings. There seemed to be no going back – no-one would have wanted him to go back – to board, though the boards had sustained the connection with the dance. I regretted that the canvases and boards were framed in a fashion that diminished the difference: the thinness of the board was not apparent and both were conventionally mounted on the wall. I had a thought that would have been too contrived for a curator to countenance: I wondered if it would have worked to have suspended the boards in the centre of the room, some vertically, some at odd angles, not in order to recreate their movement in the course of the Krill Krill,

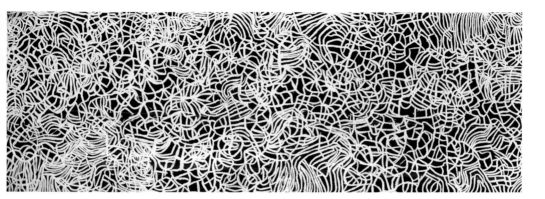

130 EMILY KAME KNGWARREYE Big Yam Dreaming, 1995

but to hint at the absence of that movement; to suggest the distance between where they were from and where they were at.

The hybrid trajectory

As I noted at the beginning of this chapter, two conflicting adjudications of indigenous Australian art are now curiously co-present. In 1995 Gabrielle Pizzi, a prominent Melbourne dealer who did much to promote important outback artists in earlier years, announced in an interview that she had become exhausted by the complications that arose from dealings with artists from remote communities, the so-called traditional milieux. Even though many of these artists were becoming increasingly famous, the fact that the role of the professional artist remained poorly defined in their communities meant that they frequently produced inferior work for quick money, and for tourist-oriented outlets, in addition to up-scale dealer galleries. This unevenness, she asserted, subverted the market, and she had accordingly decided to deal only in the works of 'urban' indigenous artists, who were becoming increasingly sophisticated and challenging. She cast the issue, in fact, not only in terms of her practical difficulties, but as an argument that the locus of creativity had shifted from the deserts to the cities.[4]

Among those who commented on Pizzi's statement was John McDonald, the astute but conservative critic for the *Sydney Morning Herald*. He has often cast harsh judgments on postmodern and post-colonial art, and thus predictably suggested that Pizzi had got it the wrong way around.[5] While in his view the 'urban' art was prone to academic sterility, artists such as the (subsequently deceased) desert painter, Emily Kame Kngwarreye (c. 1916–96) of Utopia in central Australia, seemed to proceed effortlessly from strength to strength. Whether one endorsed the negative part of his argument or not, it was hard to avoid sharing his enthusiasm for Kngwarreye, to whom a breathtaking major retrospective exhibition and two monographs were afterwards devoted.[6] Though this type of individualized celebration has often been considered foreign to the collective nature of Aboriginal sociality and art, it seemed precisely the treatment that her achievement demanded. Given that there had been many group exhibitions from this area, one could see the appreciation of Kngwarreye and other individual great painters like Thomas, Clifford Possum Tjapaltjarri and Michael Nelson not as a distortion of indigenous practice, but as a sign that indigenous art can have and must have it both ways.

I am not being flippant. Art dealers and critics are in the business of making declarations about what's hot and what's not, but I want to suggest that either the 'pro-urban' or 'pro-desert' verdicts are profoundly unhelpful if one is attempting to come to terms with the significance and power of Aboriginal art, and indeed the force of indigenous art in other colonial settler societies such as New Zealand. It could be suggested that an affirmation of 'traditional' work sustains old primitivist distinctions between 'real' natives and 'acculturated' ones. The latter, needless to say, were considered inauthentic, and were not regarded as bearers of distinct cultural traditions and values. They were not sufficiently remote from white society or from modernity to constitute figures of interest from the perspective of exoticist and primitivist imaginings. The contrary stance, however, despite its association with cultural radicalism, could be seen to echo the now discredited thinking behind assimilationist policies. By this view, indigenous cultures that are radically different, that remain resiliently other, are valued less than the cultural expressions that manifest engagement with Western traditions and debates. The artists who have entered art-world milieux, embraced cultural theory and adopted postcolonial styles of critical quotation are seen as the most 'advanced' and 'sophisticated' practitioners. The critic who is supposedly sympathetic to postcolonial indigenous art declares his or her politically progressive stance, and gestures toward an interest in cultural difference, but in fact only acknowledges the work that is most consistent with the space and time of the art world, and so is closest to his or her own aesthetic and theoretical stances.

I have already pointed out that Rover Thomas's work is unmistakably grounded in the Krill Krill and in other dimensions of the indigenous

131 ROVER THOMAS Two (White) Men, 1984

132 ROVER THOMAS Cyclone Tracy, 1991

133 SHANE COTTON Artificial Curiosities, 1993

cultures of the Kimberleys, but is also, in vital senses, a product of the present. It is no less 'contemporary' and no less 'hybrid' than the art of Gordon Bennett. But I want to set this point aside for the moment, simply because terms such as 'traditional' and 'contemporary' will not vanish simply because I say they should. Leaving aside also the powerful challenges that are indubitably present in particular works of art, such as those of Thomas and Bennett, we might suggest that neither the 'traditional' nor the 'hybrid' expressions of indigenous art *by themselves* undermine the evolutionary categories that I have discussed. That is, 'traditionalist' work may be assimilated to primitivist responses, while 'hybrid' work may be assimilated to art-world avant gardism. It is the co-presence of these tendencies that poses a more radical challenge, not only to the categories that inform art-world hierarchies, but to the invidious distinctions of settler-colonial culture itself. The simultaneity of work manifestly grounded in tradition and in cultural spaces beyond settler imaginings, and work highly engaged with international art practices, illustrates the extent to which an indigenous population can remain grounded in tradition and in ancestral practices while being fully engaged with modernity at the same time.

Obviously, individual lives and communities are located quite differently: some on their own land, experiencing many continuities with ancestral practice; others distanced in manifold respects from any mode of indigenous sociality that was not eclipsed by European settlement. What is critical, however, is that indigenous people can neither be categorically relegated to the past, to a colourful prehistory that supplies something unthreatening and culturally distinctive to a settler nation; nor can the autonomous distinctiveness of their cultures, which plainly have lives beyond as well as before the colonial impact, be denied. What can be recognized publicly of their cultural expression can only possess 'authenticity' or 'acculturation' for those who must think in such terms. The co-presence of the 'traditional' and the 'contemporary' contradicts the longstanding rhetoric of settler culture, which continually evokes indigenous signs while lamenting the passing of indigenous peoples. The native has been showcased in artifactual form while being rendered absent in human form. To note the genuinely subversive effect of the indigenous presence is to take us back to the very extraordinary phenomenon that was the success of 'Te Maori'. In the case of that exhibition, what were regarded as hallmarks of primitive art were repossessed by people who were present rather than prehistoric. By making their connection with the cultural treasures of their ancestors manifest, they also perforce exhibited their own presence.

134 SHANE COTTON Whakapiri Atu te Whenua, 1995

Art is commonly regarded as a form of 'high' culture, whose quality gives it a special status which is reinforced through its situation in the privileged spaces of national art galleries, in the private collections of the wealthy, and in similar prestigious locations. Taste, quality and prestige have always been contentious, but the critique of the class culture of art is not one that needs to be recapitulated here. My departure point is rather the obvious point that art, understood more broadly, is encountered outside galleries in many situations, not necessarily prestigious. Galleries, genres and markets are themselves heterogeneous, and this heterogeneity must be addressed if we are concerned not merely to interpret or theorize particular art movements, but to understand the public and political importance of art.

At another level, this chapter aims to reinforce the point of the previous one – that the accomplishments of indigenous art are too diverse to be contained by the terms of art criticism, and that they challenge the cultural premises of settler societies in radical ways. While these claims were based on the work of two highly accomplished Australian artists, whose works were discussed in some detail, I want in this case to review contemporary Maori art in more of a broad-brush fashion, to convey the sheer proliferation of indigenous expressions. Some of the artists I want to draw attention to are not highly regarded in elite art milieux but have a public presence that some more 'recognized' figures lack. I am also concerned to draw attention to the great variety of work and the distinct audiences it aspires to reach, or does reach. Our commonsense view of art as a branch of 'high' culture does not prepare us for the widespread and diverse visibility of a remarkable range of 'low', 'middle' and 'high' indigenous art forms, if we must use unhelpful terms that do not possess much salience for indigenous genres.

This is the point, also, at which the longer-term ramifications of the use of indigenous references in national and tourist culture become evident. As we saw, indigenous motifs and art styles were adapted widely in settler design, contributing significantly to a national visual culture. If some are concerned to condemn this in retrospect as a process of appropriation, it did at the same time give central place to emblems of indigenous culture in the imagining of the nation, notably in New Zealand and more erratically in Australia. What happens when these emblems are reconnected with indigenous people, and regarded as expressions of *their* power and prestige? If the always unstable 'and/or' of the native and/or national sign dissolves and solidifies again, how are native and nation then related?

Diary (1)

Consider the following range of examples of 'Maori art' that might be encountered over a few days in Auckland.

You are walking down Queen Street in the city centre. There are quite a few young Maori men selling bone and nephrite jewellery, spread out on pieces of cloth or on small tables. These objects could be seen as replicas of traditional artifacts, such as *tiki*, the greenstone neck ornaments that have been widely produced in cheap green plastic as tourist trinkets. If you live in New Zealand, you take the spectrum of plastic, stone and bone varieties for granted: they are simply part of the artifactual environment.

Further down the street is an upmarket Maori design store. The 'traditional' objects here are fine *kete*, or woven baskets; these examples are expensive, and may be there for display rather than sale. The merchandise consists mainly of shirts and sweaters with stylish geometric designs based loosely on weaving patterns.

Just off Queen Street, there are a several narrower lanes; cafés, bookshops, galleries and music and fashion shops are concentrated around here. Younger Polynesian and Maori people are conspicuous; shirts feature *kowhaiwhai* patterns; Polynesian design, often featuring barkcloth, is adapted on lamps, fabrics and ceramics; trendy shops display more expensive versions of the jewellery sold on the street; the bookshops have substantial sections on Maori history, craft, art, writing and spirituality. Not far from here is the Te Taumata art centre. This is the exhibition space of Te Waka Toi, the Maori arts and crafts council. Located in a somewhat unsympathetic office building, its several small galleries and shops showcase carving and weaving, paintings, prints and drawings. Some of the carvings display great technical virtuosity. They are produced by artists who would also have worked on meeting houses and other objects of continuing community significance, either for tribes outside the cities, or for pan-Maori *marae* or meeting places on

135 Printed T-shirt from Kia Kaha, Queen Street, Auckland

university campuses and elsewhere in towns. Some work of this kind strikes the outsider as innovative and dynamic, a continuation of the remarkable experimental carving and painting of the late nineteenth century. Other work disappointingly resembles the polished stuff in tourist shops.

The feel of Te Taumata, like that of any commercial gallery, changes according to what is on, although it's notable that it is always more frequented than ordinary dealer spaces, and that it is always unambiguously a Maori space. The range of work and the presence of the Maori staff give one a sense that one must, at least for the moment, defer to the principles that the work incarnates. During one visit, I was engaged by the work of Jolene Douglas, of Ngati Maru and Ngati Raukawa descent.[1] The cut-out shapes of her images of Maori women recalled the forms and patterns of weaving. As the brochure indicated, the series evoked 'the awakening and learning processes of the novice. To the knowledge and skill of the tutor. A celebration of pattern and its relevance to the natural world, and in honour of all weavers, continually revitalizing this traditional craft with new eyes.' The titles of the pastels were all bilingual, *TE KARU O TE MARAMA: eye of the moon, WHAKATUPU: growth*, and so on. The works themselves connected the forms and the architecture of weaving with the bodies of women, often tattooed, that is to say culturally-marked, women. The motifs of Maori tattooing were not reproduced; in their place were images of staining, flow and weave, vehicles for the expression of life, reproduction, genealogy and culture.

Art of this kind has little to do with current trends in avant-garde or 'international' art. It is not going to get reproduced in *Artforum*. But it clearly provides a vehicle for an affirmative self-presentation of Maori womanhood and undoubtedly also appeals to non-Maori women who are impressed if not awed by the calm presence of the woman, by the inter-weaving of the art and the body, by this validation of natural flow and growth. The relatively modest prices of Douglas's pastels make them available to women who are not art collectors in the elite sense. Images of this kind thus find a place in the households of those New Zealanders for whom the country has become Aotearoa New Zealand, a place defined by parity between indigenous and settler cultures, and which can only be enriched by the spirituality of the former. If what is at work here is the appeal of authenticity, even exotic authenticity, this is not the imposition of some kind of primitivist-colonialist gaze. This is a work of empower-ment grounded not in mystifications but in genealogical connections with ancestral strength that were as present to the antecedent art forms of weaving and tattooing as they are to this contemporary work. There is no contrivance of sanctification here, though there may certainly be a novel collusion between New Age forms of spiritual primitivism and the gentle assertions of these indigenous artists. The shortcomings of the former view of the world are perhaps not cause to dismiss the latter.

A couple of years later, and a block or two away, Auckland's enor-mous casino has been completed. The building incorporates much impressive art, including much impressive Maori art, to which manage-ment and patrons – mainly Asian tourists displaying every anxiety to lose their shirts – appear equally indifferent. One expression of this indifference is the fact that one of the largest and finest paintings has been located behind a concrete staircase, with the result that even the visitor who would go out of his or her way to see it cannot see the whole work from any vantage point and cannot see sections of it at all (figs 134, 137). Shane Cotton's painting, however, ought not be passed over, so we might imagine ourselves instead in the Auckland Art Gallery, or at his dealer's, in front of one of his rich and perplexing highly varnished paintings (fig. 133).[2] These immediately appealed to me when I saw them first, because they adapt the European tradition of representing ethno-graphic objects ('artificial curiosities') in strange spaces; these objects are therefore materially engaged, yet radically decontextualized. Cotton has also worked with coastal profiles of the kind engraved and published with the accounts of voyages by navigators such as Cook, which saw the land not from in and on it – the indigenous point of view – but as a hazily delineated distant spectacle. Yet these profiles were sketched with

136 JOLENE DOUGLAS Tewhea te Huarahi? Where is the Pathway? Self Portrait, 1995

137 SHANE COTTON Whakapiri Atu te Whenua, 1995 (detail)

ominous precision, as if they were a step toward a more precise mapping, toward colonization. Cotton's paintings are also replete with esoteric forms and motifs: objects such as soccer balls that do not immediately signify themes in colonial history or indigenous culture. They are playful rather than didactic; they exceed both short and long captions.

Cotton is one of the handful of Maori artists whose work has deservedly gained the attention of those New Zealand art critics, dealers and curators who more or less define what is valued and acknowledged. His work will thus circulate in ways that most of what is exhibited at Te Taumata will not. He has been included in exhibitions in Australia and elsewhere, for example at Sydney's Museum of Contemporary Art. And in the Auckland casino, what I imagine is his largest painting provides an unusual backdrop to a concrete staircase.

The architecture does more justice to another major work, Lyonel Grant's extraordinary vertical canoe, a densely carved ancestral embodiment. One would expect this to be harder to walk past: Grant is something of a contemporary Tene Waitere (pp. 46–7), an innovative exponent of 'traditional' sculpture who carves meeting-houses and figures, mostly for community or public situations. His work looms large, though more in Maori spaces than Pakeha ones; he happens to be highly regarded by one of Auckland's most astute dealers, though he is represented internationally in the ethnography department of the British Museum rather than in contemporary art galleries.

138 LYONEL GRANT
Te Ihingarangi, 1992

139 LYONEL GRANT
Te Ihingarangi, 1992 (detail)

140 LYONEL GRANT Pou Wairua, 1996

Within a few blocks of the Auckland casino there are many other major pieces of Maori sculpture, including a number around the Aotea Centre, an arts precinct, by senior figures such as Paratene Matchitt and Selwyn Muru. The law courts feature an elaborate metal and coloured-glass gateway work by Jacob Manu Scott representing guardians of the land.[3] There are many works of this sort around, but they index one of the contradictory features of the success of Maori art. An appropriate recognition of indigenous precedence and presence has encouraged state and corporate sponsorship for works that give buildings and situations an indigenous signature. Yet these commissions are often contentious, and when they are not they do not rate highly in the eyes of art critics and curators. Once in place, they acquire a sort of unrecognized visibility:

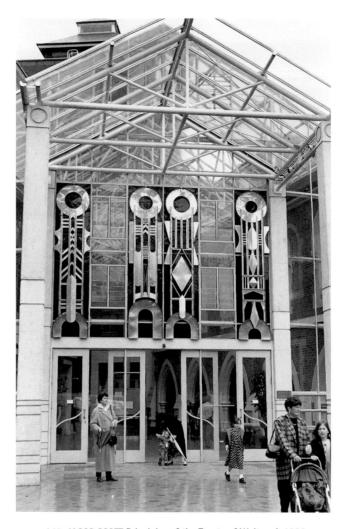

141 JACOB SCOTT Principles of the Treaty of Waitangi, 1990

thousands of people pass them every day, yet in few cases are they cited, discussed or celebrated in art literature. This may be equally true of public works by white artists, and there are of course exceptions. But in the case of indigenous art this relation between public presence and critical canonization appears to become increasingly lopsided, making it peculiarly difficult to measure what these highly visible indigenous pieces might contribute to the overall impact and efficacy of Maori art.[4]

Diary (2)

It is not far from this city centre. It is the first day of my research on questions of identity in contemporary art in Aotearoa New Zealand, in February 1993. I am not completely new to the topic; I have seen exhibitions before, both in New Zealand and in Australia. And I have corresponded with some of the artists I hope to interview. I've arrived late the night before and am staying in a bed-and-breakfast in Parnell, an all too genteel inner-city suburb; I'd recalled from the previous visit, a family holiday, that there was something of a concentration of dealer galleries in the area, and it seemed a good place to start. Feeling silly and out of place, as one does when one embarks on ethnographic field-work, which is what I thought I was doing, I walked down Parnell Road, intending to look at what was on in a few galleries. I was not quite ready for dialogue, not comfortable yet with the idea of announcing my agenda; I was not yet sure of what it was.

I was disconcerted, then, when a young woman in one of the first places I entered subjected me to a series of friendly questions, and quickly established that I was engaged in research, and especially interested in contemporary Maori art. She drew my attention to the work of Brett Graham, whom I was later to get to know well.[5] There was nothing of his up in the gallery at that particular time, but I took a catalogue brochure from a recent exhibition, and was advised that a couple of substantial works were on view in a foyer exhibition space in one of the office build-ings down in Queen Street. After this first day, my 'fieldwork' almost immediately became a breathless series of gallery visits, interviews, meetings, dinners, openings and parties – I hasten to add that it featured some long days in archives and in gallery and museum stores too – hence during my subsequent weeks on that first trip I never managed to get to the Queen Street foyer when it was open, although I did peer through the plate glass at Brett's substantial dark wooden forms.

I only gained a better understanding of his work much later in the year when I visited Auckland briefly, making sure that I didn't miss his next show. There were two things that struck me on this particular occa-sion. His work was unambiguously grounded in Maori culture in its reference to traditional forms and concepts. Yet this reference, though profound, was never literal. The connections were typically at the level of elegant translations into pure forms, not the more or less slavish replication of traditional sculpture and motifs that one encounters more often, especially among young artists anxious to exhibit their Maoriness in the most explicit and unambiguous way.

The cultural integrity of Brett Graham's work is not connected with an insularity of outlook. Although many of his sculptures embody genealogies, and refer to incidents in Maori history, he has drawn also on connections between the historical experiences of Maori and those of other indigenous peoples, particularly in Hawaii and North America. Graham studied in Hawaii during the build-up to the Columbus quincentenary, which also marked 350 years since Tasman had been the first European to visit New Zealand. The affinities between these experiences of colonization and adaptation stimulated a series of works that narrated the origins and growth of indigenous culture, acknowledging the threatening arrival of peoples who sought domination, but culminating in symbols of hope, of a future vitalized by the past.

These are certainly compelling themes for indigenous peoples in many places. Their generalized form in Graham's work marks a distinctive aspect of the process of globalization, which is so often inadequately described in the sociological literature, where it has become a fashionable topic. Although it is frequently acknowledged in principle that global flows of capital and cultural value are no longer defined by two or three centres – in Europe and North America – globalization is nevertheless all too often identified with the spread of popular Western culture, notably Hollywood films, soft drinks, jeans and so on. Yet the most cursory examination of trends in many parts of the world makes it evident that many significant transnational cultural flows – in music and film for example – proceed quite independently of 'the West'. Graham's work exemplifies a relatively new level of exchange and dialogue between native peoples that links tribal peoples of south Asia with Inuit, first Australians and Native Americans, among others. Hence at an indigenous artists' conference in Adelaide, a Queensland painter noted that the Sami of Finland possessed 'songlines' similar to his own. At no point does Graham's art efface the distinctions between particular indigenous cultures; its specifically Maori character instead empowers his pan-indigenous generalizations.[6]

I doubt that the second feature of Brett's work that struck me was of much significance to any other viewer of his work. As we walked around the small gallery, I knew that I recognized the sandstone out of which a number of his forms, suggesting canoes and growth, were made. This was Hawkesbury sandstone, the friable quartz, so often stained orange and black, that gives the low bluffs and gullies around Sydney their rough intimacy. What he used had been removed from the foundations of a demolished nineteenth-century Auckland building; I discovered subsequently that it was carried as ballast by the trans-Tasman ships which

142 BRETT GRAHAM
Waka Tumanako, 1993
(detail)

143 BRETT GRAHAM
Te Pu, 1993

took loads of fine kauri hardwood between northern New Zealand and Sydney; much of it, apparently, was simply dumped into the Hokianga Harbour. That trade, incidentally, had fostered an earlier phase of indigenous globalization; Maori, at any rate, had a good deal of experience of Sydney, among other Pacific ports, and intermarried with Aboriginal people on the New South Wales coast. Now Sydney stone, the stone of Berowra and Calabash Creek, was transformed into Maori art – into canoes and ancestral Polynesian pots that imaged the voyaging traditions of Oceanic peoples and their affinities in the deep time of prehistory. Yet part of that story – a late and small part – was my story too.

Diary (3)

South Auckland is an entirely different space from the inner city. It is a working-class area dominated by poor Maori and migrant Polynesians (from Samoa, Tonga, the Cook Islands and Niue, among other places). It is the space of the 1994 film *Once Were Warriors*. There are few shops that could be described as boutiques, and not too many art dealers. Yet 'Maori art' has presence here too, in schools, in government buildings such as public libraries, and in the design of the occasional new shopping mall. But there are few such new developments; what is striking, when you walk around the shopping centres of suburbs such as Otara, is the degree to which the cultural geography of an earlier epoch remains inscribed on the mouldings and the stucco of commercial premises that in other parts of the city have all been torn down and replaced. Here the pink and blue flaking paint announces 'Empire Buildings', 'Victoria Arcade', 'King Edward Terrace' and so on. This is all the more extraordinary since at street level the population appears to be largely Polynesian – both Maori and migrant – with some Asian shopkeepers. There is scarcely a Pakeha New Zealander to be seen.

144 ARNO GASTEIGER portrait of Black Power member with facial tattoos, Whangarei, New Zealand, 1994

145 Koru-patterned shirt from New Zealand

On the streets here one encounters gang members with full-face *moko*, usually mixed with the non-Maori tattoos that might be seen on working-class shoulders anywhere. Outside the polite spaces of galleries and cultural performances, these are intimidating, in a fashion that is arguably fully consistent with the primary purpose of such tattoos in the Maori warfare of the pre-contact and colonial periods. This was and is a technology of fear. It is also an expression of 'Maori art'.

There are shops selling fabrics with what are called islands prints, patterns based on barkcloth designs, T-shirts, cheap jeans and the like. These include shirts incorporating a New Zealand map, *koru* motifs, and various other icons of Maori and tourist culture. This would seem a classic conflation of the native and the national, one of the most kitsch of rip-offs of Maori design. And yet it is here, in a Polynesian neighbourhood, a space that seems recolonized, wholly occupied and defined by indigenous people, for all the poverty and violence of its inhabitants' colonized experience.

Diary (4)

It is a long drive east rather than south; the Fisher Gallery is in Pakuranga, I suppose a lower middle-class and working-class area, but not a solidly Polynesian one. This is a local council gallery, a space that takes smaller touring shows than those that would be seen at the main public institutions, but it has also been a distinctively vigorous place, more so than some of the self-consciously avant-garde venues elsewhere.

Shane Cotton's work is here, and so is Robert Jahnke's. It is now 1995 and I have seen a good deal of Jahnke's work, and found its virtuosity and the sophistication of its historical argument highly engaging. But what is here is new, striking for its difference despite the threads of continuity, and it takes some time to think through. Some of the works use chess pieces, and these are familiar from a previous show, which manipulated symbols of sovereignty. Jahnke's purpose, in the earlier exhibition, had been to remark on the prodigious acquisitions of land perpetrated by the Church Missionary Society in the nineteenth century; on one occasion 40,000 acres were exchanged for twelve steel axes. The metaphor of the game of chess suggested an antagonistic series of such unequal exchanges: 'pawn for bishop', 'pawn for queen' and so on. Maori, he suggested, had been pawns in the process of colonization, a process in which both church and state had been implicated, a process that had seen their lands pawned.[7]

While constructions of history, metaphorical innuendos, and arguments about the present had always animated one another in Jahnke's work, the political events of early 1995 had prompted him to make a more direct and angry statement. During visits to Aotearoa in 1994, my sense was that there was a certain stability in settler-indigenous relations, some common political ground and a widely shared commitment to the evolution of the polity toward a more genuinely bicultural reformation, whatever that might mean. Of course, there was always contention, and things were never in fact stable. But early in 1995 a new phase of activism and polarization was triggered by speculation and then confirmation of what was to become a notorious government policy: all the Maori claims for lost lands and rights that were being addressed by the Waitangi Tribunal had to be compensated for out of a fixed amount of money (a billion New Zealand dollars) over a fixed period of time. Beyond that, the process of redressing injustices, and specifically violations of the Treaty of Waitangi, would be deemed complete. For a host of reasons, the 'fiscal envelope' was explosive. Though many larger and well-organized tribes had already submitted their claims or had them settled, the lack of preparedness of others, and the enormous complexity of the historical research and the legal proceedings entailed in developing claims, meant that the time limit effectively prejudiced many groups' chances of redress. And the financial cap, the dollar figure, was incommensurable with the significance possessed by the lands in question.

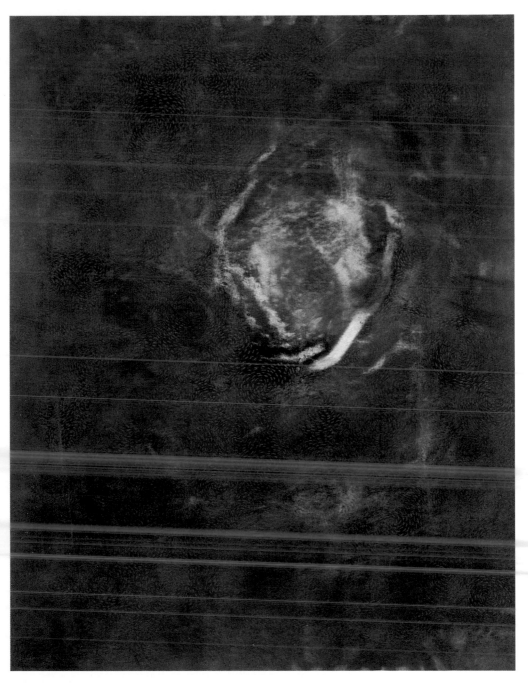

146 JUDY WATSON heartland, 1991

147   Balarinji Australia, Qantas Boeing 747 'Wunala Dreaming'

148 ROBERT JAHNKE
with his work Con-Version
3.33R, 1994

149 ROBERT JAHNKE
For King and Country,
1994

150 ROBERT JAHNKE
Ta te Whenua,
1995

The announcement of the policy led not only to intense lobbying
and activism on the part of Maori organizations and a furious debate in
the media, but also to a succession of violent incidents, including the
desecration of Maori carving, and the tree of 'One Tree Hill', something
of an Auckland symbol. There was also a protracted confrontation in the
town of Wanganui between authorities and Maori occupying the central
park; claims about sovereignty were being advanced and rejected on the
street, rather than in courts, offices and chambers. It was almost as if
there had been a sudden reversion to the politics of the 1970s, when
police and Maori had frequently been lined up against each other.

151 WILLIAM DUNNING Antipodean Embranchment, 1993

Jahnke's response was a potent but not overtly angry work. His enlarged 'Not Negotiable' stamps, *Ta te Whenua*, at once evoked the inflexible authority of the state and the inalienable status of land in indigenous imaginings. The sheer bulk of the object suggested the dead weight of government over rights to former territories, and, as the artist put it, 'Its shadow [cast] an ominous cloud over equitable consideration of outstanding land claims.'

Diary (5)

Though Wellington is the capital, it's a much smaller city than Auckland; here I meet, among other people, the veteran dealer Peter McLeavey, who represented key figures such as McCahon, Walters and Toss Wollaston, and has frequently picked out the most interesting younger artists, Maori and non-Maori. I never get around to having lunch with Peter, and feel slightly guilty because I so often drop in unannounced, only to find him all too obliging, bringing out work that I'll be interested in, a set of snapshots, reading me passages from artists' letters. He introduces me to the extraordinary and idiosyncratic work of William Dunning, a reclusive Maori artist in Christchurch, who produces intricate monochrome pencil drawings of fictive colonial monuments, posed domestic scenes of the protagonists of colonial histories surrounded by heavy furniture and colonial paintings, and objects of furniture that themselves

152 WILLIAM DUNNING Time Table, 1995

bear carved or perhaps inlaid colonial scenes. These meditations on histories, on alternative histories, and on the strange business of their artifactual commemoration strike me as extraordinarily engaging, yet as virtually untranslatable to any other context. The contemporary effect of colonial history in Aotearoa New Zealand, the sheer presence of the past, has yielded a kind of cultural introspection that is more extreme than I have encountered elsewhere. It is a postcolonial antiquarianism, an almost morbid curiosity for the intricate tracery of historical fictions and re-imagined presents.

When I saw Dunning's triptych *Antipodean Embranchment* in the 1993 Sydney exhibition, 'Localities of Desire', I felt it stuck out like a sore thumb, despite the heterogeneity of the show as a whole. Dedicated to expressions of indigenous and diasporic hybridity, 'Localities' displayed a breathtaking range of work from North America, Asia, New Zealand and Australia; yet much of it used 'locality' in a fashion that was intelligible elsewhere, that presupposed a dialogue with international avant-garde art and with the other indigenous and diasporic arts.[8] Dunning's drawings seemed the product of no such compromise; if they were brilliantly odd in the New Zealand context, they were simply incomprehensible outside it. Many artists have examined the colonial appropriation of indigenous art forms in witty, suggestive or angry ways, but I felt Dunning's visual meditation upon the issue, *Time Table*, was somehow definitive. To put it crudely, the sheer ugliness of his Victorian cabinet condemned the 'appropriation' it attempted.

I saw many other shows at Cuba Street galleries, as well as elsewhere; in the early phases of research I eagerly absorbed everything, photographing full shows, picking up catalogues indiscriminately, and talking to anyone remotely relevant who'd talk to me. As time passed I felt that there was more that I didn't need to see, more that was earnest rather than critical.

One work that stood out, and that has remained at the back of my mind for a long time, was an installation by Jacqueline Fraser at the City Gallery, Wellington.[9] Fraser, of Ngai Tahu (South Island) descent, works with fibre, but in a fashion that is wholly distinct from the work of distinguished traditionalist weavers such as Rangimarie Te Hetet and Diggeress Te Kanawa, who have produced magnificent flax and feather capes which are held as *taonga*, or treasures, by Maori communities as well as by art galleries and museums. By contrast Fraser uses electrical wire, plastic and similar materials rather than plant fibres. *He Tohu: the New Zealand Room* (1993) emulated the architecture of a Maori meeting house, yet the dominant ancestral figures, the *poupou*, were in the feminine medium of fibre rather than the masculine one of sculpture. Several translations were thus effected at once: from past to present, natural to industrial, male to female. The title alluded to the idea of a colonial cabinet, a chamber of New Zealand curiosities that was at once supplied and superseded by these delicate installations.

Yet what was so effective about Fraser's work was not its conceptual play but rather the environment it created. The constitution of forms and spaces out of a linear web made for a lightness of being, a kind of

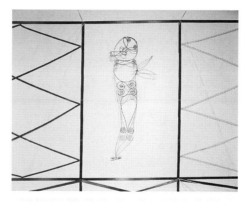

153 JACQUELINE FRASER
He Tohu: the New Zealand Room,
1993 (opposite and above)

154 JACQUELINE FRASER
He Tohu: the New Zealand Room,
1993 (detail)

breathing space, possibly a utopian domain that was structured by Maori form but unburdened by the sheer weight of tradition, in architecture and in the gendering of Maori art forms and media.

In the interplay between art and context, Fraser's room was also suggestive. It was sympathetically situated, in a light and airy space, and in a contemporary art gallery, an institution that exists to affirm and exhibit art of this type. Framed in these enabling terms, the work could be seen to take over, to define a room as a Maori room, yet to define Maoriness in turn in its own way. That redefinition empowered both the idea of Maoriness in general and a specific Maori art, an avowedly contemporary and feminine form of indigenous expression. Just as a work of religious art, framed in a particular way, exemplifies and strengthens the faith it attests to, while allowing that faith to empower its own aesthetic statement, Fraser's work – which partook of the ancestral religiosity of the architecture of the meeting-house – seemed animated by an exchange between microcosm and macrocosm, between the work and the culture, spirituality and history.

This relation between the particular and the general could be seen as an instance of the workings of indigenous art and the indigenous cultural renaissance that the latter sections of this book have charted. The prestigious space of the gallery has lent validity to indigenous claims, while the larger categories of indigenous culture and tradition have lent value to particular works, at the same time as often misframing them or framing them uneasily: indigenous art works frequently have had both less and more to say than was asked of them. The space of the art world and the gallery never *necessarily* lifts or validates the works that are framed within it. This did occur when great ancestral objects such as the *taonga* of 'Te Maori' were transposed from the domain of the museum to that of the gallery, and when Aboriginal objects were similarly recontextualized as works of art rather than ethnological artifacts; in these instances the virtuosity of the pieces carried the day. But when the 1941 exponents of white 'Aboriginal art' attempted to use Aboriginal art works to define the context of their own efforts, the framing exercise backfired: the Aboriginal pieces were rated higher than the 'applications' that were the point of the exhibition (p. 124). If the efficacy of the work of art depends in part upon the virtuosity of particular works, it depends also upon the kind of sympathetic contextualization that I felt had allowed Jacqueline Fraser's room to speak.

Not far away, the Museum of New Zealand, Te Papa Tongarewa, had enlisted other Fraser pieces, together with other contemporary Maori works, in its own effort of redefinition. A major pole commemorating the Maori navigator, Te Kupe, by the senior artist John Bevan Ford, and a number of Fraser's works were used, quite literally, to give the museum a new face, one appropriate to the bicultural moment. Fraser's major piece in this situation could be seen as a further instance of the fascination with the involuted forms of the Maori *waka* or canoe, which can be traced through generations of Maori carvers, through the early nineteenth-century drawings of Thomas Tui, and through many and mainly anonymous European engravers who gave Sydney Parkinson's eighteenth-century sketches mass circulation. Fraser's accomplishment was here to suggest curvilinear involution in an elegant and austere fashion; yet this piece was hard to see, and was

155 JOHN BEVAN FORD Ko Kupe, 1993

surely defeated by the gloomy masonry of the museum's facade. The building was, after all, not only a museum and national art gallery, but also a national war memorial; the sombre weight of the edifice, indeed the sheer dirty bulk of the stone, were hardly suited to additions of this sort. By the time this book is published, a completely new museum will have been open for almost a year. This new institution is a happier and more powerful expression of the bicultural principle that prescribes a parity of Maori and Pakeha cultures.

The celebration of indigenous art in Australia and New Zealand has hovered between such displays of superficial and awkward redefinition and the manifestation of deeper change. Whether it is more the former or the latter surely depends on the question of whether the work is sympathetically framed. Can indigenous art as a whole be seen to be placed in an enabling situation, like that of Fraser's New Zealand room in the City Gallery, which gave the work a space in which to work its magic? Or is the more general situation like that of the MONZ facade, which in the end exhibited an incompatibility between cultures and institutions, and attested to the awkwardness of combination rather than the prospects of partnership?

Diary (6)

Over several years of more or less frequent visits, I witnessed changes at Auckland Airport that entailed not only the usual extensions and renovations but also a progressive accentuation of the Maori components of its design. In more and more ways, New Zealand seemed to be becoming Aotearoa New Zealand; Maori culture, at least, was increasingly displayed.

Oddly enough, one of the most significant art works at the airport was removed over this period. In the 1960s, Ralph Hotere had produced a major fifteen-panel mural based on a Maori chant of welcome, a more colourful, lighter and indeed welcoming variation on his minimal, mainly black works of the period. This was no doubt initially well-situated in the arrivals area, but with reorganization came to be divided between sections of the immigration hall, and was mainly visible to people whose luggage was being searched by customs officials. The painting was recently moved, and deservedly displayed in a large room by itself in the Auckland Art Gallery early in 1997. Yet it is in a way regrettable that it was not simply relocated within the airport, to some conspicuous new situation which would enable this modernist Maori welcome to greet those returning or arriving.

Over the last few years woven panels (*tukutuku*), emulating those of traditional meeting houses, appeared on the columns in the departure area; a huge pair of carvings and lintel have been created around one of the exits, suggesting a threshold between the non-space of international transience and the culturally specific, and particularly Maori space, of Aotearoa; the indigenous souvenirs and the publications and videos on Maori history and culture seem to have proliferated; and there was for a period a gallery-style room featuring Maori carvings and paintings (which I took initially to be a permanent feature; on a subsequent visit I realized that it was a strangely symptomatic expression of ongoing renovation, an ephemeral museum). This room, perhaps more than any other space, seemed to manifest the uncertain and unpredictable character of public spaces into which Maori values had been inserted. Some 'traditional' clubs, adzes and *tiki*, new versions of old artifacts, were not especially different to the pieces on sale in the tourist shops; yet signs informed those entering the room that these are *taonga* and that the observance of *tapu* precludes eating, drinking or smoking. (I am not aware that the new, fully renovated airport incorporates any area defined by these cultural proscriptions.) At one time there was a model *waka*, or canoe; there were also paintings illustrating mythical scenes, produced by Maori artists in a mode reminiscent of that of the late nineteenth-century

European painters, who produced romantic versions of the arrival of canoe fleets and similar incidents of legend. Yet these works, which seemed to showcase Maori culture as Maori folklore in a fashion that had many precedents in over a century of tourist culture, were accompanied by contemporary paintings that pulled no political punches.

These included works by Emare Karaka, who belongs very much to an activist generation of Maori artists, and in particular to a cohort of strong women artists who emerged in the 1970s. Embedded in the confrontational politics of the period (which preceded the renaissance, and could not take its gains for granted), their work, particularly Karaka's, spoke violence and pain and loss. It was never slick, avant garde or comfortable, and it never received the validation that has been bestowed upon younger artists by art critics and curators. Karaka, like many other New Zealand painters, was inspired by Colin McCahon's use of writing (pp. 30–1), and, like Selwyn Muru, made this a vehicle for explicit political declaration, indeed for slogans; she was also influenced, it appears, by the more expressionist of her senior contemporaries, but again gave their painterly energy a specifically political charge. Her compositions did not simply represent the sufferings of a colonized people; they seemed rather to be a direct transcription of them, of agony and tears and blood.[10]

This particular political voice, and this expressionist style, were both to become unfashionable; though much Maori art remains critical, it often mobilizes a more subtle politics of form and irony; even its anger can be cooler, while some postmodern expressions are critical only to the extent that it is chic to be critical. Yet much of this detached, playful art speaks from the consolidation of a cultural renaissance. But the interest in biculturalism on the part of the still-dominant Pakeha majority, like the government's promises, is always provisional and insecure. The extent to which this is so became apparent with the fiscal envelope story (p. 238), which revealed how much old antagonisms that Karaka's work spoke from remain alive. If, then, interest in her work, and that of some her contemporaries, has waned, it was nevertheless as appropriate as it was entirely unexpected to find several of her tortuous and angry panels representing 'Maori art', indeed to some extent representing New Zealand, in this little showcase at the airport.

Here and in other cases, it seemed difficult to adjudicate what status this space possessed. It was a gallery of sorts, yet also one that could have been seen to display mere folk art, or souvenirs. It was identified as a Maori domain, defined by protocols that were increasingly familiar to New Zealanders and no doubt bewildering to most tourists. It was part of the nation's gateway. Its presence was at once a sign of New Zealand and an acknowledgment of the Maori presence. Despite the linoleum floor, among other unglamorous architectural features, the objects bestowed a certain gravity, even a hint of spirituality, upon the room. Yet this was also because it was quiet, because there were few visitors, because the rush and the business of the airport were just outside, yet elsewhere. To be both central and marginal, visible and off-stage, seemed once again to be the contradictory situation of indigenous art.

Diary (7)

The transformation of New Zealand into Aotearoa was marked not only in showcases of identity such as the design of airports, it was also conspicuous in the practices of white artists. Whereas the artistic vanguard from the 1960s into the 1980s was represented as 'internationalist', the pendulum was even then swinging back toward an art more avowedly connected with the peculiarities of this part of the world. This art of Aotearoa foregrounded New Zealand's Pacific affinities and situation; some work engaged with the problematic aspiration of biculturalism, and with the country's colonial history. While some of these artistic efforts took easy routes to an evocation of local culture, others responded to the contradictions and intractability of the cultural history of the place.

A good deal of popular decorative art has used beaches, plants, shells and *tapa* (barkcloth) patterns to connect the natural environment with Polynesian culture. Some such work has actually been painted on to plain *tapa*, or on to the unpainted reverse sides of large Samoan pieces, presumably purchased by the artists around Auckland markets, or on trips to the islands. In other cases, perhaps out of deference to potential Polynesian sensitivities over questions of cultural property, the barkcloth motifs are suggested rather than directly imitated. Conventional and unadventurous art of this kind is little discussed by critics other than newspaper reviewers, but is significant for its wide circulation through relatively cheap lithographs and screenprints that appeal to middle-class buyers, and through cheaper posters and postcards. As it happens, this is also literally 'airport art': a chain of galleries at New Zealand airports market landscape views, flower paintings and pretty Pacific scenes, generally as limited edition prints. These could be seen to mark the end point of an effort inaugurated by Margaret Preston in 1920s Australia to mobilize local flora toward a kind of home decor that was appropriate to our surroundings. But whereas there was rigour, risk and urgency in her visual statements, one can only find the current expressions pretty bland.

156 NIGEL BROWN Cook in Pacifica, 1993

What might be faulted is the use of Polynesian cultural traits to mark place, in the absence of any reflection upon the wider pattern of relations between Pakeha and Maori, or Pakeha and Polynesians. This could not be said of Nigel Brown, an established and prolific painter who has long addressed various aspects of common New Zealand experience. If his work had indexed middle-class New Zealand's preoccupations, including questions concerning racism and the environment, it was striking that it took a sudden historical turn in the early 1990s. Whereas Brown's earlier paintings had ranged widely in their concerns – the individual and the community, the condition of suburbia, family and estrangement, the bomb etc – the artist came to focus upon Pacific themes. Some simple images of canoes and islands scenes could be classed with the decorative Pacific prints produced by various Polynesian and non-Polynesian artists, but Brown has more consistently been interested in encounters, and in reworking Cook voyage images such as Parkinson's sketches and William Hodges' paintings. He has also produced complex composite scenes, featuring elements of many Pacific cultures, which suggest a relocation of Cook's death to New Zealand. These works attest to the palpable presence of cross-cultural history in contemporary New Zealand consciousness, and possibly also to the confusion that surrounds the legacy of that history. The enduring power of the eighteenth-century encounters to both the indigenous and European parties is conspicuous in Brown's work; what is not is any sense of where an engagement with this history takes us.[11]

The response of Michael Shepherd to the New Zealand past, and to its ramifications for personal identity, is more troubled and sophisticated. Shepherd is a highly unusual figure in contemporary New Zealand art for the depth of his scholarly and practical engagement with the techniques of seventeenth-century Dutch art, and with the European illusionist tradition. He has produced a remarkable body of still life and *trompe l'oeil* painting that has consistently used conjunctures of objects and overlaid imprints of various kinds to present historical arguments and to evoke the misconceptions, confusions and strange relativities of New Zealand's colonial past. These works have included imaginary war memorials devoted to incidents of the New Zealand wars of the 1860s; tributes to the prophet Rua Kenana, which have been included in group exhibitions featuring Maori work on similar themes; and a deceptively simple and strangely elegant distortion of the tradition of flower painting, in a series of images of New Zealand weeds – for the most part plants introduced by Europeans and so intimately connected with the history of agricultural colonization and environmental change.[12]

On the occasions that I've talked through Michael's work with him, I've been struck by his almost obsessive sense of art as historical research, which leads him into domains of arcane iconographic detail. This was manifest in a series of small works commenting on the same fiscal envelope that motivated Robert Jahnke's stamps (p. 241). Shepherd painted real envelopes, inscribing them with philological inventions, modifications and cancellations. The density of inscription is typical of his practice, which never simply reproduces a historic engraving or photograph in facsimile, but burdens it with layers of emendation, with official and unofficial graffiti. The splendid irony of the envelopes is that they are underpaid, and hence feature 'postage due' stamps, and also bear redirections and address corrections (which exploit shifting Maori and European names) and so are returned, undeliverable or simply 'too late'. As small as they are extraordinarily rich, these envelopes epitomize the ponderous formality of the colonial state, and the awkward miscorrespondence of its traffic with Maori. Like Dunning's works, these are meditative and commemorative, conscious of the past in the present, and perhaps pessimistic rather than utopian. The fraught character of the transactions between first and last nations that they image suggests no simple resolution in the future, though they do suggest that the space we inhabit is a transactional one. We are perhaps not bearers of identities, but co-inhabitants of a zone of unequal exchange.

157 MICHAEL SHEPHERD
Monuments I, 1990

158 MICHAEL SHEPHERD
Still Life for the Year of the
Comet, 1986

159 MICHAEL SHEPHERD
Five Fiscal Envelopes
(the Language of Colonialism),
1995 (detail)

Trans-Tasman

The journeys I made back and forth between Australia and New Zealand
were between two countries that I knew, and still know, imperfectly.
I lived in one but had little time to do sustained research; in the other I
did little but research, or at least I socialized with people from whom
I learned a great deal, without ever acquiring the rounded commonsense
familiarity that follows from continual, or at least longer-term, residence in a place. Yet this situation of peripheral and partial knowledge
may have its advantages; I have at any rate tried to make a virtue of its
necessity. I have never become capable of taking the extraordinary
nature of the indigenous presence in the contemporary New Zealand
nation for granted, as both Maori and Pakeha do (even though what
might be taken for granted is always changing and contentious). The
highly singular nature of the evolving bicultural polity, which has no

parallel in the evolution of any other settler nation in North America or elsewhere, has thrown the less qualified dispossession of indigenous Australia into relief, and reinforced my sense of the degree to which the 'partnership' of natives and strangers here in Australia was always more of an imposition, so that the best conversations could not proceed without a trace of bitterness.

This book has recapitulated my journeys, criss-crossing between art and settler-indigenous relations to the west and east of the Tasman Sea. It has engaged opportunistically and selectively with art works, artists, exhibitions and larger developments in both countries, attempting to keep both affinities and differences in view. This procedure would have been less defensible had many artists not themselves engaged in trans-Tasman travel, had they not responded in both places to the differences that exchange made all the more recognizable. Although Maori were part of this intermittent travelling, and indeed migration, from its beginnings – and are depicted in more than a few views of early Sydney – those artists whom we know worked in both places were mainly colonial ones. I have already discussed the work of Chevalier and von Guérard (Chapter Two); it is consistent with all the odd traffic of trans-Tasman art history that the Auckland Art Gallery declined to purchase von Guérard's finest New Zealand painting, indeed one of the finest of all his paintings, the breathtaking image of the bright, stormy, daunting, glacial precipitous-ness of Milford Sound (fig. 38). This fiord, long one of the nation's key tourist attractions, has since been endlessly painted and photographed but never with such accomplishment. It was a subject perfectly suited to von Guérard's scientific romanticism. The Auckland Gallery settled instead for the painter's indifferent view of Lake Wakatipu; the virtue that that work possessed, presumably, was its representation (in fact a misrepresentation) of a Maori canoe, copied by von Guérard from a lithograph by the earlier trans-Tasman artist, George French Angus. Though the lake's water is an unreal lurid light green, this synthesis of native and nature was evidently the ticket at the time. The unpeopled landscape of Milford Sound was right for the Art Gallery of New South Wales in the 1880s, however, and can still be seen there in Sydney.

These exchanges marked an 'Australasian' moment, when white colonists in Australia and New Zealand were conscious of their affinities. With the federation of the Australian colonies in 1901, and the separate development of the two settler nations, art histories became more provincial. White artists on both sides of the Tasman continued to look between Europe and their immediate environment, but rarely looked to the analogous situations and predicaments of their neighbours, let alone those of other settlers in British dominions like Canada. While in each place an engagement with landscape seemed to provide the route to a distinctive art appropriate to a young country, the radical differences between the nature of the land obscured the extent to which settler efforts of self-definition and cultural definition relied on the same terms. In Australia, landscape painting would increasingly mean an engagement with the bleak outback, which seemed a different world altogether to the wet pastoral hills of New Zealand. There were further affinities in artists' interests and responses which passed largely unrecognized. We can be almost certain that when James Cant and Theo Schoon copied and adapted rock paintings around 1950, they did so in ignorance of each other's efforts.

Now, however, we are coming full circle. Indigenous artists in Aotearoa and Australia are conscious of a shared historical predicament in the way that trans-Tasman settlers were in the nineteenth century. They are conscious of the similarities between the values of their cultures, and of the extent to which colonial relations and colonial iconography suggest common responses. They are also drawn together through art-world events such as conferences and residencies. They produce responses to each other's art, and occasionally collaborate. The Australian artist who has been most interested in the Pacific and in exchange with Maori is perhaps Judy Watson, who has produced a remarkable body of painting and prints over the last decade, as well as some installation works. While utterly different in appearance from the work of John Pule, discussed in the next chapter, they similarly transcend the dichotomy of the representational and the abstract. Though non-figurative, and quite extraordinary for their mistiness and liquid depth, Watson's unstretched canvases index biographies, histories and embodied pain. Works such as *heartland* and *bloodbath* are entrancingly beautiful, yet at the same time horrifying in their allusion to violence and genocide.[13]

Watson's work is also conspicuously about land, and she has often employed pigments or earth in landscape installations created during residencies in Scandinavia and elsewhere. It is notable, given the tradition of geothermal tourism around Rotorua, that participation in a Maori and Pacific artists' conference there led her not to image the site but to incorporate its volcanic mud into painting. Even if this is consistent with a wider trend toward an environmental art most popularly exemplified by Richard Long, it also reflects a basic difference between the approach of colonial artists, who have consistently appropriated the landscape through representation, and indigenous peoples, who have asserted their associations not via a distanced view, but through painting country in manifold other ways.

Judy Watson's art of earth and body happens to neatly complement the practice of Maureen Lander, a Maori fibre artist – or, perhaps more accurately, an artist of light and fibre.[14] Her translation of traditional women's practices is perhaps less radical than Jacqueline Fraser's (pp. 244–6), in that she generally uses the customary natural materials, but is no less innovative in their radical elaboration in site-specific works which in some cases engage in dialogue with colonial representations of place and artifact. An installation for the Sarjeant Gallery in Wanganui, for instance, captured the conical elegance of Taranaki or Mount Egmont, perforce referring to Charles Heaphy's famous early image, which has almost the status of an icon of New Zealand art. Again, the shift between an image of landscape and an emulation of its form is suggestive, though if Lander's work is described as a reappropriation, it is a gentle one that incorporates an acknowledgment to the Pakeha artist as much as a new evocation of the poetry of place.

In November 1995, Lander and Watson cooperated to create *Bio-luminescence*, a complex installation which formed part of 'Pacific Wave', a festival of contemporary Pacific art in Sydney. It was pieced together around, and triumphed over, an unpromising fountain situated within the precincts of a public swimming pool adjacent to the University of Sydney. (One needs to be reminded that just as Aboriginal people were seated in roped-off areas in country cinemas until the 1960s, they were barred from city facilities of this kind until around the same time.) A sailing ship in the centre of the fountain, an emblem of European trade and colonization, was surrounded by 'guardian' figures – spirit shapes that played in the wind and light. The encircling pond featured a group of delicate illuminated fibre objects, some made from recycled materials, others from combinations incorporating flax gathered by the artist and some of the Sydney Maori community. The place was defined as an indigenous historical site by Maori, Aboriginal and Samoan words inscribed in glowing chalk, and was inhabited by luminous beings that possessed their own radiance, their own movements. If the fraught contradiction of the colonial-indigenous relation was present here, it was implicit, almost literally submerged: the naturalized indigenous figures, the bearers of bioluminescence, were neither victims nor aggressors but presences. If this installation was a work toward transcendence, it was so not in the conventional aesthetic sense. The movement here seemed not one of lifting us above the commonplace, but of taking us beyond the painful contradictions of a past that remains all too alive in the present.

160 MAUREEN LANDER Ko ngaa Puna Waiora o Maunga Taranaki, 1993

161 MAUREEN LANDER AND JUDY WATSON Bioluminescence, 1996

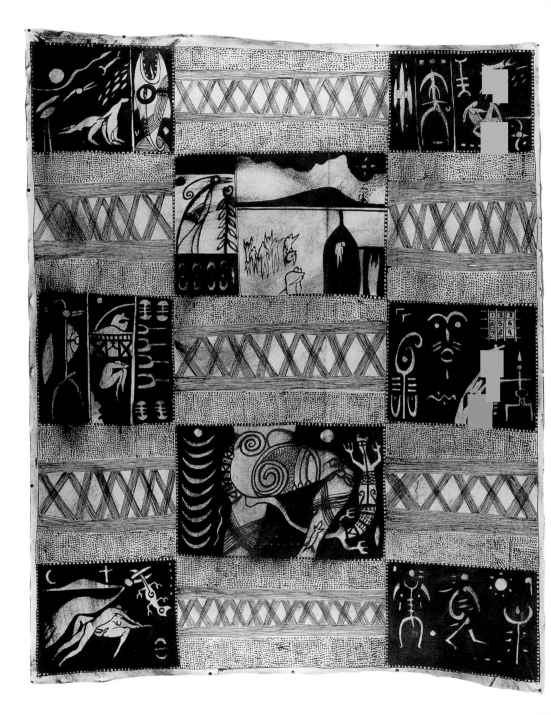

162 JOHN PULE Style with Three Moons, 1996

In hindsight, it is astonishing that the question of the significance of primitivism in European culture was neglected for so long. Although some important work was done in the 1930s, it is essentially only during the last twenty years that the extraordinary variety of fancies and fetishes concerning the exotic, the archaic and the 'savage' have been traced.[1] Research in art history, literature, anthropology and related fields has drawn attention to the ways in which the primitive or anti-modern played a formative role in the fashioning of European selfhood since Herodotus. Constructions of simple or savage societies, which possessed broad affinities with Orientalist stereotypes of other non-European cultures, have served a bewildering range of ideological and rhetorical purposes.[2] Sometimes denigrations of indigenous peoples have transparently legitimated imperial domination. In other cases, more affirmative evocations animate critiques of Western culture, economics and technology.

Nearly everything that has been written on these themes to date has presumed that the object of inquiry is a cultural relation between a 'civilized self' situated in Europe or North America and a 'primitive other' in Africa, South America or Oceania. The 'other' is fantastic, remote and generic. This book has aimed to add something to our understandings of primitivism by exploring the representation of native peoples who were (and are) *within* settler nations, not in jungles or on islands on the other side of the world. Their co-occupation of lands that Europeans were struggling to construe as their own meant that those indigenous populations had to be reckoned with, in multiple senses. As we have seen, not all colonists were comfortable with the confrontational terror that invasion and dispossession required. The archive of colonial writing and imagery is replete with misgivings, with acknowledgments of native presences that might be denied or stigmatized at the next moment. Over the longer term, this reckoning has not led to the establishment of enduring settler dominance and secure settler identities. Indigenous presences have neither been wished away, nor comfortably accommodated in unthreatening terms. Settler dominance has never become hegemonic, in the sense of securing the general acquiescence of the colonized. Settler dominance, curiously, has been reinforced and unmade again and again. The legitimacy of indigenous political claims and the power and validity of indigenous cultures are perhaps now more widely acknowledged than ever before, while questions concerning compensatory justice and sovereignty remain extraordinarily contentious and problematic.

This book's preoccupation with the many moments of stilted dialogue and non-dialogue between settler and native has entailed emphasis upon a binary relation. I have tried to show that the intimate antagonism between settlers and indigenous peoples has amounted to a fundamental contradiction, a defining contradiction, for the antipodean cultures of New Zealand – Aotearoa New Zealand – and Australia. It has been a fraught and fertile opposition, one through which aesthetic innovation, real violence, imagination and cruelty have constantly been woven together.

At this point in my story, however, it is vital that we acknowledge that these nations are not composed simply of British settlers and native peoples. There have also been subsequent waves of non-British, and non-European migrants, especially in Australia, where significant numbers of southern and eastern Europeans, and peoples from the Middle East, Southeast Asia and the Pacific make the cities of the east coast in particular among the most ethnically diverse in the world.[3] New Zealand's immigration history is rather different. The same postwar boom and demand for labour that prompted Australia to introduce Greeks, Italians and Maltese, among others, led New Zealand to encourage immigration from the Polynesian countries that were then administered by New Zealand, the Cook Islands and Niue, and those which were more informally within a neo-colonial sphere of influence, Samoa and Tonga. These Pacific Islanders display many cultural affinities with Maori, even though their situation, as migrants rather than people of the land, remains fundamentally distinct. More recently, Asians, particularly south Asians, have become visible; but New Zealand remains less ethnically heterogeneous than Australia.[4]

For many years, these non-dominant migrant populations in both nations were marginal in public life and in the arts. After multiculturalism was officially embraced by the Whitlam Labor Government in the early 1970s, various forms of sponsorship for 'ethnic' writers and artists were devised and implemented. Partly as a result of this encouragement, partly in spite of it, the Anglo-Australian dominance of high culture gave way, not only before the astonishing emergence of modern Aboriginal art, but as artists conscious of their diasporic situation became increasingly visible. For some people, and certainly for many less avant-garde dealers and consumers of art, Australian art remained an art of landscape and the outback and national myths. Yet in other domains, questions of dislocation and marginality became the hallmarks of contemporary practice. The postmodern interests in eclectic quotation and the politics of representation became intimately connected with a diasporic aesthetic.

The same theoretical currents were noticed in New Zealand but did not have the same effect. In this chapter I juxtapose the expressions of migrant art in the two countries. Needless to say, I cannot provide any sort of balanced survey, but instead aim to show that the relationship between migrants and indigenous peoples has been quite different in each, and that this difference accords with a contrast between the responses of white settler artists in Australia and New Zealand to the indigenous cultural renaissances in their respective countries. In both places, and just about everywhere else, there are anxieties about identities; yet the anxieties take different forms that may suggest the limits, or the exhaustion, of the very ideas of nation and identity. The cultural histories and contemporary predicaments that I have described, which may seem odd and atypical from the perspective of the northern hemisphere, may thus have a more universal historical importance if they suggest terms that lie beyond the language of culture, place and attachment that has long held sway in the Euro-American world and its peripheries. Before hazarding such generalities, however, the arts of the diasporas in New Zealand and Australia must be mapped out.

Let it show in your work

One younger Maori artist once complained to me that Pacific artists in New Zealand had emerged 'on the back' of the Maori renaissance. If this was unfair as an aspersion upon the creativity of individual Polynesians, it was accurate as a historical observation on the dramatic appearance of a contemporary Pacific art. Before the late 1980s, there was no visible Polynesian painting or sculpture; though Islander migrant women were certainly producing objects such as woven bags and the exuberant appliquéd quilts known as *tivaevae* which have since been acknowledged as art forms and have entered both commercial and public galleries. The situation changed rapidly. The visibility of Maori art, and its significance in the presentation and affirmation of Maori culture, suggested that there was something missing; Pacific Islanders, too, warranted recognition. A few art school students of Islander descent, and two or three older Polynesian painters who had been working more as isolated amateurs than as exhibiting artists, were prompted to take their work in a specific direction. Several of these individuals acknowledge retrospectively that they were working essentially in a European idiom, inspired by one modernist or another, until they were encouraged to make their art a vehicle for their cultural identity. Fatu Feu'u says that he was a 'Sunday painter' who emulated Gauguin until the mid-1980s, when Pakeha artists such as Tony Fomison – who had long been interested in Polynesian cultures – encouraged him to develop a style that drew upon his background. Similarly, according to his secondary school art teacher, Michel Tuffery 'was doing a lot of expressionist moody figures – Kirchner, Van Gogh. I remember saying one day, for God's sake you're a Polynesian, let it show in your work!'[5]

Feu'u is especially interesting for his deliberate and successful invention of a contemporary pan-Polynesian art. His work features bright colours, frangipani and masks; some motifs are derived from barkcloth patterns, as is a grid structure that he has employed in many paintings and lithographs. His use of motifs from Lapita pottery is especially significant, since this is not a modern but an archaeological tradition associated with the early waves of Oceanic settlers in the Pacific. The Lapita potters are understood to be the ancestors of most

163 FATU FEU'U Light of the Rainbow, c. 1989

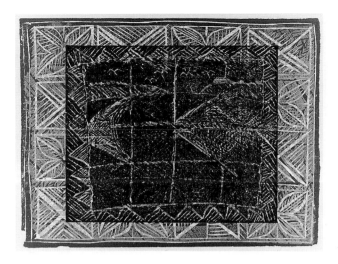

164 FATU FEU'U Tulimanu, 1991

island Melanesians and all Polynesians; this is therefore a shared tradition rather than one specific to Feu'u's own Samoan culture or the
particular art traditions of the Tongans or Cook Islanders. In a few
paintings – including an interior mural in the Aotea Centre, the central
Auckland theatre and arts complex in which work by artists including
Paratene Matchitt and Selwyn Muru is displayed – Feu'u has also
imaged a kind of national narrative for New Zealand's Polynesians.
In these works, migrating tuna and traditional motifs flow together
past two coastal profiles – Auckland's two harbours, where Polynesians
first arrived by ship and more recently by plane. Their journey is figured
as an extension of the travels of their ancestors across the Pacific.
Auckland, now the largest Polynesian city in the world, emerges as a
new centre and further point of settlement for Polynesian culture.

Feu'u has refrained from continuing to paint in this didactic fashion,
though it is worth mentioning that another version of the painting was
acquired by what was then the Ministry for Pacific Islands Affairs. Many
of his other paintings and lithographs have emphasized environmental
themes, particularly concern about the overfishing of the Pacific. This
kind of work, which makes an appeal on behalf of all of us, or our
children, rather than an assertive or angry statement, appeals broadly to
mainstream environmentalist sentiment, and has been popular. Feu'u has
worked very hard at disseminating his work through prints accessible to
more affluent buyers, and T-shirts accessible to everyone; his designs

have also appeared on ceramics, rugs and glass; his paintings have been reproduced on postcards and a few book covers. Tuffery, similarly, has produced dynamic, accessible prints, also drawing loosely on barkcloth patterns, sculptural figures, and elements of the Oceanic environment.

The success of this art not only followed in the steps of the success and proliferation of Maori art; contemporary Pacific art can be seen to have followed the model of Maori art in presuming that art was a vehicle for collective affirmation. Art objects worked as affirmations of identity by drawing upon recognizable traditional motifs, or (in the case of Pacific art) on motifs that became widely recognized. 'Pacific art' was therefore art that spoke for Pacific communities, that deployed and modernized traditional art forms, and paraded its cultural origins. It suggested that the self-realization of individuals lay in their fuller awareness of their traditions and cultures. Their 'cultures' were understood not in terms of the urban migrant milieux in which these artists generally lived, nor even those that their parents or grandparents had experienced in their island homes, but rather as their ancestral values, which were what barkcloth and pottery motifs were taken to express. This was not an unqualified traditionalism since it was taken for granted that these values required reinterpretation and novel artistic expression in the present, and connections were made with contemporary causes. What Maori art did for Maori – reinforcing a sense of collective pride, expressing continuities with ancestors and the environment – Pacific art might do for Pacific Islanders, and for those who empathized with their cultures.

If there was common ground in some of these premises between Maori and Polynesian art, it is notable that Polynesian art has generally been less overtly political than Maori art, and that claims concerning political representation have been conspicuous by their absence. Maori are defined by their situation as colonized indigenous peoples, and to varying degrees that situation is declared and renegotiated through their art. Polynesian migrants in New Zealand cities experience a good deal of racism and have much they might complain about, but at the political level, and in public cultural fora, they are generally careful to defer to Maori. Many are acutely conscious that they are on another people's land; even those who feel that their parents' lives and deaths in New Zealand give them something like the right to stand and speak that Pakeha have always presumed tend to express that point of view privately or implicitly.

All this is an effect of the unique cultural politics in Aotearoa New Zealand. Elsewhere, migrants, or descendants of migrants, have seen some form of pluralism or multiculturalism as a desirable model: the

165 MICHEL TUFFERY Pili Siva, 1988

hegemony of white Anglo-Saxon culture, accompanied by the notion
that new migrants must be assimilated or integrated, yields to a celebration of diversity that may be officially fostered through cultural
festivals, the structuring of educational and employment opportunities,
the sensitization of legal procedures to cultural differences, and the
acknowledgment of more than one official language. In New Zealand,
by contrast, while there is in fact a good deal of de facto multiculturalism, the overarching official framework, and the one that is supported in
different terms by diverse Maori and non-Maori interests, is bicultural
not multicultural. The national constitution, of which the Waitangi
Treaty is seen as the founding document, prioritizes the parity between
Maori and Pakeha, and sees the entitlements of other groups of migrants
only as following upon an equitable partnership between the people of
the land and those who negotiated the terms of their own settlement. In
general, Pacific Islander artists have deferred to this view of the polity,
and have not themselves demanded that their communities in some
sense be represented in the redefined nation.

Lost gods

This is not to say that contemporary Polynesian art lacks a critical edge. Much contemporary work in fact avoids the kind of straightforward affirmation of ethnicity and culture that artists such as Feu'u and Tuffery have achieved.

The work of Ani O'Neill, who is as much a fashion designer as an artist, typifies the practice of a group of younger Polynesians, who see themselves as creating a novel culture for Islanders in Aotearoa, one that is inspired in various senses by islands origins, but is not backward-looking or dependent in relation to them. Her most engaging and witty work to date is a reworking of figures of the Rarotongan deity Tangaroa, a rank of which featured in the major exhibition 'Bottled Ocean', which showcased innovative Polynesian work in a number of New Zealand institutions over 1995 and 1996. Tangaroa was once a principal deity, and perhaps retains spiritual importance for some Cook Islanders in the modern Christian nation. But he is familiar primarily as a national icon – appearing on coins, for instance – and as the number one Cook Islands tourist object. While the carvings in museum collections have frequently been emasculated, the outsize penis is restored in contemporary imagery, and gives the figure the appeal of a risqué souvenir, a piece of erotic airport art. This is an interesting history in itself, given that the outsider's eroticized construction of Oceania has generally been associated with an objectification of languid and inviting Tahitian women. If Tangaroa's pretty exuberant masculinity strikes a discordant note, Ani O'Neill's remaking of the figure in fabric and in the domestic form of a cuddly but inappropriately sexualized toy surely exploits the ironies of tourist culture to the hilt.

There is a notable difference of style and mode between O'Neill's feminization of a traditional god and Jacqueline Fraser's translation of sculpture into fibre (pp. 244–5). While O'Neill's piece is ironic and amusing, Fraser could be seen to restate the dignity of ancestral figures in a fresh idiom. O'Neill, on my reading, has no particular stake in Tangaroa's sanctity; she draws attention to the multiple appropriations of the god as icon, but does not denounce these as violations or assaults upon a traditional culture. The political suggestion of her work is rather that Islanders – not least younger Islanders, and those resident in Aotearoa rather than the islands – have the right to embrace and extend these appropriations in ways that may subvert tradition as much as the residual colonialism of tourist voyeurism. The calmness and the sanctity of Fraser's architecture is, of course, a matter of distinct artistic mood

166 ANI O'NEILL Tangaroa Dolls

and temperament; but it also reflects the contrasting politics of Maori art. Fraser makes a careful feminist statement as she assumes the authority to create a meeting-house environment. There is no subversion of ancestral values here, no risqué humour. The binary contest which defines Maori and Pakeha arguably precludes the labile and permissive engagement with tradition that animates the work of migrant artists such as O'Neill. Whereas a diasporic situation is conducive to a play between old homes and new, indigenous people are compelled to insist upon the enduring force and salience of the culture that defines them.

The Niuean painter John Pule also has a complex and ambivalent relation to ancestral tradition. One of the most conspicuous features of the Niuean culture of his parents and grandparents is Christianity, but his work categorically rejects the colonizing practices of missionaries, and presents the imported religion as a tragic blight. Christ is seen to have arrived in the islands as a sick man, and to have been nurtured through the lives of Islanders, as their own gods died. Pule steps away from all this and invents an extraordinary personal iconography that is suggestive of myth without being literally connected with it. His paintings are complex combinations of figurative elements and optically dynamic patterning; crosses and churches suggest missionary arrivals, canoe scenes dramatize moments of Polynesian history, and tearful masks suggest dying gods, or ancestors preoccupied with the pain of migration. Generally monochromatic, albeit in strong colour, these works also feature extraordinary

167 JOHN PULE Nofo a Koe, Fano a Au, 1995

creatures – erotic predators that suggest a world pervaded by copulation, devouring, death and reproduction.

Pule's inspiration comes in part from the nineteenth-century *hiapo* or barkcloths of Niue, whose grid patterns and motifs are often strikingly irregular, unlike those from Tonga or Samoa. Their elaborate, animated design structures are moreover often interrupted by figurative elements, including ships, small groups of figures, and white people. Pule's new *hiapo* adopt these principles loosely; though there are in fact few specific appropriations or resemblances, they almost uncannily have the look of the historic barkcloths.

The influential British artist and critic Rasheed Areen has criticized non-Western artists who foreground their cultural distinctness in their work – who 'make it show', as Feu'u and Tuffery were urged to do.

> ...this is understandable because...the only way the other artists can enter [modernist] discourse is by a cultural identity card (which is like a passbook used by blacks in South Africa during Apartheid). The cultural identity card signifies restricted entry, whatever legitimation one may give to it – cultural diversity, pluralism, post-modernism – and it should be the first priority of any artist to fight against this restriction.[6]

Pule's work, and its success, suggests that such adjudications are just too categorical. His paintings are entirely different to work being done anywhere else in the world, and are distinctively Polynesian, even distinctively Niuean. The appeal of his work, for the various institutions and private collectors who have acquired it, has no doubt inhered in its Pacific signature, as well as in the virtuosity of its highly personal sense of place, culture and history. Yet it is clear that little, if anything, has been sacrificed in order to gain and capitalize upon this 'cultural identity card'. There is no deadening preoccupation with authenticity or tradition. Nor has the circulation of the work been limited to venues or contexts in which 'Polynesia' is being exhibited (although it is true that less accomplished artists certainly find it hard to break out of that mode of art-world pigeon-holing). Most importantly, in Pule's case, his work retains a critical and mobile attitude toward any definition of Niuean culture; much of the time, in any event, that issue does not arise, because this artist claims only to represent himself, to narrate his own history and that of his family. In so far as this is a typical history, or a shared history, his images and stories are Niuean and Pacific images and stories; yet his work always amounts to both more and less than a representation of cultural identity.

The touch of the hybrid

Cultural origins figure in the work of the Greek-Australian feminist artist Elizabeth Gertsakis, but her stance toward them is more overtly critical than that of John Pule, as it is more theorized. Her position is perhaps more consonant with that of Rasheed Areen; in fact a catalogue essay for her 1994 exhibition, 'Beyond Missolonghi', was written by Nikos Papastergiardis, a contributing editor of the influential journal of diasporic culture and criticism founded by Areen, *Third Text*. 'Beyond Missolonghi' presented an extraordinary combination of Byron's poems, nineteenth-century academic paintings on Hellenic subjects that happened to have ended up in Australian art museums, photo-collages, and other combinations of image and text. The show's title referred to Byron's death at Missolonghi in 1824, and the siege there two years later that epitomizes the subjugation of Greece by the Ottoman empire. Colonialist and nationalist fantasies were traced, woven together and unravelled by Gertsakis. Byron's lubricity was linked with nationalist romance; sexual transgressions travestied romantic epics; and military heroics were shown to defend not pure or readily defined terrains and identities, but always those already constituted by an impure traffic, by outsiders' definitions, projections and fantasies.

Gertsakis's exhibition was very much a product of museum research, an excavation of history and identity that aimed not to provide a moralized narrative or an authenticating genealogy, but rather a series of incongruous juxtapositions. As she expressed her aims:

> The current varieties of resurgent nationalism, be they bloody and virulent, or sequestered by their constrained dormancy, smug in distance, perpetuate nation on the basis of metaphors often given them by the imperial and colonial west in the pursuit of its own fantasies. When the patriot Greek argues for the rightful purity of ancient Greekness, or the orthodox Serb kills and rapes as an attack against the encroaching unholy infidel; it is, paradoxically, the transmission of someone else's image metaphor that constructs the contemporary violence of identification with nation. *Beyond Missolonghi* brings together the incongruity of the sources of those image and language metaphors that have helped to construct the fictions of the Ottoman world, Greece, Macedonia, the Balkans and Islam, and attempts to distinguish between the actual conditions of past applications and their discrepancies, with our own present usages.[7]

It is difficult not to appreciate both the bizarre and amusing combination of imagery that results, and the very serious political point that underlies it. Hardly anywhere has the dark side of national 'liberation' been revealed as comprehensively as in the communal antagonism and the 'ethnic cleansing' of the Balkans in recent years. Does it follow, however, that all anti-colonial nationalisms and all movements of cultural affirmation are tainted by implication? Gertsakis's claim is that emblems of national pride may be derived from iconographies imposed by external oppressors; for her, this point in itself seems to undermine any assertion of identity or sovereignty. But this is not self-evident. The fact that there is much cross-cultural exchange, much flow in representations, does not mean that signs of history and community are necessarily inauthentic concoctions that have no genuine roots in local life. It is striking, in the Pacific, that Christianity and many other introduced practices are now entirely incorporated within the fabric of local sociality, as are dresses of the Mother Hubbard type, as Gauguin noticed long ago (p. 45). Hence, while I fully empathize with Gertsakis's irony, and with her principled hostility both to European ethnic exclusionism, and to the features of Australian politics that perpetuate various racisms within the antipodean fragments of Europe, I believe that we need to avoid taking an attitude to affirmations of identity *in principle*. Maori culture is not invalidated by

168 ELIZABETH GERTSAKIS Words Can Never Speak So Well, 1994, juxtaposed on the cover of the 'Beyond Missolonghi' catalogue with Byron's poem 'Maid of Athens, Ere We Part'

169 ELIZABETH GERTSAKIS The Face of Such a Tragedy, 1994, juxtaposed in the 'Beyond Missolonghi' catalogue with this quotation from Kemal Ataturk: 'Gentlemen, I pray you, put back your handkerchiefs in your pockets; don't weep. Weeping is only fit for women. If you are men, instead of weeping roar like lions in the face of such a tragedy. Show by your actions the sublimity of Islam!'

the fact of its historical evolution through its relation to other cultures. I have tried to show, on the basis of 'Te Maori', that contemporary affirmations of indigenous culture capitalize upon primitivist values in the dominant cultures and in the audiences for exhibitions of this type. But those affirmations do not leave those values unchanged; they do not simply collude in them. Maori insist upon the presence and the particular values of their cultures, including the tribal variety of Maori culture, even as they evoke spirituality and their embeddedness in myth and the world of the ancestors.

Gertsakis dedicated 'Beyond Missolonghi' 'to all those who have about them the touch of the hybrid.' This is seductive – I would want to count myself in. But I sense also that some are excluded, that some

170 IMANTS TILLERS The Nine Shots, 1985

171 IMANTS TILLERS Paradiso, 1994 (above)

Maori would exclude themselves, not because they would deny the complex historical interactions that shape their own culture, nor even the bicultural elements in their backgrounds as individuals, but because they would see their own claims to the integrity of Maori space, culture and selfhood as being disallowed. Indigenous people could, all too easily, be disparaged again for being too traditional, for failing the test of hybrid sophistication. Whereas the migrant Polynesians in Aotearoa seem directly or indirectly to sustain Maori art, or to acknowledge the precedence of Maori, as a consequence of the affinities between their cultures, diasporic Australian artists' projects at best seem to ignore those of Aborigines, and may in fact subvert them.

The work of Imants Tillers, one of Australia's best-known contemporary artists, indicates at once the promises and the risks of this trend. Tillers is one of Australia's strongest postmodernist artists, who in fact fashioned his own art of appropriation before this strategy became a hallmark of postmodernism internationally.[8] The postmodern understanding of culture as a process of eclectic quotation and reformation is highly apt to the diasporic situation, marked as it is by complex dislocations and relocations of nomadic identity. Tillers' art has been increasingly energized by his liminality relative to both the Latvian heritage of his

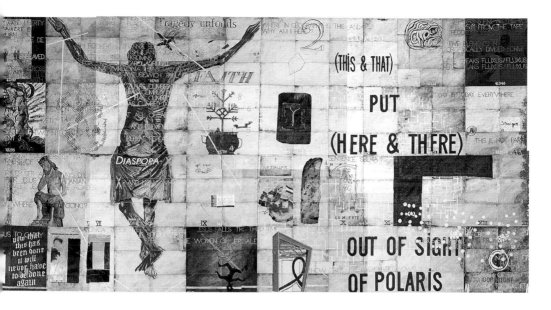

parents and the formerly hegemonic British values of white Australia, and increasingly framed by the questions of diaspora and identity.

Earlier, in works such as *The Nine Shots* (1985), the painter's avowedly postmodern approach led him to appropriate paintings by Michael Nelson Jagamara, and other examples of Aboriginal art, as he drew also on many elements of white Australian and international painting. These quotations were perhaps productively contentious, for they prompted a debate in the Australian art world around the values of postmodernism which drew attention to the differences between borrowing from well-known works of international art, and from Aboriginal creative expressions that, it was insisted, remained fundamentally attached to local landholding, myth and culture. The use of the latter seemed not so much simply an ironic comment on the detachment and confusion of identities in the current epoch as a careless negation of the enduring significance of place and tradition for indigenous Australians.[9] As Ian McLean has recently noted, Tillers' appropriations of Papunya paintings 'were designed to supersede their Aboriginality, transforming them into a postmodernism.'[10] Though Tillers trenchantly defended his own position at the time, he subsequently appeared to back away from the use of work by remote Aboriginal artists. It is notable, however, that a series of large-scale works from the early and mid-1990s, which were drawn together in a major touring exhibition in 1995, seem nevertheless to amount to an increasingly categorical vindication of the notion that globalization amounts to 'the main game', from which art practice can only be diverted by spurious deference to anachronistic 'indigenous' cultures.

It is difficult not to respect the baroque virtuosity of Tillers' accomplishment, which has proceeded from strength to strength in direct correlation with the extent to which he borrows from Colin McCahon in particular. Yet the relation here is a little like that between the appropriating work and the Aboriginal reference in Margaret Preston's painting. Like Preston, Tillers engages not in the kind of covert assimilation of modernist art, but in a practice of explicit appropriation which marks the original works out and acknowledges the business of quotation and the complexity of indebtedness. Yet, as we have seen, the effect of Preston's work superseded her intentions. If she intended to synthesize Aboriginal and European, she failed; instead, she drew attention to the stubborn and resilient presence of the Aboriginal art that had perforce been diminished and miscontextualized in her adaptation.

Tillers commendably draws attention to his source material and even subtitled the 'Diaspora in Context' show and catalogue 'Imants Tillers makes a painting by George Baselitz, Joseph Beuys, Bernhard Blume, Carlo Carra, Giorgio de Chirico, Mike Kelley, Vytautas Landsbergis, Colin McCahon, Arnulf Rainer, Nicholas Roerich and Isidore Tillers'. (He neglected to list two Gordons – Walters and Bennett – whose work was apparently also included.) The fact that many of these source works were exhibited with the show, including McCahon's deceptively simple but magnificent set of *Numerals* (1965), made it all too easy for Tillers' combination to be upstaged by his sources. If Preston's viewers were pointed away from her work toward art that was obscure and hard to locate, Tillers' audience needed only to glance from one side of the room to the

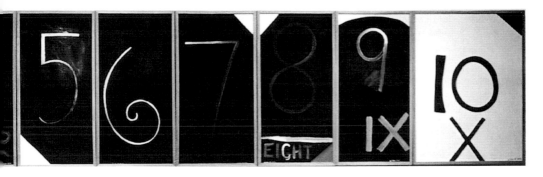

172 COLIN McCAHON Numerals, 1965

other to see the strong originals that he had reproduced with considerable verve, yet nevertheless diminished.

Of course, this is a matter of opinion; it must be conceded that views of the relative accomplishments of Tillers and McCahon certainly vary. However, in a theoretical sense, the 'postmodernization' of McCahon's work arguably entails precisely the same reduction of significance as Tillers' appropriation of Papunya painting, and for that matter, the borrowing of Aboriginal forms by Preston and by the white exponents of 'Aboriginal art'. McCahon's *Numerals* makes a range of complex statements concerning the place and contribution of art. The blackboard, the deft suggestion of hastily rubbed-out chalk, and the numbers themselves indicate that we are in a teaching situation, that the painting is a 'teaching aid'. We are being taught, or perhaps the artist is learning with us, not how to count, but how to look at art, and how to make something of it. Maybe this is as simple a matter as learning to count; but we are immediately compelled to realize that it is not a static act. Just as counting is a process, that starts at a certain point and leaves off at another, looking at a painting is a process. One has to walk past this work, begin at a certain point and leave off where it perhaps arbitrarily ends. Maybe the work is not on the walls but in the walk, in a journey with pauses, which viewers conscious of McCahon's interest in Christianity would associate with stations of the cross, but which we could also identify with any other halting motion – that of settler-colonial history, for example. The Christian allusion does not so much implicate us all in a religion we may or may not subscribe to, it implicates that religion's notion of a spiritual journey in other practices, and in ordinary practices such as the learning that children engage in, and the walking past works of art that engages adults. There is much more in this work that might be remarked upon. The co-presence of the Roman and Arabic numerals suggests the relation between the classical and the demotic, a contrived and hierarchical relation between ignorance and cultivation that might be inverted here by the limited representation and subordinate position of the Roman figures. And there is the suggestion of the *koru* motif at the end of McCahon's number 2 – a device that can be recognized through its more explicit realization in other word and number paintings. If this is a small acknowledgment, in this particular painting, of Maori culture and the Maori presence, it is one that is magnified and elaborated upon in other McCahon works in extraordinary, albeit enduringly contentious ways. (Maybe even this too is 'just another fucking colonial painting'.) What the complexity of McCahon's engagement points toward is neither the integrated completeness of a nation, nor the unlocated hybridity of a diaspora. We are drawn rather toward another paradigm of identity altogether, one of an imbalanced relationship of learning and teaching, of giving and taking. The settler-indigenous predicament is a transaction, and a fraught and unfinished one.

It is not self-evident that these meanings and arguments are anachronistic, nor that they gain a lot or even a little from 'postmodernization' – the stances of Gertsakis and Tillers respectively. The antipodean specificity of McCahon's ultimately limited if complex and respectful engagement with indigenous culture may ironically be vindicated through the 'postmodernization' of Tillers' appropriation. Tillers' accomplishment is perhaps best understood as an inadvertent revelation not of the gain but of the loss that goes with globalization. Like McCahon, he teaches us a little arithmetic, but in this case the lesson is that addition is a disguised form of subtraction. When we put many art works and locations together, we end up with something that is less than the sum of its parts. The global calculus of diasporic reference involves juggling figures that are resonant in themselves, even visually compelling, but that ultimately bear only one value. They all tell us the same thing: that we are all nomads and hybrids. Hence the banality of many of the propositions in the *Diaspora in Context* catalogue: 'The times of globalization are also times of movement'. Tillers' work is much richer than this, and is poorly served by framing commentary of this kind. Yet it is not Tillers' but McCahon's painting that suggests that it is just possible that the idea of movement can be rescued from banality. We start at a certain point and leave off at another. Wherever we live, we are burdened by our points of departure and may pause at points of irresolution. But if we inhabit the injured, bicultural and multicultural landscapes of Aotearoa and Australia, we find no shortage of such points that give us pause.

Chapter Nine

The chief steward on a Qantas flight from London to Sydney informs passengers that they are travelling in 'one of the largest works of modern art in the world'. We are in one of two Boeing 747s that have been fully painted in an exuberant neo-Aboriginal iconography designed for the airline by the indigenous fashion company, Balarinji. This extraordinary object brings us in a kind of circle. I noted earlier that while Air New Zealand opted for a logo derived from indigenous culture – the *koru* motif, mediated by Gordon Walters' formalization – Qantas preferred native fauna to native culture. But the kangaroo once confined to the tailfin has taken a leap forward and assumed an Aboriginal guise. In the lead-up to the 2000 Olympics, Aboriginality is in fact written all over the face that the nation presents to tourists, not only over the national airline, but in Olympic logos and in many other contexts. The indigenous fashion promoted by Balarinji and others is hardly ubiquitous – indigenous signs have never quite gained the pervasiveness they have long had in New Zealand – but it is nevertheless becoming steadily more conspicuous.

Nonetheless, the business of collective definition and redefinition in Australia is not only uneasy but probably purely contradictory. Anyone who took the Qantas aircraft design as proof of some novel level of regard for indigenous culture among Australians in general would be half right, but certainly also half wrong. The increasing number of exhibitions of Aboriginal art, the wide-ranging discussion of indigenous questions in the news media, and the visibility of signs of Aboriginality in public culture – which are now not generally rip-offs but works for which Aboriginal artists and designers are credited and rewarded – reflect considerable changes in public opinion since the 1960s. There is now a much deeper consciousness of historical injustices, of the validity and complexity of Aboriginal culture, and of the urgent need to redress the continuing disadvantage suffered by indigenous Australians. When the Labor Prime Minister Paul Keating acknowledged the history of violent dispossession in a speech inaugurating the United Nations Year of Indigenous Peoples, and the Australian High Court's historic Mabo

173 Balarinji Australia, 'free time clothing'
summer catalogue, 1994

decision overturned the doctrine that Australia constituted a *terra nullius*, thereby acknowledging native title to the land, it appeared that dramatic progress was possible. The history of dispossession and racism that haunted both black and white Australians might, it seemed, be conclusively redressed and transcended through national reconciliation. The painful story of settler colonialism appeared close to an end.

It has become increasingly apparent that any such hopes were utopian. It is vital that the many large and small gains effected through legal reform and shifting public attitudes not be discounted. But the 1995 change of government sparked off a racist backlash and a drift toward polarization on indigenous questions. During a 1997 conference intended to achieve some reconciliation, which took place just as a Royal Commission report on the assimilation-era practice of forcible adoption was released, Keating's successor John Howard felt unable to deliver an apology on behalf of the nation to Aboriginal Australians over the 'stolen children' issue. In New Zealand, too, the pattern has been one of two steps forward, two steps back. The way in which the Treaty has become central to much political and cultural rhetoric, and to the Waitangi Tribunal process itself, has given Maori claims much greater purchase than those of Aboriginal Australians within the nation and the process of compensatory justice. Yet the fiscal envelope (p. 238) could be seen to subvert the Tribunal process, or at least to diminish its effect, leaving many Maori in the marginal and disadvantaged situations they have long suffered.

This is not the place to review these current, rapidly changing developments. My point is simply that there is a huge mismatch between celebrations of indigenous culture in certain domains and continuing inequality and antagonism in others. Many politicians' statements, and many art works, suggest a movement toward a transcendence and a permanent resolution of the conflict between settler and indigenous populations. To describe these projections as utopian is not necessarily to find the politicians insincere or the artists naive. It is the business of those engaged in political debate to hold up ideals and to imagine desirable futures, and it is part of the work of art to represent conditions that should exist, but do not, as well as those that do exist, but should not. Yet if this history of the dialogue of the mutual invention and mutual rejection of first and last nations points toward any general thesis, it is this: that the intimate estrangement characteristic of the relations between native peoples and settlers is intractably persistent. The ebbs and flows in these relations exhibit dramatic change, but even as new things become possible, old tensions find new expression. Sovereignty and dispossession, inclusion and exclusion, affirmation and denigration: the realities of cultural and political life in these settler societies are always somewhere in the muddy and uncertain no-man's-land between these contradictory conditions.

The idea that Australia and New Zealand might constitute the 'last of the great pastoral nations' no longer makes sense. But if we know what we are stepping away from, we do not have a clear sense of what we are stepping toward. Some white settlers indulge their primitivism and invent a culture grounded in European, particularly Celtic, spirituality that mimics indigenous identity. This is a curiously recursive phenomenon: ideas of a mystical and archaic tribal condition, once imposed by Western rationalists upon indigenous cultures, are now reappropriated by envious neo-pagans. For others, the fixity and integrity of all national and indigenous cultures is superseded by the sheer energy of postmodern globalization. Diasporic aesthetics mobilize their own primitivist metaphor: that of the nomad, a figure marked by partial engagement with culture everywhere, and attachment nowhere. This vantage point at once rejects the idea of the nation and reinstates it, since it defines us all as hybrids, bearers of hyphenated identities: Italian-Australian,

Malaysian-New Zealander, Japanese-American, and so on. As we all assume this common form, our differences are reduced to content, to distinct Latvian, Japanese or Samoan ensembles of icons and traditions that are as equivalent in their difference as meals in a restaurant. The fact that some people, some cultures, might not understand their identities in these terms at all, or might, like Rover Thomas, image cyclones rather than cultures, is obscured. In all becoming nomads, we ironically dispossess the actual nomads and their descendants. The claims to place and history of Aboriginal Australians, Maori and Native Americans differ from those of diasporic hyphens, and are suppressed so long as the hybrid hyphen is taken as the norm.

There is perhaps another way of imagining all this, which does not depend on the extension of European notions of culture and nationhood to the colonized. One could, instead, attempt to imagine identity and history on the basis of the principles of exchange and sociality sustained by Oceanic peoples such as the Maori. In the indigenous Pacific world – if I can be allowed momentarily to speak very generically – there were no societies; there were only gifts and debts, relations of descent and marriage, only a dialectic between genealogy and alliance, locality and exchange. If social life is governed by exchange, identity is never a possession, never something people have, never framed by an entity such as a nation or a culture. It is rather a relation or a transaction. This could be expressed not by acknowledging two, or many, cultures in place of one nation, but instead by acknowledging each other's different situations, by giving and taking, by expressing our critical respect for gifts, works, performances and presentations. This is no utopian projection: we need to imagine ourselves through relations rather than identities not because this is the way things might or should be, but because this is the way they are and have been. Transactions are not necessarily mutually beneficial. In indigenous sociality, it is well known that the gift is often competitive, that people try to outdo one another. But exchange also entails many nuanced political statements, which may be mutually sustaining and affirmative, but are more often rivalrous. If the gift is rarely poisoned, it often carries at least a taint, a debt or a complication. The artistic exchanges that this book has charted have been of this kind. Sometimes they have been impositions, incommensurable expressions that co-existed in one land without really entering into meaningful exchange. Sometimes these exchanges have been highly imbalanced, and have caused injury and deprivation. Sometimes they have enabled treasures to be shared, things to be gained as well as lost. If there has been cultural gain, in the affirmation of indigenous identities, there has also been loss, in the generalization of the very idea of identity, which is modelled on the tired category of the nation. What we might gain from a relational understanding of history and sociality is exactly what we would lose: a sense of bounded and integrated community, of beginnings and endings, of first and last. Exchanges only ever produce new irresolutions, and leave us with business that remains unfinished.

Hence there aren't endings so much as points, like those in McCahon's progressions, where one must pause, or leave off. Somehow the most appropriate stopping-point is provided by Rover Thomas's great painting, *Roads Meeting* (1987, frontispiece). This may be seen simply as a descriptive work concerning a particular place that images the intersection of a bitumen and a gravel road and makes hands stand for stop signs. At the very least, it exemplifies the extent to which the arteries of a new order of travel and interconnection are incorporated into the Aboriginal imagining of place that is so richly and suggestively presented in Thomas's corpus. His world, I argued earlier, is not a 'globalized' one in which we are all different, yet somehow different in the same way. Thomas's work suggests not only that he occupies another kind of apparently anachronistic reality, but that we do too. Though we regard the frontier as the marker of an earlier stage of history, the conditions associated with that disorderly, shifting border appear to be with us still. We pursue a morally and politically uncertain traffic in cultural forms, whose characters are unstable, and indeed prone to corruption, as they move from one culture to another, between the statuses of high art and trinkets, between public, domestic, national and international frames. The paradox of a frontier situation is that closely connected things can remain utterly different.

This is why the conventional views of the interplay between modernism and 'primitive art' leave just too much out. Successive efforts to incorporate indigenous art into colonial culture and into colonial nationalities have generated extraordinary and unprecedented works of art on both sides. But those works are remarkable in part because they express something other than cultural synthesis. In the world in general, as well as in the art world, such efforts of incorporation ironically have revealed their own impossibility. They point toward the enduring character of cultural differences, and the persistence of awkward if not antagonistic intimacy. There has been no trend from one-sided exploitation toward two-sided exchange. Colonial histories were not so simple to start with. Nor do their current 'endings' promise reciprocity. For a resolution of the story we may need to wait for the next set of endings, or the ones that succeed those.

Notes and Sources

Author, title, and date and place of publication are given in full when a source is first cited; subsequent references give author's surname and short title only

Chapter One

Notes to pages 6–49

1. Robert Goldwater, *Primitivism in Modern Art*, Cambridge, Mass., Harvard University Press, 1966; William Rubin, ed., *'Primitivism' in 20th Century Art*, New York, The Museum of Modern Art, 1983.

2. See the debate in *Artforum* inaugurated by Thomas McEvilley's essay, 'Doctor, lawyer, Indian, Chief', *Artforum*, November 1984. A more positive alternative argument was presented by James Clifford, emphasizing that cultural influences and appropriations flowed in both directions, hence that the tribal world was as much a location of creative dynamism as the modernist West. J. Clifford, 'Histories of the Tribal and the Modern', *Art in America*, April 1985, pp. 164–77, republished as Chapter 9 in Clifford, *The Predicament of Culture*, Cambridge, Mass., Harvard University Press, 1988. For a recent survey, see Colin Rhodes, *Primitivism and Modern Art*, London and New York, Thames and Hudson, 1994.

3. Julius Lips, *The Savage Hits Back: Or, The White Man Through Native Eyes*, London, Lovat Dickson, 1937, a compendium of mainly African but also other tribal images of white men, was well ahead of its time in documenting this dimension of indigenous creativity.

4. See particularly Thomas McEvilley, *Fusion: West African Artists at the Venice Biennale*, New York, Museum for African Art/Munich, Prestel, 1993; N. Thomas, 'Cold Fusion', *American Anthropologist*, no. 91, 1996, pp. 9–16; and Annie E. Coombes, 'Inventing the "Postcolonial": Hybridity and Constituency in Contemporary Curating', *New Formations*, no. 18, pp. 39–52.

5. I draw here on Johannes Fabian's formulations in *Time and the Other: How Anthropology Makes its Object*, New York, Columbia University Press, 1983.

6. See, for example, Tim Bonyhady, *Images in Opposition: Australian landscape Painting, 1801–1890*, Melbourne, Oxford University Press, 1985; Wally Caruana, *Aboriginal Art*, London and New York, Thames and Hudson, 1993; and Bernard Smith and Terry Smith, *Australian Painting*, Melbourne, Oxford University Press, 1991. The most comprehensive resource for the period before 1870 is Joan Kerr, ed., *Dictionary of Australian Artists... to 1870*, Melbourne, Oxford University Press, 1992; more specialized studies on Aboriginal artists include Vivien Johnson's *Art of Clifford Possum Tjapaltjarri*, Sydney, Craftsman House, 1994, and *Michael Jagamara Nelson*, Sydney, Craftsman House, 1997. For New Zealand, see Leonard Bell, *Colonial Constructs: European Images of Maori 1840–1914*, Auckland, Auckland University Press, 1992; Michael Dunn, *A Concise History of New Zealand Painting*, Auckland, David Bateman, 1991; Sidney Moko Mead, ed., *Te Maori: Maori Art from New Zealand*, New York, Harry N. Abrams Inc. and The American Federation of Arts; Francis Pound, *The Space Between: Pakeha Use of Maori Motifs in Modernist New Zealand Art*, Auckland, Workshop Press, 1994; and Sandy Adsett and Witi Ihimaera, eds, *Mataora: The Living Face*, Auckland, David Bateman Books, 1996.

7. Francis Pound, *The Space Between: Pakeha Use of Maori Motifs in Modernist New Zealand Art*, Auckland, Workshop Press, 1994, p. 87.

8. Gordon H. Brown, *Colin McCahon: Artist*, 2nd ed., Auckland, Reed, 1993, p. 1.

9. Roger Eady, 'The visions of Alan Taylor', *Art New Zealand*, no. 49, 1988–9, p. 44. The comment on McCahon prefaces discussion of Alan Taylor's paintings relating to the nineteenth-century prophet Te Kooti.

10. Ngahuia Te Awekotuku, 'Ngahuia Te Awekotuku in Conversation with Priscilla Pitts and Elizabeth Eastmond', *Antic*, no. 1, 1986, p. 49.

11. The view of a prominent New Zealand critic and curator.

12. Conversely, one might point to the presence of Maori words on some earlier landscapes, such as the

Northland Panels (1958). This major work arguably encapsulates the contradictions of McCahon's sense of place: on the one hand, this is a 'landscape with too few lovers', one that breeds 'despair'; on the other hand, the native bird whose call seems to echo incompletely in the sixth panel is identified by its Maori name, which is inscribed with greater solidity than the painting's other texts. The latter look like captions, while the Tui are solid presences within the work.

13. David Collins, *An Account of the English Colony of New South Wales* [1798], Sydney, A.H. & A.W. Reed, 1975, vol. 1, p. 2.
14. Resistance not only to invasion but 'sociability' had arguably been manifest at the time of first contact; Cook reported in 1770 that when Lieutenant Hicks endeavoured to make gifts to the Aborigines around Botany Bay, 'all they seem'd to want was for us to be gone'. *The Journal of Captain James Cook*, J.C. Beaglehole, ed., Cambridge, Hakluyt Society, 1955, vol. 1, p. 306.
15. David Collins, *Account of the English Colony*, vol. 1, p. 4.
16. *Ibid.*, p. 487.
17. *Ibid.*, p. 32.
18. *Ibid.*, p. 4.
19. *Ibid.*, p. xxxix.
20. See generally Helen Topliss, *The Artists' Camps: 'Plein air' Painting in Australia*, Alphington, Victoria, Hedley Australia Publications, 1992.
21. It's important to note, however, that there has been much debate about the extent and nature of human-induced environmental change in Australia. See James L. Kohen, *Aboriginal Environmental Impacts*, Sydney, University of New South Wales Press, 1995; and Lesley Head, 'Both Ends of the Candle? Discerning Human Impact on the Vegetation', *Australian Archaeology*, 39, 1994, pp. 82–6. Head among others has also challenged the claims of Tim Flannery's bestseller, *The Future Eaters: An Ecological History of the Australasian Lands and People*, Chatswood, NSW, Reed, 1994; see her article, 'Meganesian Barbeque', *Meanjin*, vol. 54, no. 4, 1995, pp. 702–9,
22. See particularly Renato Rosaldo, 'Imperialist Nostalgia', *Representations*, 26, 1989, pp. 107–22.
23. Alan Moorhead, *The Fatal Impact: An Account of the Invasion of the South Pacific, 1767–1840*, London, H. Hamilton, 1966, p. 95.
24. Ian Cameron, *Lost Paradise: The Exploration of the Pacific*, London, Century, 1987, p. 225.
25. See Stephen Eisenman, *Gauguin's Skirt*, London and New York, Thames and Hudson, 1997.
26. See Roger Neich, 'Historical Change in Rotorua Ngati

Tarawhai Woodcarving Art', MA thesis, Victoria University, Wellington; Neich, 'The Veil of Orthodoxy: Rotorua Ngati Tarawhai Woodcarving in a Changing Context', in S.M. Mead and Bernie Kernot, eds, *Art and Artists of Oceania*, Palmerston North, Dunmore Press, 1983.
27. Sydney F. Hoben, 'Some Examples of Maori Art', *Art and Architecture*, no. 2, 1905, pp. 70–80.
28. I draw loosely on Michael Taussig's notion of history as sorcery. See his book, *Shamanism, Colonialism, and the Wild Man: A Study in Terror and Healing*, Chicago, University of Chicago Press, 1987.

Chapter Two

Notes to pages 50–93

1. My own understanding of these broader questions draws particularly on Bernard Smith, *European Vision and the South Pacific*, 2nd ed., New Haven, Yale University Press, 1985; Michael Rosenthal, *British Landscape Painting*, Oxford, Phaidon, 1982; John Barrell, *The Dark Side of the Landscape*, Cambridge, Cambridge University Press, 1980; and W.J.T. Mitchell, ed., *Landscape and Power*, Chicago, University of Chicago Press, 1994.
2. See generally Jocelyn Hackforth-Jones, *Augustus Earle: Travel Artist*, Canberra, National Library of Australia, 1980. Earle also spent time in Europe and North America. Unfortunately, work arising from these travels is not known.
3. George French Angas, *Savage Life and Scenes in Australia and New Zealand*, London, Smith, Elder & Co., 1847, vol. 1, pp. 320, 329–30.
4. Augustus Earle, *A Narrative of a Nine Months' Residence in New Zealand*, London, Longman, 1832, pp. 21, 138; cf. pp. 10, 22, 65 and similarly p. 111 for observations on the rich ornamentation of canoes and the quality of carving. Although the 'ingenuity' of Maori sculpture and design was frequently noted, this suggestion that the products might be classed among the 'fine arts' is unusual.
5. *Ibid.*, p. 65, cf. p. 161.
6. *Ibid.*, pp. 37–8.
7. This work is discussed in complementary terms by W.J.T. Mitchell, 'Imperial Landscape', in Mitchell, ed., *Landscape and Power*, pp. 24–7.
8. See, for instance, the *Wye Matte Waterfall* (1827–8, National Library of Australia), and the lithographs 'Village of Parkuni', 'Kororadika Beach' and 'Native Village and Cowdie Forest' in Earle's *Sketches Illustrative of the Native Inhabitants and Islands of New Zealand*, London, R. Martin & Co., 1838.

9. Earle, *Narrative*, p. 38.
10. *Ibid.*, pp. 40, 61.
11. [Untitled review of Earle's *Narrative*], *Quarterly Review*, no. 48, 1832, p. 133.
12. Earle, *Narrative*, p. 111.
13. Cf. Asa Briggs, *Age of Improvement*, London, Longman, 1953.
14. Earle, *Narrative*, p. 133.
15. For general background, see J.M.R. Owens, 'New Zealand Before Annexation', in W.H. Oliver, ed., *The Oxford History of New Zealand*, Wellington, Oxford University Press, 1981, pp. 50–3.
16. Some of Earle's Aboriginal portraits are more sympathetic, as has been pointed out with respect to *Desmond, a New South Wales Chief* (NK 12/61, fig. 77 in Hackforth-Jones, *Augustus Earle*). It is notable, however, that Desmond looks sideways toward some indefinite point in the distance, and thus does not challenge or engage the viewer in the way that the Aboriginal men depicted by the Port Jackson painter, for instance, do. The attitude of fixation upon a remote object already implied loss and dispossession in some anti-slavery works; if Earle is unlikely to have had these in mind, he seems to have adopted a similar technique to indicate melancholy. The *Man* and *Woman of New South Wales* (figs 69 and 70 in Hackforth-Jones, *Augustus Earle*) are certainly more cheerful, as are the situated figures of Aboriginal men before their shelters (figs 72 and 74).
17. See J. Russell Harper, *Paul Kane's Frontier*, Austin, University of Texas Press for the Amon Carter Museum and the National Gallery of Canada, 1971.
18. For an insightful survey, see Frances K. Pohl, 'Old World, New World: The Encounter of Cultures on the American Frontier', in Stephen Eisenman et al., *Nineteenth Century Art: A Critical History*, London and New York, Thames and Hudson, 1994.
19. Tim Bonyhady, *Images in Opposition: Australian Landscape Painting 1801–1890*, Melbourne, Oxford University Press, 1985, p. 8; Hackforth-Jones, *Augustus Earle*, p. 114.
20. The sketches were presumably similar to the *Bay of Islands, New Zealand* (NK 12/75, plate 118 in Hackforth-Jones, *Augustus Earle*) and others such as her plates 108 and 112. Given that the particular drawings on which the panorama was based were probably not returned to Earle, it is not surprising that no sections of the panorama correspond obviously with the extant watercolour collection, which was held by his descendants.
21. For the background to the panorama and the dimensions, see Gordon Bull, 'Taking Place: Panorama and Panopticon in the Colonisation of New South Wales', *Australian Journal of Art*, 12, 1994–5, pp. 78–81. The panorama after Earle appears to have been displayed in Burford's upper room, the smaller of the two.
22. Robert Burford, *Description of a View of the Bay of Islands, New Zealand, Now Exhibiting at the Panorama, Leicester Square, Painted by the Proprietor, Robert Burford, from Drawings taken by Augustus Earle, Esq.*, London, G. Nichols, 1838, p. 4.
23. *Ibid.*, pp. 5, 11 (transposed).
24. See Hilary Ericksen, 'Unworldly Places: Myth, Memory and the Pink and White Terraces', MA thesis, University of Melbourne, 1997.
25. Bonyhady, *Images in Opposition*, p. 25.
26. John McPhee, *The Art of John Glover*, Melbourne, Macmillan, 1980, p. 38; Ian McLean, 'Your Own Land is the Best: The Limits of Redemption in Australian Colonial Art', *Australian Journal of Art*, 12, 1994–5, p. 129.
27. Lyndall Ryan, *The Aboriginal Tasmanians*, Brisbane, University of Queensland Press, 1981, especially chapters 8 and 9; for a wide-ranging reappraisal of the mission, see Henry Reynolds, *Fate of a Free People*, Ringwood, Penguin, 1995, especially chapter 5.
28. Joan Kerr, 'Somersaults in the Antipodes', *Australian Journal of Art*, 11, 1993, pp. 22–3.
29. Quoted in McPhee, *The Art of John Glover*, p. 30.
30. Glover's title label for *Mills Plains* may have read in part 'Natives to show their mode of enjoying the country formerly…', *ibid.*, p. 91.
31. McLean, 'Your Own Land is Best', p. 128.
32. Leo Schofield, 'A Private Arcadia', *Sydney Morning Herald*, 6 January 1995.
33. Marjorie Tipping, *An Artist in the Goldfields: The Diary of Eugène von Guérard*, Melbourne, Currey O'Neil, 1982, p. 77. The painting has also been published as *The Barwon River, Geelong*, which does not seem illuminating. On the confusion concerning the titles of this work and *Australian Aborigines in Pursuit of Their Enemies* (1854) see Bonyhady, *Images in Opposition*, p. 161, notes 54 and 56.
34. Candice Bruce, *Eugen von Guérard*, Canberra, Australian Gallery Directors' Council/Australian National Gallery, 1980, p. 33.
35. Edward M. Curr, *Recollections of Squatting in Victoria*, Melbourne, George Robertson, 1883, p. 170.
36. Bonyhady, *Images in Opposition*, p. 42, quoting Charles Daley, 'Angus McMillan', *Victorian Historical Magazine*, 1927, p. 151.
37. *Ibid.*, quoting James Bonwick, *Western Victoria: Its Geography, Geology and Social Condition*, Melbourne, Heinemann, 1970, pp. 31, 43.

38. A typical height to width ratio in von Guérard's wilderness and homestead landscapes is about 7:10. Each of the Bushy Park canvases is about 4:10 or 2:10 together.

39. See von Guérard's 'Australian sketchbooks', Dixson Library, Sydney, DGB16, vol. 11, ff. 7, 37 (incorrectly cited as vol. 2 in the otherwise extremely useful catalogue by Candice Bruce et al., *Eugen von Guérard, 1811–1901: A German Romantic in the Antipodes*, Martinborough and Sydney, Alister Taylor, 1982).

40. One sketch (DGB f. 5) depicts Aboriginal men in a canoe at Bushy Park; the details of the paddles suggest a level of ethnographic interest not frequently encountered in von Guérard's sketches. I am most grateful to Mary Eagle for information concerning John King and the related work, *Mr John King's Station*, 1861 (private collection, Melbourne), see Bruce et al., *Eugen von Guérard*, p. 217.

41. Henry Reynolds, *The Other Side of the Frontier*, pp. 128–38.

42. Edward J. Eyre, *Journals of Expeditions of Discovery*, London, 1845, vol. I, f. 167; quoted in Henry Reynolds, *Dispossession: Black Australians and White Invaders*, Sydney, Allen and Unwin, 1989, p. 29.

43. Arthur W. Jose, *Australasia, the Commonwealth, and New Zealand*, London, Dent, 1901, p. 136.

44. The phrase is Edward Curr's, *Recollections*, p. 87.

45. Eugen von Guérard, 'Australian sketchbooks', DGB16, vol. 3, ff. 29, 31 [a], [b].

46. Hugh Jamieson to Bishop Perry, in response to questions about the living conditions of Murray-Darling Aboriginal people, 10 October 1853, in Thomas Francis Bride, *Letters from Victorian Pioneers*, ed. C.E. Sayers, Melbourne, Heinemann, 1969, p. 380.

47. Most notably through the Australian National Travel Association's magazine, *Walkabout*, published from 1934.

48. Jamieson to Perry, pp. 379–80.

49. *Bushy Park* itself was acquired by Rex Nan Kivell and was part of his bequest to the Commonwealth of Australia. It was exhibited, possibly for the first time, as part of the 1956 Arts Festival of the (Melbourne) Olympic Games.

50. *Argus*, 1 February 1855, p. 5, quoted in Bruce et al., *Eugen von Guérard*, p. 185.

51. *Age*, 8 December 1857, p. 5, quoted in Bruce et al., *Eugen von Guérard*, p. 195.

52. *Illustrated Journal of Australasia*, January 1858, pp. 35–6, quoted in Bruce et al., *Eugen von Guérard*, p. 199.

53. *Argus*, 29 December 1862, p. 5, quoted in Bruce et al., *Eugen von Guérard*, p. 221, transposed.

54. It is notable in this context that von Guérard's *Weatherboard Falls* (discussed below), a view in the Blue Mountains of New South Wales, was commended as an appropriate foundational acquisition for the new public gallery then mooted in Victoria; *Argus*, 29 December 1862, quoted in Bruce et al., *Eugen von Guérard*, p. 222.

55. For New Zealand, see especially Gordon Brown and Hamish Keith, *An Introduction to New Zealand Painting*, Auckland, Collins, 1969. This line of argument has been ably documented and contested by Francis Pound, for example, 'The Words and the Art: New Zealand Art Criticism, *c.* 1950–1990', in Mary Barr, ed., *Headlands: Thinking Through New Zealand Art*, Sydney, Museum of Contemporary Art, 1992, pp. 185–202.

56. *The Ballarat Miner*, 14 August 1863, p. 5, quoted in Bruce et al., *Eugen von Guérard*, p. 224.

57. *Illustrated Australian Mail*, 22 February 1862, quoted in Bruce et al., *Eugen von Guérard*, p. 209. Quoted lines of verse from Alfred Tennyson's 'Mort D'Arthur', lines 200–1.

58. *Otago Witness*, 2 December 1865, quoted in Melvin N. Day, *Nicholas Chevalier: Artist*, Wellington, Millwood, 1981, p. 97.

59. *Otago Witness*, 28 July 1866, quoted in Day, *Nicholas Chevalier*, pp. 98–9.

60. Bonyhady, *Images in Opposition*, p. 2.

61. Bernard Smith, *Australian Painting 1788–1970*, 2nd edition, Melbourne, Oxford University Press, 1971, p. 59.

62. *Australasian*, 17 November 1866, misquoted in Day, *Nicholas Chevalier*, p. 100.

63. The most significant exception is *Stony Rises, Lake Corangamite* (1857, illustrated in Bonyhady, *Images in Opposition*, plate 5). This evening scene can be interpreted as a melancholy work, but hardly as positively gloomy as some the Glover paintings discussed above.

64. The associated sketches (DGB 16, vol. 9, ff. 14–17; 'Head of the Grose', DG XV 1B/1, Dixson Library, State Library of New South Wales) include no human figures.

65. *Argus*, 29 December 1862, p. 5, quoted in Bruce et al., *Eugen von Guérard*, p. 221.

66. Bonyhady, *Images in Opposition*, p. 102.

67. *Eugen von Guérard's Australian Landscapes*, Melbourne, Hamel and Ferguson, 1857–8, text accompanying plate VII.

68. *Ibid.*, text accompanying plate III.

69. *Souvenir Views of Melbourne and Victorian Scenery by Eminent Artists*, Melbourne, Charles Troedels,

c. 1865, plates 9 and 10. A more jarring set of images appears in a rarer collection of *Views of Australia, c.* 1865 (NLA pictorial shelves, 504); this includes both *The Buffalo Mountains [sic]... (From the Prize Painting by N. Chevalier)* and a stark depiction of a distribution of blankets to Aborigines in Queensland.

70. Curr, *Recollections of Squatting*, p. 425.
71. Smith, *Australian Painting*, p. 84.
72. See particularly Bernard Smith, *Place, Taste and Tradition; Australian Painting*, rev. 2nd ed., Melbourne, Oxford University Press, 1979, chapter 5; Bonyhady, *Images in Opposition*, chapter 8; Leigh Astbury, *City Bushmen: The Heidelberg School and Rural Mythology*, Melbourne, Oxford University Press, 1985; and Jane Clark and Bridget Whitelaw, *Golden Summers: Heidelberg and Beyond*, Melbourne, International Cultural Corporation, 1986. I have found Ian Burn's 1980 article, 'Beating about the Bush', very helpful, reprinted in Ian Burn, *Dialogue: Writings in Art History*, Sydney, Allen and Unwin, 1991; see also his *National Life and Landscape*, Sydney, Bay Books, 1991.
73. For example, Smith, *Australian Painting*, p. 82. I nevertheless often hear this view reiterated in the conversation of viewers of Heidelberg paintings in public institutions, guides' talks, and so on.
74. Burn, 'Beating about the Bush', pp. 21–3.
75. Helen Topliss, *Tom Roberts 1856–1931: A Catalogue Raisonné*, Melbourne, Oxford University Press, 1985, pp. 19–20, cat. nos 156, 176, 177, 179, 180, 183, 229–31. Topliss mentions three further untraced portraits of Murray Islanders. On Roberts' interest in Glover, see McPhee, *The Art of John Glover*, p. 51.
76. Topliss, *Tom Roberts*, cat. no. 156, p. 116; *Sydney Morning Herald*, 2 September 1892, quoted in cat. no. 183, p. 123.

Chapter Three

Notes to pages 94–125

1. Francis Adams, *The Australians: A Social Sketch*, London, T. Fisher Unwin, 1893, p. 84.
2. Margaret Preston, 'Aboriginal Art', *Art in Australia*, 1 June 1941, p. 46.
3. J.C. Beaglehole, ed., *The Endeavour Journal of Joseph Banks, 1768–1771*, Sydney, Angus & Robertson/Public Library of NSW, 1962, vol. II, p. 24. It is not clear now which 'two styles' Banks could have had in mind.
4. Owen Jones, *The Grammar of Ornament*, London, Day & Son, 1856, pp. 13–17, plates 1–3. Jones

notes that voyagers such as Cook 'repeatedly' and 'constantly' commented upon the 'taste and ingenuity' of Pacific islanders. His inclusion of Polynesian art in a global narrative was anticipated by Sir James Hall, whose 1813 *Essay on the Origins, History and Principles of Gothic Architecture* (London) cursorily noted 'Tahitian' canoe and adze design among other ornamental traditions that imitated nature.

5. Roger Neich, 'The Veil of Orthodoxy: Rotorua Ngati Tarawhai Woodcarving in a Changing Context', in *Art and Artists of Oceania*, Sidney M. Mead and Bernie Kernot, eds, Palmerston North, Dunmore Press, 1983, p. 254.
6. Roger Neich, *Painted Histories: Early Maori Figurative Painting*, Auckland, Auckland University Press, 1993, pp. 19–21 (on the Maori ranking of painting below carving); p. 29ff. (on the neglect of *kowhaiwhai* in Maori art studies).
7. Another New Zealand composer, Douglas Lilburn, has recently suggested that Hill was not 'really a nationalistic composer in the older meaning of the term—his interest in Maori music seems to have been transient, not deeply rooted in his psyche' (quoted in John Mansfield Thomson, *A Distant Music: The Life and Times of Alfred Hill*, Auckland, Oxford University Press, 1980, p. ix). This may or may not be valid as an account of Hill's creativity, but neglects the point that the enthusiasm with which his work was generally received in New Zealand responded particularly to its adaptation of indigenous legends and subjects; see Thomson, pp. 60–3, 72–7.
8. John Mansfield Thomson, *The Oxford History of New Zealand Music*, Auckland, Oxford University Press, 1991, pp. 217–19. For a brief but interesting comment on *Rewi's Last Stand* by the Maori director Merata Mita, see her essay, 'The Soul and the Image', in Jonathan Dennis and Jan Bieringa, eds, *Film in Aotearoa New Zealand*, Wellington, Victoria University Press, 1992, p. 43. The now-standard account of the wars is James Belich's highly readable *The New Zealand Wars and the Victorian Interpretation of Racial Conflict*, Auckland, Auckland University Press, 1986.
9. See entry under 'Lulu Shorter' in Joan Kerr, ed., *Heritage: the National Women's Art Book*, Roseville, New South Wales, Craftsman House/Art and Australia, 1995, p. 277 and plate 466.
10. Anyone now asking after pieces from this set in New Zealand shops is likely to be put on a waiting list; several dealers claimed that interest in this material, and in some considerably more kitsch pictorial treatments of Maori warriors and scenes, had

mounted steadily over the last decade, one attributing its allure to a 'revival of national spirit'. The example illustrated here (fig. 67) is from the 'Maori Art Ware'; 'Kia Ora Ware' had been launched slightly earlier, at the 1906 Christchurch International Exhibition, and was distinguished by the use in relief of tiki figures, tattooed faces, and the carving features that were reproduced with diminished emphasis in the 'Maori Art Ware'. For brief discussion, see Jennifer Quérée, *Royal Doulton: Illustrated Treasures from New Zealand and Australia*, Christchurch, Canterbury Museum, 1993, pp. 72–3.

11. A good deal might be said about the more sporadic but nevertheless significant appropriations of Maori design in architecture that appear to have been most in vogue in the 1930s. *Kowhaiwhai* appear around the ceiling in at least one provincial town hall, and carved faces appear occasionally on houses. More recently, forms associated with meeting-houses have been widely reintroduced into airports, tourist centres, museums, and some educational institutions and public buildings.

12. Effectiveness in war is cited as the basis for a widespread belief in Maori nobility as early as 1889 by a cynical writer who argued for a much harsher assessment: though conceding the 'undeniable courage' of the Maori, Phil Robinson deplored their arts, folklore, standards of cleanliness, and so on, and presented a wildly exaggerated picture of cannibalism; 'The Maori', *Centennial Magazine*, vol. 1, no. 11, 1889, pp. 753–6. The idea that Maori were treated better than Aborigines because of the former's propensity for military resistance was frequently aired by Australian schoolteachers, at least between the 1950s and 1970s, but was also reiterated by scholars; see, for example, C.D. Rowley's influential survey, *The Destruction of Aboriginal Society*, Harmondsworth, Penguin, 1972, pp. 15, 23.

13. For the best general accounts, see Henry Reynolds, *The Other Side of the Frontier*, Ringwood, Penguin, 1982, and *Frontier: Aborigines, Settlers, and Land*, Sydney, Allen and Unwin, 1987.

14. Edward Tregear, *The Maori Race*, Wanganui, A.D. Willis, 1926, pp. 6–7. On Tregear's attitudes, see K.R. Howe, *Singer in a Songless Land: A Life of Edward Tregear, 1846–1931*, Auckland, Auckland University Press, 1991.

15. The censorious contrast of Rome and not-Rome, turning upon German valour and chastity, was generally understood as the principal rhetorical point of Tacitus's essay; see, for example, Edward Gibbon, *The Decline and Fall of the Roman Empire*,

ed. David Womersley, London, Allen Lane, 1994, vol. 1, p. 243 – which of course influenced many subsequent readers.

16. Simon Schama, *Landscape and Memory*, London, HarperCollins, 1995, pp. 76–86.

17. Tregear, *The Aryan Maori*, Wellington, Government Printer, 1885, pp. 31, 35.

18. Tregear, *The Aryan Maori*, p. 105. The diffusionist literature is incisively surveyed by M.P.K. Sorrenson in *Maori Origins and Migrations: The Genesis of Some Pakeha Myths and Legends*, Auckland, Auckland University Press, 1979. Not too much weight should be placed upon the fact that Tregear's book was issued by the Government Printer: though significant in so far as it was consistent with an official effort to promote Maori ethnology – a much larger work, John White's *Ancient History of the Maori* also went through the press between 1887 and 1891 – it does not seem that Tregear's somewhat extreme speculations received any explicit official endorsement. For further information, see Howe, *Singer in a Songless Land*, pp. 39–60.

19. Sorrenson, *Maori Origins and Migrations*, p. 30. Howe rejects the suggestion that this passage provides a charter for racial amalgamation on the grounds that Tregear was 'notably disinterested in contemporary race relations issues' and never otherwise advocated assimilation or amalgamation (Howe, *Singer in a Songless Land*, p. 209). This seems too literal; whether or not Tregear advocated a specific policy of racial admixture, he evidently sought to graft a white settler history on to indigenous tradition, and the two were certainly rendered more compatible by an original shared ancestry. As Howe notes, Tregear hoped that his ethnological studies would one day be valued 'in New Zealand as sacredly as the modern American treasures relics of those who "came over in the Mayflower"' (*Singer in a Songless Land*, p. 11). It is suggestive, moreover, that in other texts of the period the Aryan link, and imagined prior affinities between Britain and New Zealand, were more explicitly drawn into nationalist argument. See, for example, J.C. Firth, *Nation Making: A Story of New Zealand: Savagism v. Civilization*, London, Longman, Green & Co., 1890, pp. v–vi, 6–8.

20. Quoted in Hamilton, *Maori Art*, p. 120.

21. Johannes C. Andersen, *Maori Life in Ao-tea*, Christchurch, Whitcombe and Tombs, n.d. [c. 1907], p. xi. The volume itself consists of nearly seven hundred pages of imaginatively adapted folklore, much of it drawn from earlier writers such as John White.

22. Patrick Wolfe, 'Nation and MiscegeNation: Discursive Continuity in the Post-Mabo Era', *Social Analysis*, 36, 1994, p. 94.
23. Frontispiece illustrating work by Lucien Henry, *Centennial Review*, vol. 2, no. 3, 1889.
24. Eirene Mort, 'Arts and crafts and Australian design', *Art and Architecture*, vol. 4, no. 2, 1907, 62–5; 'An Australian artist-craftsman' (editorial) *Art and Architecture*, vol. 4, no. 3, 1907, 113–15. The 'artist-craftsman' discussed was George Taylor, who had written 'A Plea for National Character in Architectural Decoration' in the inaugural volume of the same journal, then titled *Journal of the Institute of Architects*, 1, 1904, pp. 29–32; the arguments presented were highly generalized but it appeared that, in the Australian case, the expression of national character entailed recourse to what was novel and suggestive in 'Nature in Australia'. For further information on Mort, see Kerr, ed., *Heritage*, pp. 410–11.
25. It is suggestive that Henry Lawson was urged by another writer, his younger contemporary Mary Gilmore, to take up the Aborigines in his stories; he responded that he was unable to do so, fearing that any effort to romanticize or heroize them could only be ridiculous. The implication is that the fiction of the period was simply unable to accommodate Aboriginal experience. See Gilmore, quoted in J.J. Healey, *Literature and the Aborigine in Australia*, St Lucia, Queensland, University of Queensland Press, 1978, p. 179. Katharine Susannah Pritchard's *Coonardoo*, 1929, has been cited, with some justification, as the first Australian novel to deal with Aborigines as complex and fully human characters.
26. A.W. Grieg, 'Aboriginal Art', *The Lone Hand*, 1 May 1909, p. 46.
27. As late as 1949, it was taken as an accepted fact that the Wandjina paintings were 'obviously not the work of Aborigines'; Herbert Badham, *A Study of Australian Art*, Sydney, Currawong Publishing, 1949, pp. 4, 7. Speculations of this kind may be traced back to George Grey's early illustration of a Wandjina in *Expeditions in Western Australia, 1837–1839*, London, T. & W. Boon, 1841, vol. 1, facing p. 202.
28. D.J. Mulvaney and J.H. Calaby, *'So Much that is New': Baldwin Spencer 1860–1929*, Melbourne, Melbourne University Press, 1985, pp. 303–4.
29. *Ibid.*, quoted p. 326.
30. The printmaker, painter and art educator Frances Derham did however later cite Spencer's lecture as a point of inspiration; she began to make prints with Aboriginal motifs, some derived from Spencer's publications, in the mid-1920s. See entries by Barbara Piscitelli in Kerr, ed., *Heritage*, pp. 284–5, 342 and plate 479.
31. 'Arts for Crafts: Aboriginal Art Artfully applied', *The Home*, 1 December 1924, pp. 30–1.
32. 'The Indigenous Art of Australia', *Art in Australia*, March 1925.
33. *Sunday Pictorial* (Sydney), 6 April 1930, p. 22.
34. 'Arts for Crafts', p. 31.
35. For references to some of the artists and a valuable review of the context, see Grace Cochrane, *The Crafts Movement in Australia: A History*, Kensington, University of New South Wales Press, 1992, pp. 48, 50, 60, 88–9, 136–8; most of the white 'Aboriginal' art she discusses dates from the 1950s and '60s.
36. 'At last – Australian Designed Fabrics', *Australia: National Journal*, 1 December 1940, pp. 26–8.
37. Margaret Preston, 'Paintings in Arnhem Land', *Art in Australia*, 25 November 1940, pp. 61, 63; cf. 'Aboriginal Art', *Art in Australia*, 1 June 1941, p. 46; 'Aboriginal Art of Australia', *Art of Australia* (1941 catalogue of an exhibition toured to the United States by the Carnegie Corporation), pp. 16–17.
38. Diana Nemiroff, 'Modernism, Nationalism, and Beyond', in *Land, Spirit, Power: First Nations at the National Gallery of Canada*, Ottawa, National Gallery of Canada, 1992, pp. 20–5. A major exhibition contemporary with the Sydney show, *Indian Art of the United States*, at the Museum of Modern Art in 1941, proceeded from the notion that the values of indigenous culture and art were relevant to the American future, but included only the indigenous work, and hence featured no argument that American art needed to draw on native designs or styles.
39. Ernest Wunderlich to A.B. Walkom, 7 March 1941, file 1941/123, Archives, Australian Museum, Sydney.
40. F.D. McCarthy, 'Australian Aboriginal Art and its Application', *Australian Museum Magazine*, 1 September 1941, pp. 355–60; *Exhibition of Australian Aboriginal Art and its Application*, exhib. cat., Sydney, 1941. The lecturers included McCarthy and Preston and several well-known anthropologists from the University of Sydney, A.P. Elkin, Phyllis Kaberry and Ian Hogbin.
41. McCarthy, 'Australian Aboriginal Art', pp. 355–6.
42. 'Abo. Art', *Australia: National Journal*, 1 September 1941, p. 76.
43. 'Aboriginal Art', *Sydney Morning Herald*, 12 August 1941. Though the writer proceeded to commend some of the fabric and pottery, the overall adjudication was clearly mixed.

Chapter Four

Notes to pages 126–163

1. Frederick McCubbin, 'Some Remarks on the History of Australian Art' [1916], in Bernard Smith, ed., *Documents on Art and Taste in Australia*, Melbourne, Oxford University Press, 1975, pp. 270, 275.

2. Margaret Preston in a radio interview, *c.* 1947, quoted in Roger Butler, *The Prints of Margaret Preston*, Canberra/Melbourne, Australian National Gallery and Oxford University Press, 1987, p. 41; see also Humphrey McQueen, *The Black Swan of Trespass*, Sydney, Alternative Publishing Cooperative, 1979, p. 154.

3. *Art of Australia* (1941 catalogue of an exhibition toured to the United States by the Carnegie Corporation), p. 28.

4. See, for example, Ada Rainey, 'Australian Art at National Gallery', *Washington Post*, 5 October 1941; Butler, *The Prints of Margaret Preston*, p. 22.

5. The layout is unclear and implies that Preston only wrote the first section of the text, which dealt with Aboriginal art. Acknowledgment is made to William Moore's *The Story of Australian Art*, Sydney, Angus and Robertson, 1934, for what follows, but the style is typical of Preston's directness. The passage immediately preceding that quoted endorses the work of Donald Friend, said to have been inspired by indigenous art in Nigeria, in terms consistent with Preston's thinking.

6. The support of Sydney Ure Smith, who at one time or another published *Art in Australia, The Home* and *Australia: National Journal*, was not only crucial to the promotion of Preston's art, but no less vital to her writing career: about fifty of the sixty or so essays she published appeared in one or other of his journals. See Nancy D.H. Underhill, *Making Australian Art, 1916–49: Sydney Ure Smith, Patron and Publisher*, Melbourne, Oxford University Press, 1991.

7. But see Roger Butler, *The Prints of Margaret Preston*, for the fullest biographical discussion; Ian North, ed., *The Art of Margaret Preston*, Adelaide, Art Gallery Board of South Australia, 1980; McQueen, *The Black Swan of Trespass*; and Elizabeth Butel, *Margaret Preston: The Art of Constant Rearrangement*, Ringwood, Victoria, Penguin, 1985.

8. 'Society of Artists: The Modern Influence', *Daily Telegraph*, 9 September 1927.

9. Margaret Preston, 'The Indigenous Art of Australia', *Art in Australia*, March 1925, unpag.

10. See, for example, Daniel Miller, *Material Culture and Mass Consumption*, Oxford, Basil Blackwell, 1987; Arjun Appadurai, ed., *The Social Life of Things: Commodities in Cultural Perspective*, Cambridge, Cambridge University Press, 1986.

11. For the identification of the vase and Reynell, see Roger Butler, *The Prints of Margaret Preston*, pp. 8–12, 149.

12. Introduced northern hemisphere flowers are typically conspicuous in Preston's earlier still lifes (such as *Summer*, 1915, AGNSW). She turned toward native plants fairly abruptly in about 1925, exotics appearing only occasionally after 1930.

13. P.R. Stephenson, *The Foundations of Culture in Australia: An Essay Toward National Self-Respect*, Gordon, NSW, W.J. Miles, 1936, pp. 11, 12.

14. McQueen, *The Black Swan of Trespass*, pp. 126–9.

15. Preston, in Ure Smith, ed., *Margaret Preston's Monotypes*, Sydney Sydney, Ure Smith, 1949, p. 11.

16. Preston, in Smith, ed., *Margaret Preston's Monotypes*, caption to plate 5.

17. On Counihan, see Bernard Smith, *Noel Counihan: Artist and Revolutionary*, Melbourne, Oxford University Press, 1993; paintings with Aboriginal subjects include *Aboriginal Family Outside Swan Hill*, 1960, reproduced in Max Dimmack, *Noel Counihan*, Melbourne, Melbourne University Press, 1974. On Bergner, see Nissim Aloni and Rodi Bineth-Perry, *Yosl Bergner: Paintings 1938–1980*, Jerusalem, Ketter Publishing House, 1981, especially pp. 24–5, 206–7. On Mahood, see entry by Peter Timms and Joan Kerr in Joan Kerr, ed., *Heritage: The National Women's Art Book*, Sydney, Craftsman House, 1995, pp. 401–2.

18. See Colin Rhodes, *Primitivism and Modern Art*, London and New York, Thames and Hudson, 1994, pp. 84–6, and J. Lloyd, *German Expressionism: Primitivism and Modernity*, New Haven, Yale University Press, 1991.

19. Generalized titles not only reflect, but arguably produce, a delocalization of reference. Even when a modernist work is closely based on an indigenous source, as is Modigliani's *c.* 1911 *Head of a Woman* (on an Ivory Coast mask, in this case), his title suggests universality. See Robert Goldwater, *Primitivism in Modern Art*, Cambridge, Mass., Harvard University Press, 1966, figs 54 and 55.

20. The caption to the plate itself noted that it was 'on the principle of some of the early Italian painting, in which primitive landscapes are painted in conjunction with figures in the clothes of the painter's own period.' Preston, in *Margaret Preston's Monotypes*, p. 15, and caption to plate 16.

21. Butel, *Margaret Preston*, p. 53.

22. Ann Stephen, 'Margaret Preston's second coming', *Art Network*, no. 2, 1980, pp. 14–15.

23. On the nature and politics of appropriation, which I discuss more extensively below, see the valuable anthologies, Bruce Ziff and Pratima V. Rao, eds, *Borrowed Power: Essays on Cultural Appropriation*, New Brunswick, New Jersey, Rutgers University Press, 1997 (which emphasizes North American and particularly Canadian examples), and Rex Butler, ed., *What is Appropriation?*, Sydney, Power Publications, 1996 (concerned with Australia).

24. *Bulletin*, 1 April 1942.

25. *Bulletin*, 17 August 1949.

26. Herbert Badham, *A Study of Australian Art*, Sydney, Currawong Press, 1949, pp. 79–80.

27. *Ibid.*, p. 80.

28. Leonard Bell, 'Putting the record straight: Gordon Walters', *Art New Zealand*, no. 27, 1983, pp. 42–5; Ngahuia Te Awekotuku, interview, *Antic*, no. 1, 1986, pp. 50–2; Rangihiroa Panoho, 'Maori: At the Centre, on the Margins', in Mary Barr, ed., *Headlands: Thinking Through New Zealand Art*, Sydney, Museum of Contemporary Art, 1992, pp. 123–33.

29. It is important to stress that there is much debate about these issues within indigenous milieux. The range of questions and debates cannot be fully reviewed here, but see Ziff and Rao, eds, *Borrowed Power*, and Butler, ed., *What is Appropriation?*, for more extensive discussion.

30. Francis Pound, 'The Words and the Art: New Zealand Art Criticism, *c.* 1950–*c.* 1990', in Barr, ed., *Headlands*, p. 187. See also Pound's 'Walters and the canon', in James Ross and Laurence Simmons, eds, *Gordon Walters: Order and Intuition*, Auckland, privately published, 1989.

31. Gordon Walters, undated notes, MS 90/8, Archives, Museum of New Zealand Te Papa Tongarewa, Wellington.

32. Among positive early notices, see 'Between Op and Geometry', *New Zealand Herald*, 11 March 1966; 'One Man Op Art Show', *Dominion*, 9 May 1969; 'Modern Art Exhibition', 14 May 1969; Hamish Keith, 'Painting in the Sixties', *New Zealand Listener*, 11 July 1969; Keith, *Dominion*, 30 June 1970; and 'Top Painter Exhibiting at Festival', *New Zealand Herald*, 8 May 1972.

33. New Vision Gallery, catalogue brochure for Gordon Walters' 'New Paintings and Drawings', May–June 1968, Walters file, Auckland City Art Gallery.

34. 'Maori Motif', letter from Arene Teira, *New Zealand Herald*, 10 June 1968.

35. McLeavey to Walters, 16 August 1971, MS 90/6/1, Museum of New Zealand.

36. Francis Pound, *The Space Between: Pakeha Use of Maori Motifs in Modernist New Zealand Art*, Auckland, Workshop Press, 1994, p. 110.

37. Quoted in Michael Dunn, *Gordon Walters*, Auckland, Auckland City Art Gallery, 1983, p. 125.

38. 'Gordon Walters: An Interview', *Salient*, 7 May 1969.

39. Michael Smythe to Walters, MS 90/1/7, Museum of New Zealand.

40. Hamish Keith, 'Painting in the Sixties', *New Zealand Listener*, 11 July 1969.

41. Leonard Bell, 'Walters and Maori Art: The Nature of the Relationship?', in Ross and Simmons, eds, *Gordon Walters*, p. 16.

42. See MS 90/1/1, 1/3, and 1/6, Museum of New Zealand, for correspondence concerning various commissions and reproductions.

43. Anna Moszynska, *Abstract Art*, London and New York, Thames and Hudson, 1990, p. 211.

44. Pound, *The Space Between*, p. 74.

45. Quoted in Dunn, *Gordon Walters*, p. 39.

46. See Geoffrey Smith, *Russell Drysdale*, Melbourne, National Gallery of Victoria, 1998.

47. See Daniel Thomas, 'An Introduction to Tony Tuckson', in Daniel Thomas, Renée Free and Geoffrey Legge, *Tony Tuckson*, Sydney, Craftsman House, 1989, pp. 38–9.

48. See W. Jackson Rushing, *Native American Art and the New York Avant-Garde*, Austin, University of Texas Press, 1995, chapter 6.

49. Serge Guilbaut, *How New York Stole the Idea of Modern Art: Abstract Expressionism, Freedom, and the Cold War*, Chicago, University of Chicago Press, 1983.

Chapter Five

Notes to pages 164–195

1. A.B. Walkom, 'Preface to the Second Edition', in F.D. McCarthy, *Australian Aboriginal Decorative Art*, 2nd ed., Sydney, Australian Museum, 1948, p. 5.

2. A.P. Elkin, 'Forward', in McCarthy, *Australian Aboriginal Decorative Art*, pp. 8–9.

3. For the best overview, see Howard Morphy, 'Audiences for Art', in Ann Curthoys, A.W. Martin and Tim Rowse, eds, *Australians From 1939 (Australians: A Historical Library)*, Sydney, Fairfax, Syme & Weldon, 1987, pp. 166–75. A more detailed analysis of developments under Labor was provided by Fred Myers, 'The Wizard of Oz', paper presented to the 'Re-Imagining the Pacific' conference, Canberra, August 1996.

4. Andrew Sayers, *Aboriginal Artists of the Nineteenth Century*, Melbourne, Oxford University Press, 1994.

5. Bull also however completed a major mural during a period of incarceration in Melbourne's Pentridge

prison, which clearly affirms an Aboriginal identity through a canonical camp scene. See Sylvia Kleinert, 'Blood From a Stone: Ronald Bull's Murals in Pentridge Prison', paper presented to the Art Association of Australia conference, Canberra, October 1997.

6. Norma L. Davis, 'The Artist (for Albert Namatjira)' in *Corroboree: Aboriginal Cartoon Fun*, by Eric Jolliffe, Sydney, 1946, p. 19.

7. Cf. Ian McLean, *White Aborigines*, Cambridge, Cambridge University Press, 1998, pp. 98–104.

8. Colin Simpson, *Australian Images*, Sydney, Legend Press, 1956, p. 6.

9. Or this at least was on the complete bound volume; the fasicules initially published separately had carried the more hesitant title, *The Art Workmanship of the Maori Race in New Zealand*.

10. T.J. McNamara, 'Real Thought Lacking', *New Zealand Herald*, 20 November, 1967; Harry Dansey, 'Balancing Two Cultures', *Auckland Star*, 28 January, 1967.

11. See Judith Binney, *Redemption Songs*, Auckland, Auckland University Press, 1995.

12. Nikitin Sallee, 'Te Maori: A Move Upmarket', *Metro*, 29 September 1984, p. 20.

13. *Auckland Star*, 22 June 1987.

14. *Auckland Star*, 22 June 1987.

15. Bernie Kernot, 'Te Maori Te Hokinga Mai: Some Reflections', *AGMANZ Journal*, vol. 18, no. 2, 1987, p. 7; see also Hirini Moko Mead, *Magnificent Te Maori /Te Maori Whakahirahira*, Auckland, Heinemann, 1986.

16. Andrew Sharp, *Justice and the Maori*, Auckland, Oxford University Press, 1990, pp. 74–81.

17. See Fred Myers, 'Culture-Making: The Performance of Aboriginality at the Asia Society Galleries', *American Ethnologist* 21:4, 1994, pp. 679–99.

18. 'Glow from Taonga no Magic Wand', *New Zealand Herald*, 28 June 1987.

19. Rangihiroa Panoho, *Whatu Ahu Rua: Two Threads Intertwined*, exhib. cat., Wanganui, Sarjeant Gallery, 1990, pp. 12–13.

Chapter Six

Notes to pages 196–223

1. Works from this series are reproduced with Gordon Bennett's text, 'Notes on Perception', in Nicholas Thomas and Diane Losche, eds, *Double Vision: Art Histories and Colonial Histories in the Pacific*, Cambridge, Cambridge University Press, 1999. See also Ian McLean and Gordon Bennett, *The Art of Gordon Bennett*, Sydney, Craftsman House, 1996, for the most extensive publication of Bennett's work to date.

2. Citing Piet Mondrian, 'Plastic Art and Pure Plastic Art', in Herbert Henkels, ed., *Mondrian: From Figuration to Abstraction*, exhib. cat., Tokyo, Tokyo Shimbun, 1987, p. 22.

3. Most of the information in this section is drawn from Rover Thomas, Kim Akerman, Mary Macha, Will Christensen and Wally Caruana, *Roads Cross: The Paintings of Rover Thomas*, Canberra, National Gallery of Australia, 1994.

4. Simon Kronenberg, 'Why Gabrielle Pizzi has Changed Her Mind about Aboriginal Art', interview, *Art Monthly Australia*, no. 85, November 1995, pp. 7–9.

5. John McDonald, 'Back to the Bush: Kngwarreye, like Monet, feels nature', *Sydney Morning Herald*, 10 June 1995, p. 20A. John McDonald was responding to a radio interview with Gabrielle Pizzi, in which she expressed similar views to those published later in the *Art Monthly Australia* interview cited in note 4.

6. See Margo Neale et al., *Emily Kame Kngwarreye: Alhakere–Paintings from Utopia*, South Brisbane, Queensland Art Gallery/South Yarra, Vic., Macmillan, 1998.

Chapter Seven

Notes to pages 224–257

1. See Sandy Adsett and Cliff Whiting, eds, *Mataora: The Living Face. Contemporary Maori Art*, Auckland, David Bateman, 1996, pp. 40–1; this is a Te Waka Toi publication, and provides the broadest survey available of contemporary Maori art.

2. Shane Cotton's work is discussed by Jim and Mary Barr in, 'Mana from History', *World Art*, no. 15, 1997, pp. 58–62.

3. Jacob Manu Scott has written of this work (fig. 142): 'I thought it appropriate that the principles be acknowledged and remembered by those who pass into and out of this High Court building under this lintel after all these are the people who make, exercise and test our laws. This work consists of four main panels representing guardians who are Tangata Whenua of this land.'

4. For Grant, Scott, Muru and Matchitt see, again, Adsett and Whiting, eds, *Mataora*.

5. See James Ritchie, 'Through the Eye of a Needle: Recent Work by Brett Graham', *Art New Zealand*, 76, 1995, pp. 58–61.

6. These affinities were extended and performed through subsequent works, notably *Pallawah*, a joint installation by Graham and the Polynesian artists Jim Vivieaere and Michel Tuffery in Tasmania in October 1994, that involved the indigenous

Australian photographer, Destiny Deacon, among other local artists. It is important to add to this account of Graham's work that pan-indigenous reference has not been a constant theme in more recent installations, though it certainly remains significant to his understanding of his practice.

7. This wording draws on Robert Jahnke's exegesis of the work in an unpublished lecture delivered at the Canberra School of Art, August 1996. For a more extended discussion of his earlier work, see my essay 'A Second Reflection: Presence and Opposition in Contemporary Maori Art', *Journal of the Royal Anthropological Institute*, 1, 1995, pp. 23–46.

8. See Bernice Murphy, ed., *Localities of Desire: Contemporary Art in an International World*, Sydney, Museum of Contemporary Art, 1994.

9. The associated catalogue was: Jacqueline Fraser, *He Tohu: The New Zealand Room: A Commemorative Project*, Wellington, City Art Gallery Te Waka Toi, 1993. On Fraser's work, see also Wendy Vaigro, 'Totally Wired: Jacqueline Fraser's Poetics of Space', *Art Asia Pacific*, vol. 3, no. 2, 1996, pp. 76–80.

10. For Karaka's early work, see Bruce Birdling, 'Emily Pace', *Art New Zealand*, 26, 1983, pp. 38–9.

11. See Denys Trussell and Tony Martin, *Living Here Aotearoa: Nigel Brown Survey Exhibition*, Palmerson North, Manawatu Art Gallery, 1992.

12. For more detailed discussion, see Nicholas Thomas, 'Weeds and Monuments: The Paintings of Michael Shepherd', *Art Asia Pacific*, vol. 2, no. 3, 1995, pp. 102–7.

13. See *Judy Watson*, exhib. cat., Green Point, Victoria, Moët and Chandon, 1996.

14. Maureen Lander's work is discussed together with that of other fibre artists in Megan Tamati-Quennell, *Pu Manawa*, Wellington, National Museum, 1993.

Chapter Eight

Notes to pages 258–276

1. Arthur O. Lovejoy, *Primitivism and Related Ideas in Antiquity* [1935], New York, Octagon, 1965 (this was the inaugural volume of a series of 'contributions to the history of primitivism', which later incorporated work on the Middle Ages, the eighteenth century and other periods).

2. For references to the very extensive literature, and discussion, see Nicholas Thomas, *Colonialism's Culture: Anthropology, Travel and Government*, Cambridge, Polity Press, 1994.

3. On migration and cultural politics in Australia, see Gill Bottomley and Marie De Lepervanche, eds, *Ethnicity, Class and Gender in Australia*, Sydney, Allen and Unwin, 1984, and Gillian Bottomley, *In Another Place: Migration and the Politics of Culture*, Cambridge, Cambridge University Press, 1992.

4. See Paul Spoonley, *Racism and Ethnicity*, Auckland, Oxford University Press, 1993. For an affirmative survey of the Polynesian presence in contemporary New Zealand culture, see Graeme Lay, *Pacific New Zealand*, Auckland, David Ling, 1996.

5. For lengthier discussion of contemporary Polynesian art in New Zealand, see my articles 'The Dream of Joseph' and 'From Exhibit to Exhibitionism', *The Contemporary Pacific*, 6, 1996, pp. 291–317 and 319–48. Most recent issues of *Art New Zealand* include relevant material on specific artists and exhibitions.

6. Hou Hanru, 'Interview with Rasheed Areen', *Art and Asia Pacific*, vol. 2, no. 1, 1995, p. 106.

7. Elizabeth Gertsakis, *Beyond Missolonghi*, exhib. cat., Melbourne, University of Melbourne, 1994, p. 7.

8. Tillers' work has been extensively discussed in art journals, but for an overview and insightful interpretation, see Wystan Curnow, *Imants Tillers and the 'Book of Power'*, Sydney, Craftsman House, 1997.

9. Many of the key statements of this debate are reproduced in Rex Butler, ed., *What is Appropriation?*, Sydney, Power Publications, 1996.

10. Ian McLean, 'Racism and Postmodernism: Australian Art and its Institutions', *Art Monthly Australia*, no. 103, September 1997, p. 17.

Bold entries signify colour plates. Measurements are in centimetres followed by inches, height before width.

24   George Catlin, *The Last Race, Part of Okipa Ceremony* (Mandan), 1832, oil on canvas, 58.8 x 71.3 (23¹/₈ x 28¹/₈), National Museum of Art, Smithsonian Institution, Washington DC, USA, gift of Mrs Joseph Harrison Jnr

25   Augustus Earle, *A Bivouack, Daybreak, on the Illawarra Mountains*, 1827, watercolour, 25.7 x 17.5 (10 x 7), National Library of Australia, Canberra, Nan Kivell collection

26   Augustus Earle, *A Bivouack of Travellers in Australia in a Cabbage-Tree Forest, Daybreak*, c. 1838, oil on canvas, 118 x 82 (46¹/₂ x 32¹/₄), National Library of Australia, Canberra, Nan Kivell collection

27   From Robert Burford, *Description of a View in the Bay of Islands, New Zealand, now exhibiting at the Panorama, Leicester Square, painted by the Proprietor Robert Burford, by drawing taken by Augustus Earle Esq.* (London: G. Nichols, 1838)

28   Charles Blomfield, *White Terraces, Rotomahana*, 1897, oil on canvas, 81.9 x 133 (32¹/₄ x 52³/₈), Auckland Art Gallery Toi o Tamaki, gift of Mr D.L. Murdoch

29   Charles Blomfield, *Panoramic view of the White Terrace, Rotomahana*, 1885 (detail), oil on canvas, 60 x 100 (23⁵/₈ x 39³/₈), private collection, courtesy of the Ferner Gallery, Auckland

30   John Glover, *A Corroboree of Natives in Mills Plains* (also known as *A Corrobery of Natives in Mills Plains*), 1832, Deddington, Tasmania, oil on canvas on board, 56.5 x 71.4 (22¹/₄ x 28¹/₈), Art Gallery of South Australia, Adelaide, Morgan Thomas Bequest Fund 1951

31   Benjamin Duterrau, *Mr Robinson's First Interview with Timmy*, 1840, oil on canvas 113 x 142 (44¹/₂ x 55⁷/₈), National Gallery of Australia, Canberra

32   John Glover, *The Last Muster of the Tasmanian Aborigines at Risdon*, 1836, oil on canvas, 121.5 x 182.5 (47⁷/₈ x 71⁷/₈), Queen Victoria Museum and Art Gallery, Launceston, Tasmania

33   John Glover, *Figures in the Landscape*, c. 1834, pen and ink, 17.8 x 26.5 (7 x 10³/₈), from the sketchbooks of John Glover, National Library of Australia, Canberra, Nan Kivell collection

34   Benjamin Duterrau, *Trucanini, Wife of Warreddy*, 1835, bas relief, oil on plaster, 33 x 26 x 10 (13 x 10¹/₄ x 4), Museum of Tasmania, Hobart

35   Eugen von Guérard, *Panoramic View of Mr Angus McMillan's Station, Bushy Park*, c. 1861, oil on pair of canvases, each 35.9 x 93.9 (14¹/₈ x 36⁷/₈), National Library of Australia, Canberra, Nan Kivell collection

36   Eugen von Guérard, *Bushy Park, Gippsland, Australia*, 1860, pencil sketch, 32.6 x 52.4

(12³/₄ x 20⁵/₈), Alexander Turnbull Library, National Library of New Zealand, Te Puna Matauranga o Aotearoa, Wellington

37   Eugen von Guérard, *Ferntree Gully in the Dandenong Ranges*, 1857, oil on canvas, 92 x 138 (36¹/₄ x 54³/₈), National Gallery of Australia, Canberra

38   Eugen von Guérard, *Milford Sound, New Zealand*, 1877–9, oil on canvas, 99.2 x 176 (39 x 69¹/₄), The Art Gallery of New South Wales, Sydney

39   Eugen von Guérard, *The Weatherboard Falls, NSW*, 1863, oil on canvas, 45.5 x 75.8 (18 x 29⁷/₈), Geelong Art Gallery, Victoria, gift of Alfred Felton, 1900

40   Eugen von Guérard, *Weatherboard Falls, NSW*, hand-coloured lithograph, 32.5 x 51 (12³/₄ x 20¹/₈), published in *Eugen von Guérard's Australian Landscapes* (Melbourne: Hamel and Ferguson, 1867), National Library of Australia, Canberra

41   Eugen von Guérard, *View of Lake Illawarra, NSW*, hand-coloured lithograph, 32.5 x 51 (12³/₄ x 20¹/₈), published in *Eugen Von Guérard's Australian Landscapes* (Melbourne: Hamel and Ferguson, 1867), National Library of Australia, Canberra

42   François Cogné, *Merri Creek, Plenty Ranges*, lithograph, 26 x 36.5 (10¹/₄ x 14¹/₄), published in *Souvenir Views of Melbourne and Victorian Scenery* (Melbourne: Charles Troedel, c. 1865), National Library of Australia, Canberra

43   Arthur Streeton, *The Selector's Hut: Whelan on the Log*, 1890, oil on canvas, 76.7 x 51.2 (30¹/₈ x 20¹/₈), National Gallery of Australia, Canberra

44   Frederick McCubbin, *The Pioneer*, 1904, oil on canvas (triptych) 222.5 x 86 (87¹/₂ x 33⁷/₈); 224.7 x 122.5 (88¹/₂ x 48¹/₄); 223.5 x 85.7 (88 x 33³/₄), National Gallery of Victoria, Melbourne, Felton Bequest, 1906

45   Tom Roberts, *Aboriginal Head – Charlie Turner*, 1892, oil on canvas on paperboard, 39.4 x 29.8 (15¹/₂ x 11³/₄), The Art Gallery of New South Wales, Sydney

46   Phil May, *A Curiosity in Her Own Country*, published in the *Bulletin*, 3 March 1888, National Library of Australia, Canberra

47   Charles Goldie, *The Calm Close of Valour's Various Days*, 1906, oil on canvas, 127 x 101.6 (50 x 40), Auckland Art Gallery Toi o Tamaki, bequest of Emily and Alfred Nathan, 1952

48   Anton Seuffert, Secretaire, c. 1870, New Zealand wood, glass and whalebone, 161 x 127 x 73 (63³/₈ x 50 x 28³/₄), National Gallery of Australia, Canberra, Founding Donor Fund 1984

49   Carved-wood lintel or *pare* from the Ngati Whatua (Kiataia region), 81.5 (32) wide, Auckland Institute and Museum

50   Engraved hunting boomerang from Coopers Creek, 78 (30³/₄) long, South Australian Museum, Adelaide

84 Theo Schoon, rock carving design on the cover of *Arts Yearbook 6: Annual Review of the Arts in New Zealand* (Wellington: The Wingfield Press, 1950)

85 Bridget Riley, *Fall*, 1963, acrylic on board, 141 x 140.3 (55^1/$_2$ x 55^1/$_4$), Tate Gallery, London

86 Gordon Walters, *Untitled*, 1958, cut and pasted paper, 61 x 45.7 (24 x 18), private collection. © Gordon Walters Estate

87 Gordon Walters, *Genealogy 5*, 1971, acrylic on canvas, 152.3 x 152.3 (60^1/$_8$ x 60^1/$_8$), private collection, Auckland. © Gordon Walters Estate

88 Gordon Walters' banner design for the New Zealand Film Commission. © Gordon Walters Estate

89 *Mobil New Zealand Travel Guide, South Island* (Auckland: Heinemann Reed, 1990)

90 Namau mask, Gulf Province, Papua New Guinea, painted bark cloth and cane, 244 (96^1/$_8$) high. © National Museum of Ireland, Dublin

91 Tattoo designs, published in W.C. Handy, *Tattooing in the Marquesas* (*Bishop Museum Bulletin*, no. 1, 1922)

92 New Vision Gallery displaying works by Gordon Walters (first from left: *Kahukura*, 1968, PVA and acrylic on canvas, 114 x 154 (44^7/$_8$ x 60^5/$_8$), Victoria University, Wellington), courtesy of Auckland Art Gallery Toi o Tamaki

93 Gordon Walters, *Untitled Painting*, 1952–3, oil on canvas, 38.2 x 36 (15 x 14^1/$_8$), Auckland Art Gallery Toi o Tamaki, gift of the patrons of the Auckland Art Gallery, 1994. © Gordon Walters Estate

94 Gordon Walters, *Transparency 7*, 1991, acrylic on canvas, 71.5 x 91.5 (28^1/$_4$ x 36), private collection. © Gordon Walters Estate

95 Ralph Balson, *Constructive Painting*, 1951, oil on cardboard, 63 x 78.8 (24^3/$_4$ x 31), National Gallery of Australia, Canberra, bequest of Grace Crowley 1980

96 James Cant, *Mimi-Figure Variation*, 1949, colour monotype on thin wove paper, 50.6 x 39.9 (20 x 15^3/$_4$), National Gallery of Australia, Canberra

97 Tony Tuckson, *White on Black with Paper*, 1970–3, acrylic and paper collage on hardboard, 244 x 122 (96^1/$_8$ x 48), Ballarat Fine Art Gallery, Victoria. © Tony Tuckson, 1973/VI$COPY, reproduced by permission of VI$COPY Ltd, Sydney, 1998

98 John Coburn, *Western Desert Dreaming*, 1987, oil on canvas, 183 x 304 (72 x 119^5/$_8$), private collection. ©DACS 1999

99 Cover of *DYN* 'Amerindian Number', nos 4–5 (December 1943), with drawing of a killer whale by Kwakiutl artist James Speck

100 Will Barnet, *Janus and the White Vertebra*, 1955, oil on canvas, 104.4 x 60.7 (41^1/$_8$ x 23^7/$_8$) (1986.73), National Museum of American Art, Smithsonian Institution, Washington DC, gift of Mr Wreatham E. Gathright

101 Otto Pareroultja, *Totemic Rhythm*, 1963, watercolour, 53.2 x 74.5 (21 x 29^1/$_4$), Gayle Griffiths and Robin Batterbee collection

102 Hans Heysen, *The Land of the Oratunga*, 1932, Hahndorf, South Australia, watercolour, 47.5 x 62.5 (18^3/$_4$ x 24^5/$_8$), Art Gallery of South Australia, Adelaide, South Australian Government Grant, 1937

103 Fred Williams, *Landscape with Goose*, 1974, oil on canvas, 183.5 x 152.5 (72^1/$_4$ x 60), National Gallery of Australia, Canberra. © Lyn Williams

104 'Take a good look at New Zealand', Teal Airlines advertisement, published in *Walkabout*, January 1961, courtesy of the National Library of Australia, Canberra

105 Clifford Whiting, *Te Wehenga o Rangi Raua ko Papa*, 1969–76, mixed-media mural, 259 x 755 (102 x 297^1/$_4$) National Library of New Zealand, Wellington

106 Arnold Wilson, *He Tangata, he tangata*, 1956, totara, 117 x 360 x 30 (46^1/$_8$ x 141^3/$_4$ x 11^3/$_4$), Auckland Art Gallery Toi o Tamaki, purchased 1993

107 Flag of the Maori leader Te Kooti from Te Porere 1869, Museum of New Zealand Te Papa Tongarewa, Wellington, negative number B.016237

108 Paratene Matchitt, *Flag*, 1984, mixed-media wall relief, 91 x 333 x 105 (35^7/$_8$ x 131^1/$_8$ x 41^3/$_8$), Sarjeant Gallery, Wanganui, New Zealand

109 Ralph Hotere, *Vidyapati's Song – a poem by Bill Manhire*, 1979, oil and enamel on unstretched canvas, 304 x 91.2 (119^5/$_8$ x 36), private collection, Auckland, courtesy of Gow Langsford Gallery, Auckland

110 Ralph Hotere, *A Black Union Jack*, 1989–90, mixed media on steel, 233 x 123.5 (91^3/$_4$ x 48^5/$_8$), Congreve collection, Auckland

111 Ralph Hotere, *A Black Union Jack*, 1989–90 (detail), mixed media on steel, 233 x 123.5 (91^3/$_4$ x 48^5/$_8$), Congreve collection, Auckland

112 **Albert Namatjira**, *The Western MacDonnell Range, Central Australia*, c. 1957, watercolour and pencil on thick wove paper, 25.2 x 35.8 (10 x 14), National Gallery of Australia, Canberra. © Legend Press Pty Ltd

113 **Paratene Matchitt**, *Taunga Waka*, 1971, wood and oil paint, 228.5 x 229.5 x 745 (90 x 90^3/$_8$ x 293^3/$_8$), 2ZG Radio Station collection, Gisborne, courtesy of Museum of New Zealand Te Papa Tongarewa, Wellington, negative number B.042176

114 **Ralph Hotere**, *O Africa*, 1981, acrylic on fabric, 280 x 150 (110^1/$_4$ x 59), Govett-Brewster Art Gallery, New Plymouth, New Zealand, photo: Bryan James

115 Maori protesters at Bastion Point, Auckland, in May 1978. © *New Zealand Herald*

116 *Uenuku*, wood carving from the Waikato area, 267

National Gallery of Australia, Canberra, gift of the National Heart Foundation (ACT Division) 1993

147 **Balarinji Australia, Qantas Boeing 747 'Wunala Dreaming'**, courtesy of Qantas Airways Limited

148 Robert Jahnke with his work *Con-Version 3.33R*, 1994, wood, axes, lead and metal solder, 300 x 120 x 22 (118^1/$_8$ x 47^1/$_4$ x 8^5/$_8$), Chartwell collection, Auckland Art Gallery Toi o Tamaki, courtesy of Waikato Museum of Art and History Te Whare Taonga o Waikato, Hamilton, New Zealand

149 Robert Jahnke, *For King and Country*, 1994, wood, lead and solder, 200 x 120 x 22 (78^3/$_4$ x 47^1/$_4$ x 8^5/$_8$), McDougall Gallery, Christchurch

150 Robert Jahnke, *Ta te Whenua*, 1995, exotic timber, custom board, photographic paper and rubber, 200 x 200 x 150 (78^3/$_4$ x 78^3/$_4$ x 59), Auckland Art Gallery Toi o Tamaki, purchased 1995

151 William Dunning, *Antipodean Embranchment*, 1993, charcoal and acrylic on paper, 3 panels 132 x 100 (52 x 39^3/$_8$), Bell Gully Buddle Weir collection, Wellington, photo: Julia Brooke-White

152 William Dunning, *Time Table*, 1995, pencil, charcoal, acrylic wash on paper, 75 x 106.5 (29^1/$_2$ x 42), Peter and Hilary McLeavey collection, Wellington, photo: Julia Brooke-White

153 Jacqueline Fraser, *He Tohu: the New Zealand Room*, 1993, installation, City Gallery Te Whare Toi, Wellington, photo: Michael Roth

154 Jacqueline Fraser, *He Tohu: the New Zealand Room* (detail), 1993, installation, City Gallery Te Whare Toi, Wellington, photo: Michael Roth

155 John Bevan Ford, *Ko Kupe*, 1993, wood and paint, 900 (354^3/$_8$) high, Museum of New Zealand Te Papa Tongarewa, Wellington

156 Nigel Brown, *Cook in Pacifica*, 1993, lithograph, 32 x 50.1 (12^5/$_8$ x 19^3/$_4$), private collection, Canberra, photo: Neal McCracken and Stuart Hay

157 Michael Shepherd, *Monuments I*, 1990, oil on board, 45 x 60 (17^3/$_4$ x 23^5/$_8$), private collection, photo: Mark Adams

158 Michael Shepherd, *Still Life for the Year of the Comet*, 1986, oil on board, 85 x 165 (33^1/$_2$ x 65), private collection, Auckland, photo: Michael Shepherd

159 Michael Shepherd, *Five Fiscal Envelopes (the Language of Colonialism)*, 1995, 1 of 5 panels, oil on board, installed dimensions 46.5 x 62 (18^1/$_4$ x 24^3/$_8$), University of Canterbury collection, Christchurch

160 Maureen Lander, *Ko ngaa Puna Waiora o Maunga Taranaki*, 1993, flax-fibre and mixed-media installation, exhibited at the Govett-Brewster Gallery, New Plymouth, New Zealand, December 1993

161 Maureen Lander and Judy Watson, *Bioluminescence*, water, light and mixed-media installation, exhibited at Victoria Park Lake, Pacific Wave Festival, Sydney, November 1996

162 John Pule, *Style with Three Moons*, 1996, oil on unstretched canvas, 224 x 182.5 (88^1/$_8$ x 71^7/$_8$), Gow Langsford Gallery, Auckland, photo: John Petit

163 Fatu Feu'u, *Light of the Rainbow*, c. 1989, mural, Aotea Centre, Auckland

164 Fatu Feu'u, *Tulimanu*, 1991, lithograph, 37 x 49 (14^5/$_8$ x 19^1/$_4$), private collection, Canberra, photo: Neal McCracken and Stuart Hay

165 Michel Tuffery, *Pili Siva*, 1988, lithograph, 56.6 x 75.5 (22^1/$_4$ x 29^3/$_4$), artist's collection, Wellington

166 Ani O'Neill, *Tangaroa Dolls*, fabric and shell, as exhibited in 'Bottled Ocean', Auckland Art Gallery Toi o Tamaki, December 1994, photo: John McIver

167 John Pule, *Nofo a Koe, fano a au*, 1995, woodcut, 39 x 84 (15^3/$_8$ x 33^1/$_8$), private collection, Canberra, photo: Neal McCracken and Stuart Hay

168 Elizabeth Gertsakis, *Words Can Never Speak So Well*, 1994, colour bubble-jet print, vinyl lettering, 150.6 x 210.6 (59^1/$_4$ x 83), artist's collection, courtesy of the Sutton Gallery, Melbourne. Juxtaposed on the cover of the *Beyond Missolonghi* catalogue with Byron's poem *Maid of Athens, Ere We Part*

169 Elizabeth Gertsakis, *The Face of Such a Tragedy*, 1994, colour bubble-jet print, vinyl lettering, 138 x 156 (54^3/$_8$ x 61^3/$_8$), artist's collection, courtesy of the Sutton Gallery, Melbourne. Juxtaposed in the *Beyond Missolonghi* catalogue with this quotation from Kemal Ataturk: 'Gentlemen, I pray you, put back your handkerchiefs in your pockets; don't weep. Weeping is only fit for women. If you are men, instead of weeping roar like lions in the face of such a tragedy. Show by your actions the sublimity of Islam!'

170 Imants Tillers, *The Nine Shots*, 1985, oilstick and synthetic polymer paint on 91 canvas boards, 330 x 266 (130 x 104^3/$_4$), private collection, courtesy of the Sherman Galleries, Sydney

171 Imants Tillers, *Paradiso*, 1994, oilstick, gouache and synthetic polymer paint on canvas boards, 300 x 912 (118^1/$_8$ x 359) (entire work), Chartwell collection, Auckland Art Gallery Toi o Tamaki, courtesy of Waikato Museum of Art and History Te Whare Taonga o Waikato, Hamilton, New Zealand, photo: Stephanie Leeves

172 Colin McCahon, *Numerals*, 1965, acrylic on board, total 13 panels, 2 panels 122 x 92 (48 x 36^1/$_4$), 11 panels 122 x 61 (48 x 24), Auckland Art Gallery Toi o Tamaki, presented by the McCahon family, 1988. © Colin McCahon Research and Publication Trust

173 Balarinji Australia, 'free time clothing' summer catalogue, 1994, photo: Graham Monro

Research connected with this book has, over the last six years, involved many visits to public institutions, museum stores, libraries, archives, private collections, art dealers and antique shops. I have received an enormous amount of help from dealers, curators and archivists, and should not fail to mention much practical assistance from collection management, photography and registration staff in many institutions. Although I cannot mention everyone here, I would like to thank Roger Blackley, Ron Brownson and William McAloon of the Auckland Art Gallery; Megan Tamati-Quennell, Tim Walker and John Walsh at Te Papa (formerly the Museum of New Zealand/Te Papa Tongarewa); Roger Neich and Louis LeVaillant at the Auckland Institute and Museum; Ann Stephen at the Powerhouse Museum, Sydney; and Tim Fisher at the National Gallery of Australia. Kim Akerman, Peter Bellas, Anna Bibby, Kate Darrow, Jenny Gibbs, John Gow, Peter McLeavey, Ann Morrison, Maud Page, Jane Sanders, Jane Sutherland, Irene Sutton, and William Wright have all helped with access to collections, contacts, information and images.

I could not have commenced the project without the support of the Australian Research Council, which provided me with a Senior Fellowship (1993–6) and grants that supported travel and research assistants. Giselle Byrnes traced material in Auckland and Wellington libraries, while Jenny Newell and Hilary Ericksen have undertaken the onerous job of obtaining reproductions and permissions; I am especially indebted to Hilary for her help in getting the final version of the book to the publisher. The Centre for Cross-Cultural Research at the Australian National University provided a challenging environment and much support.

The book has benefited from many discussions with anthropologists, art historians and other scholars and curators, including Leonard Bell, Roger Butler, Wystan Curnow, Mary Eagle, Jocelyn Hackforth-Jones, Margaret Jolly, Jonathan Lamb, Nigel Lendon, Jonathan Mané-Wheoki, Margo Neale, Bridget Orr, Rangihiroa Panoho, Francis Pound, Andrew Sayers and Jeff Sissons. Special thanks to Annie Coombes; and to two senior colleagues, Jeremy Beckett and Anne Salmond, whose support has meant more to me than I am sure either would realize. I am grateful to Stephen Eisenman and Joan Kerr for detailed written responses to the penultimate draft, and to Nikos Stangos at Thames and Hudson for his enthusiasm regarding the project.

I am indebted especially to Margaret Jolly and Anna Jolly for their support. I also owe a great deal to a number of artists, especially Mark Adams, Gordon Bennett, Jacqueline Fraser, Brett Graham, Robert Jahnke, Michael Shepherd, and Jim Vivieaere. One of the most precious rewards of my time in Aotearoa was getting to know John Pule: we have shared more good conversation and good wine than I really care to recall, in Australia, Hawaii and New Caledonia, as well as in various places in New Zealand. I am more grateful than I can say to him and Sofia Tekela for their generosity and hospitality.